The International Library of Sociology

ADOPTED CHILDREN
HOW THEY GROW UP

Founded by KARL MANNHEIM

The International Library of Sociology

THE SOCIOLOGY OF GENDER AND THE FAMILY
In 15 Volumes

I	Adopted Children	*McWhinnie*
II	Britain's Married Women Workers	*Klein*
III	Families and their Relatives	*Firth et al*
IV	The Family and Democratic Society	*Folsom*
V	The Family and Social Change	*Rosser et al*
VI	The Family Herds	*Gulliver*
VII	Family Socialization and Interaction Process	*Parsons et al*
VIII	Foster Care	*George*
IX	From Generation to Generation	*Eisenstadt*
X	The Golden Wing	*Yueh-Hwa*
XI	In Place of Parents	*Trasler*
XII	In Retirement	*Bracey*
XIII	Middle Class Families	*Bell*
XIV	Nation and Family	*Myrdal*
XV	Women's Two Roles	*Myrdal et al*

ADOPTED CHILDREN
HOW THEY GROW UP

A Study of their Adjustment as Adults

by
ALEXINA MARY MCWHINNIE

Foreword by
EILEEN YOUNGHUSBAND

LONDON AND NEW YORK

First published in 1967 by
Routledge

Reprinted 1999, 2000, 2001 by
Routledge
2 Park Square, Milton Park, Abingdon, Oxon, OX14 4RN

Simultaneously published in the USA and Canada by Routledge
711 Third Avenue, New York, NY 10017

Transferred to Digital Printing 2007

Routledge is an imprint of the Taylor & Francis Group, an informa business

First issued in paperback 2013

© 1967 Alexina Mary McWhinnie

All rights reserved. No part of this book may be reprinted or reproduced or utilized in any form or by any electronic, mechanical, or other means, now known or hereafter invented, including photocopying and recording, or in any information storage or retrieval system, without permission in writing from the publishers.

The publishers have made every effort to contact authors/copyright holders of the works reprinted in *The International Library of Sociology*. This has not been possible in every case, however, and we would welcome correspondence from those individuals/companies we have been unable to trace.

British Library Cataloguing in Publication Data
A CIP catalogue record for this book
is available from the British Library

ISBN 978-0-415-17640-8 (hbk)
ISBN 978-0-415-86841-9 (pbk)

Publisher's Note
The publisher has gone to great lengths to ensure the quality of this reprint but points out that some imperfections in the original may be apparent

TO
JAMES

FOREWORD

DR McWhinnie has undertaken an important pioneer study into the life history of people adopted in childhood; indeed this is the first study in this country of an unselected sample of adults who were adopted as children. Dr McWhinnie procured her 58 cases through the cooperation of a number of family doctors who referred to her any patient they knew to be adopted and who was willing to take part in the enquiry. This was an ingenious way of avoiding the obvious disadvantages of follow-up studies of those who later find themselves in psychiatric clinics, the courts or the children's department. None of Dr McWhinnie's cases had come to light through a breakdown in adoption. They all belong therefore to the large group of adopted children about whose happiness or unhappiness, success or failure in life, nothing is known in any systematic way.

Inevitably when knowledge is at a minimum prescriptions grow up based upon intuition and hallowed by time. Dr McWhinnie looks at these against the findings from her 58 cases (six of whom were long term foster-children) and finds that there is some truth in some clichés and no proof in others. Thus for example, fewer children did well where the adoptive mother was over 50 when the order was made—partly because this aroused other people's suspicions about the relationship. On the other hand, 13% of such adoptions were a success. Family patterns, for example whether or not there were natural children of the adoptive parents, material conditions and class status had no invariable significance in themselves. As Dr McWhinnie says: '. . . it emerged that much more important than family pattern as such were the basic attitudes in the family to all the children whether adopted or not'. In other words: spontaneous and real love for children for their own

Foreword

sakes was the only sure safeguard against all the foreseen and unforeseen hazards of adoption.

On the searching criteria which she applied to each case, Dr McWhinnie found that 15 of the adopted adults had made a successful and happy adjustment to life. 10 others were at the opposite end of the scale. And there were a further 21 who had had or were still struggling with severe emotional problems related to their adoption situation.

The detailed case histories which are an invaluable part of the study show the efforts made to employ objective criteria in the largely uncharted field of child nurture, where there are comparatively few studies that clarify norms in different social groups and at different periods. Dr McWhinnie rightly stresses that these histories are both introspective and retrospective. Nonetheless common elements emerge, for example the first doubts about the biological relationship and the lengths to which some children went to discover the truth. And then, as might be expected, the crucial importance of the good or poor relationship with the adoptive parents when the child discovered his adoptive status. If these parents were in the psychological sense indeed father and mother to the child the discovery of adoption was a passing episode rather than the traumatic or isolating experience which it became for children who were already oppressed by impossible demands and lack of love. To the reader these vivid histories of sad or happy childhoods bring out starkly the dependence of the child upon his small adult world, a world in which some of these boys and girls experienced warmth, love and freedom, while others were caught in the web of adult neurosis, self-centredness, possessiveness and rigidity—and marked for life by it. Naturally this invites the further question of whether these experiences were any different from the range to which children in their natural families are subject. Dr McWhinnie is emphatic that the hazards of adoption are different from and greater than those for the child in its own family.

Dr McWhinnie's substantial experience as a social worker in the child care field, coupled with her wide reading and scrupulous regard for evidence, resulted in a level of interviewing skill and capacity for conceptualisation unfortunately rare at present in this country. This exploratory study is as

Foreword

important for its pointers as for its findings. It reinforces the acknowledged need for wide ranging further discussion and scientific enquiry to help dispel the terrifying blindness in which at present society sets its legal seal upon adoptive parenthood and then leaves the child to his fate.

EILEEN YOUNGHUSBAND

CONTENTS

Foreword by Eileen Younghusband, D.B.E. *page* vii

Acknowledgments xv

Introduction 1

1 PREVIOUS RESEARCH STUDIES IN RELATION TO THE PRESENT RESEARCH PROJECT 36

2 METHOD OF RESEARCH USED IN THIS STUDY 47

   1 Conceptual Framework 47
      Methodology in Social Research 47
      Heredity and Environment 52
      Principles of Social Casework 54

   2 Method of Referral 57

   3 Details of the Interview Technique. Manner of History Recording 71

3 DESCRIPTION OF HISTORIES 85

   Group A—Good Adjustment 95
   Group D—Poor Adjustment 111
   Group C—Intermediate Adjustment 138
   Group B—'Fairly Good' Adjustment 175
   Group E—Adjustment of Foster Children 185

4 ANALYSIS OF HISTORIES AND OF ADOPTION SITUATION 195

   1 Analysis of Histories 197
      Age of Adoptive Mother at Placement 198
      Adoption by one Adoptive Parent (a Mother) 200
      Death of Adoptive Parent and Known Health of Adoptive Parents related to Adjustment Classification 201

Contents

	page
Financial Circumstances related to Adjustment Classification	203
Occupational Classification related to Adjustment Classification	205
Religion in the Adoptive Home related to Adjustment Classification	209
Age at Placement related to Adjustment Classification	211
Experience Prior to Placement and Separation from Adoptive Home and changes of Mother-Figure	215
Family Pattern in Adoptive Home related to Adjustment Classification	215
Relatedness and Personal Knowledge of Biological Parents related to Adjustment Classification	218
Attitude in the Home Area to Adoption	220
Patterns which emerged	220
Histories in Group A	221
Histories in Group D	225
Histories in Group C	229
Histories in Group B	236
Histories in Group E	238
2 Analysis of Adoption Situation in 58 Histories	240
How and When the Adopted Person Learned of Being Adopted	240
How Much Information was Wanted by the Adopted Person about the Details of his or her Adoption	243
Communication regarding Adoption within the Adoptive Family	246
Some Adoptive Parental Attitudes in the Adoption Situation	251
Physical Resemblances and Differences	253
5 CONCLUSIONS	257
Notes	271
Bibliography	281
Appendix: Annual Figures of Legalised Adoptions in England and Scotland	289
Index	291

TABLES

1 OCCUPATIONAL CLASSIFICATION OF THE ADOPTED PERSON *page* 86

2 AGE OF ADOPTIVE MOTHER AT PLACEMENT RELATED TO ADJUSTMENT CLASSIFICATION 199

3 KNOWN HEALTH OF PARENTS DURING CHILDHOOD OF ADOPTED PERSON TO AGE OF 18 RELATED TO ADJUSTMENT CLASSIFICATION 202

4 FINANCIAL CIRCUMSTANCES DURING CHILDHOOD OF ADOPTED PERSON TO AGE OF 18 RELATED TO ADJUSTMENT CLASSIFICATION 204

5 OCCUPATIONAL CLASSIFICATION RELATED TO ADJUSTMENT CLASSIFICATION 206

6 OCCUPATIONAL CLASSIFICATION OF ADOPTIVE FATHER RELATED TO ADJUSTMENT CLASSIFICATION 207

7 RELIGION IN THE ADOPTIVE HOME RELATED TO ADJUSTMENT CLASSIFICATION 210

8 AGE OF CHILD AT PLACEMENT RELATED TO ADJUSTMENT CLASSIFICATION 213

9 FAMILY PATTERN IN ADOPTIVE HOME RELATED TO ADJUSTMENT CLASSIFICATION 216

ACKNOWLEDGMENTS

THIS study and book became possible only because of the willing cooperation of many people and I should like to express my sincere thanks to them.

First, I want to say how very grateful I am to all the 58 adopted adults who agreed to participate in this research. They did so on the understanding that in due course I would write a Thesis and then publish a book about my interviews with them. In accordance with the permission they gave me, details about their lives are given anonymously in the chapters which follow. Although, as far as possible, all specific identifying information has been omitted from the case-histories which have been quoted, it remains feasible that some of the people referred to, although no one else, might be able to recognise themselves. Should this occur, I know that these adopted people will understand that only by having a good deal of personal information given about them was it possible to present a total picture to illustrate the unique situation of their adjustment to being adopted. From such detailed descriptions, however, they were aware that their own life experience could become of value to others, and I know from them that this was why they agreed to participate in this study, and I am greatly indebted to them for their consistent cooperation.

I owe thanks, too, to the many medical practitioners who gave of their time and thought to effecting introductions for me to grown-up people adopted as children. Since all were busy men and women, their active cooperation was all the more appreciated. I should like to express particular thanks to the following:

Professor R. Scott, of the General Practice Teaching Unit, University of Edinburgh; Dr Lowell Lamont, of Edinburgh;

Acknowledgments

Dr A. E. Cormack, of Edinburgh; Dr John T. Baldwin, previously of Penicuik; Dr R. M. McGregor, of Hawick; and medical officers in the Department of Health for Scotland.

My thanks are also due to those who assisted in the initial planning stages of this research. These were the late Miss Marjorie Brown, Miss Margaret Browne, and Professor R. Scott, all of the University of Edinburgh. To the late Miss Marjorie Brown I was particularly grateful since throughout all the vicissitudes of this research study, its inevitable setbacks and its ultimate compilation, she was always available with advice, support and encouragement. This research study was presented and accepted for the degree of Ph.D. at the University of Edinburgh in 1960. The present book is a shortened and edited version of the original thesis. The latter contains all the case histories as well as the detailed charts used in the interviewing and analysis.

I am also deeply indebted to the Carnegie Trust for the Universities of Scotland for the award of a Carnegie Scholarship for three years to assist me to undertake this research.

There are others in my more personal life without whom I would neither have embarked on this research and book nor completed it. Emeritus Professor Sir Alexander Gray supported my initial endeavours, and professional colleagues and others facilitated my continuing with it after returning to professional employment. Professor Sprott has given invaluable advice in connection with the editing and abridgement of the original thesis, while Dame Eileen Younghusband kindly read both the original and edited versions and made many helpful suggestions. The person, however, to whom I owe most is my husband. He inspired me to embark on this research and then was an active collaborator and constructive critic throughout, as well as being a continuing source of encouragement and support.

ALEXINA M. McWHINNIE

Edinburgh, 1966

INTRODUCTION

CHILD adoption is a practice which can be found in many cultures and its origins go far back into antiquity. The earliest formal record of adoption is a cuneiform tablet dated as early as 2360 B.C. There are familiar examples in ancient mythology and throughout history. In the legend of Oedipus, the ill-fated King of Thebes, he was stated to be found lying on a mountainside, and Sophocles described his adoption as follows: 'The Corinthian, a servant of Polybus, King of Corinth, brought the child to his royal master, who, being childless, gladly welcomed the infant and adopted it as his own.'[1] In Olympus too child adoption was practised, and the gods viewed it as a bond as close as true birth. Thus Diodorus stated that 'when Zeus persuaded his jealous wife, Hera, to adopt Hercules, the goddess got into bed and, clasping the baby hero to her bosom, pushed him through her robes and let him fall to the ground in imitation of real birth'.[2]

Both Greeks and Romans practised adoption and frequently did so to ensure an heir for property and a son to perform the rites at the ancestral graves. Such adopted children had a secure legal status in their families and the birth of subsequent legitimate children did not deprive them of their rights.

In Hebrew history, the most famous adoption was that of Moses. As Ellison[3] observes, it is interesting to consider that the Ten Commandments, one of the foundations of western social conduct, came to us through the medium of an adopted child abandoned in infancy.

In eastern countries where ancestor worship was and still is practised, the presence of a son in the family was essential. If there were no biological son, a son would be adopted. Male child adoption in China was thus a religious rite, as it was also amongst the Hindus. Equally concerned with ancestral worship were the Eskimos and they too would acquire a son by adoption.

Closely allied to the question of child adoption is that of the

Introduction

future of the child born out of wedlock. Under Roman Law he had a defined status, and when a bastard was born in royal families he was given special privileges. No sense of shame or of inferiority was associated with his status. As illustrations of such social attitudes, Ellison[4] quotes Theodoric I, the natural son of Clovis, who shared the kingdom of the Franks with other sons born in wedlock, and, the first Norman King of England, who was openly called 'William the Bastard'.

Child Adoption in England and Scotland—
Historical Review of Community Attitudes and Legislative Provision

In England in feudal times the bastard of lowly origin had no legal rights but under the feudal system there were no unwanted children in the modern sense. The lord of the manor had obligations to all his people and this included legitimate, illegitimate and orphaned children. Furthermore, labour, together with land, were the two forms of wealth in those days and so future potential labour was valuable. A further factor was the universal influence at that time of the Roman Catholic Church which, although hierarchical and feudal in administrative structure, yet viewed all its members as having an equal right to the sacrament and to eternal salvation.

In Tudor and Shakespearean England, bastardy was more or less socially acceptable. By this time, however, society in England was much less static and was also becoming much more secularised. With the decline of the influence of the Roman Catholic Church, and so of its charitable functions, Poor Law legislation was introduced, which could not be described either as charitable or as merciful. During the Puritan régime, with its strict adherence to a moral code, a social stigma began to be clearly attached to illegitimacy. Despite a less rigid attitude during the Restoration period, the general attitude in the centuries that followed was to view the illegitimate child, like the pauper child, as socially inferior. The community was critical and hostile towards such children throughout their lives, and stigma was attached both to the child and to the unmarried parent.

During the eighteenth and early nineteenth centuries, with the disrupting influences on society of the industrial revolution,

Introduction

and the resulting conditions of work, particularly as they affected women and children, there was no social conscience about the care of the illegitimate child, which was frequently abandoned by its mother and died. Anthony Trollope, who referred to such a child as a 'nameless child', illustrates the attitude of Victorian respectability. Charles Dickens, however, who stirred the public conscience about the plight of children in workhouses, in foundling hospitals and the like, clearly identified with the illegitimate child in making Esther Summerson his heroine in *Bleak House*. In the second half of the nineteenth century there was a growing concern for children, with the beginnings of such organisations as Dr Barnardo's Homes, the London Society for the Prevention of Cruelty to Children, the Waifs and Strays Society, and the Homes for Catholic Destitute children. Although, however, there was this growing concern for children, only very gradually did a more enlightened attitude develop towards the problems of the illegitimate child, and infanticide was still common.

Regarding the adoption of children, another significant influence in England was that of the English Common Law with its emphasis on the rights of the natural parents. This tended to discourage the adoption of children, although in fact this was done in an informal way, as *de facto* adoptions and on the basis of wards in Chancery. This practice is reflected in literature by such examples as Little Effie in *Silas Marner*, Rose Maylie in *Oliver Twist* and Henry Fielding's *Tom Jones*. In Scotland there has for long been a tradition of fostering and *de facto* adoption. Child adoption on the whole, however, was viewed as rather unconventional and as appropriate only for the working classes until the First World War brought a change in many previously accepted social standards. Any adoption arrangements prior to this had been made informally and usually directly between the individuals concerned. There was no method of giving legal status to such arrangements and in fact the whole practice had been open to much abuse.

In the second half of the nineteenth century the evils of 'baby farming', the caring of babies for a premium, became recognised; it was estimated[5] that 60% to 90% of all such babies died. A famous case[6] in 1870, brought this practice to the public notice. Publicity was then also given to the fact

Introduction

that babies were offered with a premium for adoption through public advertisement. Child welfare legislation as such can be said to have begun in 1872 with the first Infant Life Protection Act by which all those receiving two or more infants under one year 'for hire or reward', had to register with the local authority. Although this 1872 Act was widely evaded, the passing of the Births and Deaths Registration Act of 1874 was the 'first step in eradicating the anonymous destruction of infants born in unregistered maternity homes. These homes, however, were not compulsorily registered by local authorities until 1927.'[7]

A further Infant Life Protection Act was passed in 1897 and incorporated in the amending Children Act, 1908, or the 'Children's Charter'. From 1908, the age of supervision for children kept for hire or reward was now raised to 7, and life insurance of the child was prohibited. In 1932[8] the age of supervision was raised to 9, and in 1948[9] to cover all of compulsory school age. The 1908 Act was important in that through its operation, baby-farming was gradually eradicated. This was confirmed by the Tomlin Committee's[10] third report in 1926, which stated that the Committee was satisfied that the legislation, introduced largely as a police measure, had eradicated the mischief and, as this had diminished, the value of the legislation as a welfare measure became apparent. This indicates the growing emphasis in legislation on the welfare of the child.

Coinciding with this growing concern for the welfare of children, there was a changing attitude towards the illegitimate child and its mother. In Victorian times the emphasis in social work with unmarried mothers was in providing penitentiaries. The first two of these appears to have been the Dalston Refuge and the London Female Penitentiary, opened in 1805 and 1807 respectively. Others followed and their names show the same emphasis, for example, The School of Discipline for Destitute Girls (1825), The Oxford Penitentiary (1839), and The British Penitent Female Refuge (1840).

In the 1870s and 1880s it was viewed as not respectable to know anything of immorality, nor was it considered possible for an unmarried mother to regain social status if she kept her child. Such children went into an institution or to a 'baby farm'. In 1871 the first home[11] was opened which would

Introduction

accept a mother with her child. In the 1880s, Josephine Butler[12] was agitating for reformed legislation, and by 1912, the first hostel, the Day Servants' Hostel in Chelsea, was opened which enabled a mother to retain and care for her child. Many other mother and baby homes opened after this, until now at least one is to be found in nearly every area of the country. The theory behind such new emphasis in keeping mother and child together was that in this way the unmarried mother was likely to become more responsible and less likely to have a second illegitimate child. Reinforcing this argument was the discovery, after the provision of maternity services, that the infant mortality rate was lower amongst breast-fed compared with bottle-fed babies. It was argued then that the unmarried mother should be encouraged to keep her child both on moral or religious grounds, and on such grounds of health. This was in fact the official policy of the National Council for the Unmarried Mother and her Child. This Council was founded in 1918, largely out of concern to improve provisions for the unmarried mother and the illegitimate child, as the infant mortality rate[13] amongst illegitimate children was twice that amongst legitimate children. It also became the policy of most moral welfare organisations. These, because they were usually affiliated to religious denominations, have also commonly approached the problem of the unmarried mother and her child from a religious point of view.[14]

Gradually, however, there has been a change in attitude to social work with the unmarried mother. Annual reports in 1900 described some unmarried mothers as unruly and it was commented that it was no wonder that parents would not have such girls at home. By 1930, however, some reports emphasised how unhappy she was and how little understood. There was evidence that a change was gradually occurring, since there was less emphasis on sins to be erased and more on good qualities to be developed.[15] The policy, however, of most moral welfare organisations is still to have a bias towards encouraging an unmarried mother to keep her child rather than insist on an attempt at an objective appraisal of each case and each situation. The objects of the National Council for the Unmarried Mother and her Child are stated in approximately the same terms in 1963 as they were in 1918.[16]

Introduction

The development of child welfare legislation in the pre-1914 era had helped to emphasise the importance and value of the child. The earlier legislation, however, derived its motive from pity for the helpless and innocent. The Boer War with its revelation about the nation's poor health produced a crop of legislation aimed to improve the future health and fitness of the nation. The School Medical Service was inaugurated at this time and systematic medical inspection of children at elementary schools[17] was followed by provision for certain forms of treatment.[18] The 1914–18 war with its heavy loss of life, gave further impetus to child welfare legislation,[19] which now began to focus much more on the value of the child as such, although opposition to legislation for the welfare of children still came from those who felt it would detract from parental responsibility. This community attitude coincides with the emphasis of English Common Law, already mentioned, where the rights of the natural parents are stressed. Thus under an Act of 1886,[20] dealing with the guardianship of infants, it was stated that, in cases of divorce and where there was a dispute about the custody of the child, regard was to be paid to the welfare of the child and also to the conduct of both parents. By 1925, however, in the Guardianship of Infants Act of that year, the courts were given a clear directive. A court in deciding about the custody of a child . . . 'shall regard the welfare of the child as the first and paramount consideration'. Reinforcing this growing concern for the health and welfare of children was the rapidly falling birth-rate.[21] This fell in England and Wales from 29·9 in the last decade of the nineteenth century to 14·8 by 1939. The equivalent figures for Scotland were 31·4 to 17·3.

It is against this general background of community attitudes to the illegitimate child, of social work attitudes to the unmarried mother, and of developing legislation for child welfare, that the developments in child adoption in the twentieth century in this country must be viewed. Previously, as already mentioned, many *de facto* adoptions were arranged but these placements were made informally and directly between the parties concerned. The growth of adoption societies undertaking to place children in adoptive homes dates from the 1914–18 World War, and the legalisation of adoption place-

Introduction

ments became possible in England and Wales only in 1926 and in Scotland in 1930.

The organisations which pioneered adoption work in this country were all voluntary societies. The first Children's Society to do this work was the National Children's Home and Orphanage, which was making such placements as early as the 1890s. The real impetus, however, to adoption work came from the need for homes for many children, orphaned or born out of wedlock, during the First World War. This led to the setting-up of two large national adoption societies in London, The National Adoption Society and the National Children Adoption Association. These organisations believed that it was better for a child to be brought up in a home rather than in an institution. Since 1918 there has been a great growth in child adoption work in this country. Such growth was gradual during the 1930s. The Horsburgh Committee Report,[22] 1937, when referring to adoption societies, mentioned eight organisations.[23] There was a rapid expansion in the years of the Second World War, when the illegitimate birth-rate rose again as it had done during the First World War.[24] Some of the large English children's organisations officially became adoption societies during this time. For example, Dr Barnardo's Homes became a registered adoption society in 1946.

In Scotland, there is a fairly similar picture of the gradual development of adoption societies. The first, the Scottish Association for the Adoption of Children, was founded in Edinburgh in 1923, and other adoption societies gradually grew up in other centres, such as Glasgow and Perth. There was also an increase in the number of adoption societies in the 1940s.

The picture now for the country as a whole is that gradually most of the organisations concerned with the care of children have started to place children for adoption, and many of the 'rescue' organisations primarily set up to help unmarried mothers and women having illegitimate pregnancies have also become adoption societies. In England and Wales in 1964 there were 65 registered adoption societies, whilst in Scotland the figure was 8. Adoption placements have also been made over the years by the Public Assistance Departments of the local authorities. After the 1948 Children Act, which set up a special and separate Children's Department for each local

Introduction

authority, many, though not all, of such departments interpreted this Act as allowing them to arrange adoptions. The Adoption Act of 1958, however, gave them specific 'power to make and participate in arrangements for the adoption of children',[25] since when an increasing amount of adoption work has been undertaken by local authorities. Throughout all this time, adoptions were also arranged by many people in the community who came into contact with unmarried mothers, illegitimate children, and childless couples or others wishing to adopt children. This practice of third party placements still continues. This growth of child adoption reflects a gradually changing attitude in the community both to becoming an adoptive parent and to the illegitimate or other child offered for adoption. It has also arisen or become possible because of changes in the law. An examination of the laws and of the reports of the various government committees relating to child adoption illustrates and reflects how public opinion over the years has changed and how it has both influenced and been influenced by the law.

The first government committee on child adoption,[26] which reported in 1921, reviewed the provisions for the legal adoption of children in other countries and considered that it was now urgent that legal provision for this should be made in this country. It saw the increasing desire for this legal provision as partly arising out of family losses in the First World War and partly out of the increasing interest in child welfare. It considered that family life was better for children than institutional life, but it pointed out that, in the *de facto* adoptions currently being arranged, the natural parents could claim the adopted child back when he or she was of earning age. In advocating provision for the legalisation of adoption, the report stated:

> In all cases no doubt the welfare of the child is the question of paramount importance; but it is right also to recognise that if the natural desire of many persons, who have no children of their own, to have the care and bringing up of some child could have legitimate satisfaction, that, too, is a proper object to aim at. Such a desire is often one of the strongest feelings of human nature and is in itself the best guarantee for the welfare of the adopted child.'[27]

This report, however, also stated as a guide for future legislation

Introduction

that, 'Nothing should be done to impair the sense of parental responsibility or, unless where essential, to prevent injury to the child, to interfere with the rights and duties based on the natural tie between parent and child.'[28] Mother and child, whether legitimate or illegitimate, should not be separated unless there were very strong reasons for this, 'in order to secure the true welfare of the child, and all possible encouragement should be given to the efforts of philanthropic persons who seek to avert such severance taking place on economic grounds.'[29]

A further committee, the Tomlin Committee,[30] in its first report in 1925, stated that it had been unable to ascertain the effective demand for a legal system of adoption. It considered that it was doubtful if the lack of such a system deterred those who considered adopting from so doing. It pointed out that the 1914-18 war had led to a great increase in the number of *de facto* adoptions but that this increase had not been maintained. It also commented that, 'The people wishing to get rid of children are far more numerous than those wishing to receive them . . .',[31] and it considered that the problem of the unwanted child was a serious one which the introduction of legal adoption might not do much to solve. These comments of the Tomlin Committee correspond with the reported experience of adoption societies at that time. Anyone applying to adopt a child was welcomed by the adoption societies. Most applicants were from the working class group in the community and it was assumed that the desire for parenthood was enough to guarantee the welfare of the child.

In spite, however, of these reservations on the part of the Tomlin Committee it considered that there was a case for the alteration of the law to give community recognition to adoption. Its attitude to adopting parents was to view them as in the position of a special guardian. It did not therefore consider, for example, that inter-marriage between the ward and guardian should be prohibited. It presumed that all legally adopted children would take the surname of the adoptive parents. It also considered that this, together with the date of birth, could appear on the certificate of adoption which could then be produced instead of a birth certificate. At the same time, however, it deprecated the policy of complete

Introduction

secrecy followed by many adoption societies who thereby 'deliberately seek to fix a gulf between the child's past and future.'[32] The Committee considered that this arose partly from a fear that the natural parent might later 'seek to interfere with the adopter, and partly in the belief that if the eyes can be closed to facts, the facts themselves will cease to exist so that it will be an advantage to an illegitimate child who has been adopted if in fact his origin cannot be traced'.[33] This comment reflects the attitude already referred to that illegitimacy was something socially unacceptable and which one could hide or ignore simply by not referring to it. This emphasis too of the early adoption workers on secrecy coincided with the feelings of many adopters that they would not tell the child of his or her adoption. It also indicated that the adoption workers themselves had the same moralistic attitude towards illegitimacy that was still prevalent in the community. They saw adoption as a cloak for illegitimacy. It is interesting to note that with the passage of time and as child adoption has become a relatively common practice in all social groups, prejudices when referring to the adopted child have become often of a kind somewhat different from those expressed towards the child more obviously illegitimately born. Adoption in fact has provided the cloak which the early workers hoped that it would.

It should, however, be noted that since the attitudes of each generation reflect and derive at least in part from the attitudes they observed in their parents, so, over thirty years after the Tomlin Committee report, there is still evidence that people feel uncomfortable when illegitimacy is mentioned or when they find themselves in a position of having to explain to a child that its parents were not lawfully married.

The Tomlin Committee Report was followed by the Adoption of Children Act, 1926, and the Adoption of Children (Scotland) Act, 1930. These two Acts have formed the basis of all subsequent legislation and many of the main provisions are still part of current legislation. The effect of the granting of an adoption order by a court in respect of any particular child, who had never been married and was under the age of twenty-one, was to make the official relationship between the adopting parents and the adopted child similar to that between

Introduction

a parent and 'a child born to the adopter in lawful wedlock',[34] with the one exception that the adopted child had no legal right to inherit from his or her adoptive parents but continued to have a right of inheritance from his or her natural or biological parents.

These Acts prescribed certain conditions for those who could adopt. No applicant must be under 25 years of age, and an applicant, without the prohibited degrees of consanguinity, must not be less than 21 years older than the child. Where the sole applicant was a male, he would not be allowed to adopt a female child unless under special circumstances, and one spouse could not adopt without the consent of the other, unless he or she could not be found, or was incapable of giving consent, or the spouses were permanently separated. The reasons for these provisions in relation to the protection of the child are obvious, as, too, is the provision which forbade any payment in respect of the adoption of the child, except such as was sanctioned by the court. An adoption order could not be made 'except with the consent of every person or body who is a parent or guardian of the infant . . . or who has the actual custody of the infant or who is liable to contribute to the support of the infant'.[35] A court could dispense with any such consent if it was satisfied that:

> the person whose consent is to be dispensed with has abandoned or deserted the infant or cannot be found or is incapable of giving such consent, or being a person, liable to contribute to the support of the infant, either has persistently neglected or refused to contribute to such support or is a person whose consent ought, in the opinion of court and in all the circumstances of the case, to be dispensed with.[36]

Before making an order the court had to be satisfied that all appropriate consents had been obtained and that, if made, the order 'will be for the welfare of the infant, due consideration being for this purpose given to the wishes of the infant having regard to the age and understanding of the infant. . . .'[37] This Act also made it possible for *de facto* adoptions to be legalised. This could be done without requiring the consent of any parent or guardian of the infant, provided the infant had been with its new parents for at least two years before the

Introduction

commencement of the Act, and upon the court being satisfied that in all the circumstances 'it is just and equitable and for the welfare of the infant that no such consent should be required and that an adoption order should be made'.[38] The court was to appoint 'some person or body to act as guardian *ad litem* of the infant . . . with the duty of safeguarding the interests of the infant before the Court'.[39]

The Registrar-General was to establish and maintain a register to be called the *Adopted Children's Register* in which entries would be made following every adoption order.[40] A certified copy of this entry would be accepted as evidence of the adoption and where the entry also included the date of birth this copy would be accepted '. . . in all respects as though the same were a certified copy of an entry in the Registers of Births'.[41] The Registrar-General would keep an index of the *Adopted Children's Register* which would be open to public search in the usual way. He would also, however, keep a register, or book, in such a way as to make traceable the connection between an entry in the register of births which had been marked 'adopted' and any corresponding entry in the *Adopted Children's Register*. Such registers or books, however, would not be open to inspection or search nor would any information by given from them 'except under an order of a court of competent jurisdiction. . . .'[42]

The Adoption of Children (Scotland) Act, 1930, was similar in its provisions to the 1926 Act, with one important exception. The same registers were to be kept as in England, and also, as in England, only the index of the *Adoption Register* itself was to be open to public inspection and search. Information, however, from the register which gave the connection between any entry in the *Adopted Children's Register* and the original birth entry was available to the adopted persons themselves after they had attained the age of seventeen years. It was not available to anyone else except under an order of the Court of Session or a Sheriff Court.

Although these two Acts were introduced to regularise what was already happening, they gave a great impetus to child adoption in both England and Scotland, and subsequent history seemed to show that the forecast of the Tomlin Committee in this respect was incorrect.

Introduction

The next important historical landmark was the report of the Horsburgh Committee[43] of 1937. This committee, primarily concerned 'to inquire into the methods of adoption societies and other agencies engaged in arranging for the adoption of children', commented that, although there was an increasing use of legal adoption,[44] *de facto* adoption still existed and although it was difficult to estimate the extent of it, 'it must also be large'.[45] The report also commented that of the placements made by one of the largest adoption societies in 1935, 30% were not subsequently legalised. It considered, however, that this was not typical of adoption societies. Although this committee received evidence from some witnesses that, because of the risks in adoption, it was better to place a child in an institution, or with foster-parents, it supported the view of the early adoption workers that 'for the child a good family life is to be preferred to life in an institution however excellent, and adoption has the additional advantage that a child brought up as a member of the adopter's own family enjoys a sense of security which otherwise it might not acquire'.[46] From the figures available, the Committee concluded that at that time adoption societies were arranging a large proportion of the legal adoptions,[47] in some courts over 50% and in others about 25%.

The report also obtained evidence about the adoptions arranged by local authorities. Under section 52(7) of the Poor Law Act of 1930, Public Assistance departments could consent to the adoption of children deemed to be maintained by them. Although most departments insisted on an adoption order in such cases, they were not obliged to do so. The report commented that 'in view of the considerable demand from would-be adopters and the advantage of adoption in suitable cases, it is perhaps surprising that greater use is not made of section 52. . . .'[48] The most active local authority in this respect was the London County Council,[49] and later in the report the committee commended the method of careful investigation used by this local authority. To those adoptions arranged for children actually maintained by the local authority, had to be added those where officers of the public authorities brought prospective adopters into touch with children, although they had no statutory authority for 'rendering this friendly service'.⁵⁰ The committee understood that this was done by infant life protection visitors and health visitors, and by officers of local education authorities who were asked for advice by unmarried mothers and would-be adopters.

The report stressed . . . 'It appears to us beyond question that the first duty of the adoption society is to the child . . . and the society should take every reasonable step to satisfy itself as to the suitability of the prospective adopters on all grounds. . . .'⁵¹ By this it stated that it meant more than simply social and economic circumstances. It discussed the difficulties and hardships involved in rejecting applications, but stated: 'The child and not the would-be adopter should be given the benefit of the doubt.'⁵²

It further stated that although some of the adoption societies made thorough enquiries, some dispensed with full personal enquiries, either because some items were missing from their application form, or because they dispensed with a personal interview or a home visit, or failed to verify statements. It further commented that even in societies which made full enquiries, it doubted 'whether in practice they are always sufficiently thorough or whether the persons who carry them out possess the qualifications to perform what should be a very thorough social investigation. Thus none of the chief adoption societies appears to possess on its staff trained social workers.'⁵³ It gave details of the appalling results for the child of the haphazard methods of enquiry used by some societies. Children were placed with elderly, deaf, blind, unreliable, mentally unstable people who might ill-treat them, or be totally unsuited in other ways to care for a child. It also gave details of the monetary charges made by some societies to the natural mother.

This report also advocated that . . . 'an attempt should be made as far as possible to place the right child in the right home',⁵⁴ and that it should not simply be a question of deciding in general whether a child is suitable for adoption. It advocated medical and mental examination of the child. 'Inquiries should also be made into the social and medical history of the child's parents and the adopters informed of any circumstances of which it is desirable that they should be aware and which may require special consideration in the upbringing of the child.'⁵⁵

Introduction

It found that some adoption societies insisted on a medical examination of the baby but others dispensed with this in a considerable proportion of the cases and the fitness of the child was judged on sight by the officials of the society. In other cases the medical report on the child could be completed by the mother herself. In some instances the briefest of details were obtained about the biological mother.

The report observed that, although under the 1926 and 1930 Acts, the name and address of the adopters had to be inserted on the consent form signed by the natural parents, anonymity and secrecy were achieved by adoption societies either by leaving this section of the consent form blank or else by covering over the name and address while the natural parent signed. There were also instances of adoption societies which did not assist the guardian *ad litem* to get in touch with the biological mother even when the society knew her address. Adoptions arranged by private agents were also described in this report. These were open to severe abuse and there was evidence of quite considerable sums[56] of money being paid for negotiating adoptions, and of the intermediary using threats of disclosure to the biological unmarried mother.

It is hardly surprising that this report strongly recommended that adoption societies should conform to certain prescribed forms of procedure, for example, that all their placements should be legalised, that all applicants should be interviewed, their home visited and references for them obtained, that there should be a probationary period of three to six months after the placement of the child and before legalisation took place, and that any charges made should be adjusted to the parents' ability to pay and should require the approval of the Court. It recommended that adoptions of British children by foreign nationals should be prohibited and that private persons should not receive any payment for negotiating an adoption except with the leave of the Court. It also recommended that it should no longer be lawful for a private person, other than an adoption society, to advertise that a baby was available for adoption.

The recommendations of the Horsburgh Report were incorporated into the Adoption of Children (Regulation) Act 1939, but because of the outbreak of the Second World War this Act did not come into force until 1943. This Act prohibited

Introduction

any body of persons other than a registered adoption society or local authority from making arrangements for adoption. It provided for the supervision of children under 9 years of age who were placed for adoption through the agency of a third party, but any arrangements made directly between the natural parents and adoptive parents were unaffected. Adoption societies were to operate only if registered by the local authority, which was to be satisfied, amongst other things, that any person employed by the society for the purposes of making adoption arrangements should be a fit person to be so employed, and that the number of competent persons so employed should be sufficient to carry out the activities of the society in this respect. The Adoption Society Regulations 1943 also prescribed the appointment of a case committee to consider the case of every child to be placed with an adopter, and also the points[57] on which enquiry must be made, and reports obtained in the case of every child proposed to be so placed.

By the end of 1945, the Curtis Report[58] stated that in England, of the 16,357 adoptions legalised since the passing of the Adoption of Children Act 1926, 'approximately 4,000 were effected through registered adoption societies'.[59] This report in its comments about adoption stated: '... Adoption is a method of home-finding specially appropriate to the child who has finally lost his own parents by death, desertion or their misconduct, and in a secondary degree to the illegitimate child whose mother is unable or unwilling to maintain him. If it is successful it is the most completely satisfactory method of providing a substitute home.'[60] This shows a great change in emphasis from the view expressed in the Tomlin Committee Report of 1925 where it was considered that the introduction of legal adoption was likely to do little towards solving the problem of the unwanted child. This new official acceptance of adoption as a satisfactory solution for such a child contrasts also with the emphasis of the Hopkinson Report 23 years earlier that everything should be done to preserve the natural tie between parent and child.

The Children Act 1948 arose out of the Curtis Report for England, and the Clyde Report[61] for Scotland. These two inter-departmental committees had been set up 'to enquire into existing methods of providing for children who, through loss

Introduction

of parents or from any other cause whatever, are deprived of a normal home life with their own parents or relatives. . . .'[62] This Act provided for the setting up of a Children's Department in all local authorities, whose whole work should be focused on the welfare of children, and whose Children's Officer, according to the Curtis Report, should be 'an executive officer of high standing and qualification who would be a specialist in child care'.[63] The Curtis Committee thus recognised that administrative machinery would not in itself solve the complex and very personal problems of deprived children and through its recommendations an 'Advisory Council in Child Care' and a 'Central Training Council in Child Care' were established.

Such a comprehensive administrative provision for children contrasts with the early piece-meal child welfare legislation already mentioned. With specific regard to adoption practice, this Act was also important since many of the Children's Officers viewed the placement of children, whether officially in the care of the local authority or not, as one of their duties. Thus, although many Public Assistance Departments before the 1948 Children Act did place children for adoption, this Act brought more local authorities actively into this work. It also introduced a new group of workers into the field of adoption placements, side by side with those working in adoption societies and moral welfare organisations. Some of this group were workers transferred to the new Children's Departments from other local authority departments, and brought with them the tradition of local authority work with its emphasis on administration, whilst others, trained social workers, came to these new departments from other fields of social work and brought with them the emphasis of the social caseworker.

Frequently in England the Court hearing an adoption petition had appointed the local authority as the guardian *ad litem*. With the implementation of the 1948 Children Act, this work was usually undertaken by the Children's Department. In Scotland the tradition has been somewhat different. Although in many areas, the local authority has been appointed curator *ad litem*, in other areas, notably Edinburgh and the Lothians, a lawyer has always been the person appointed.

Introduction

The Adoption of Children Act, 1949, with the consolidating Adoption Act, 1950, introduced certain amendments to the 1926 Act, and it ended any legal differences between placements made by adoption societies and by third parties, by requiring that there should be a three months' probationary period prior to every adoption order being made. During this three months' probationary period the adoptive home, into which the child was placed, was to be supervised by the local authority Children's Department. The amendments to the 1926 Act allowed adopted children in England to inherit property, but not a title, from their adoptive parents, but this only became the case in Scotland in 1964.[64] A further emphasis on an adopted child having a status similar to that of a biological child was the introduction of the same consanguinity prohibitions as for biological children. Evidence too of a change of emphasis in the law towards favouring adoption as opposed to emphasising the rights of the natural parents was the introduction of the concept that the consent of the natural parent could be dispensed with if it were 'unreasonably withheld'. . . . 'Refusal by a parent is regarded as unreasonable only if his or her attitude is one unreasonable for a parent, whether or not the welfare of the infant would be promoted by the adoption.'[65] A natural parent, however, could not normally give consent to an adoption until the child was at least six weeks old. The aim of this provision was to try to ensure that the natural parent had had time fully to consider the implication of adoption. A further amendment was the introduction of a serial number allotted by the Court where the adoption petition was to be lodged, by which device the adopters could conceal their identity from the natural parents.

The statutory instruments following the Adoption Act of 1950 governed closely the courts in hearing applications to adopt a child and also clarified and made more explicit the functions of the guardian *ad litem*. In England and Wales an adoption petition can be heard in the High Court, a County Court or a Juvenile Court, whilst in Scotland these generally come before a Sheriff Court, but can also be presented in the Court of Session or a Juvenile Court. Although hearings in England and Wales are heard *in camera*, sometimes the natural mother as well as the adopters are asked to attend Court.

Introduction

This happens particularly in Juvenile Courts where the legal position is such that evidence of any doubtful point cannot be taken by way of an affidavit, as in the County Court, but only by the personal testimony in the court of the person concerned. Where a serial number is used to preserve anonymity, the adopters and respondents are asked to appear at different times, but there is always the possibility that they may meet while waiting in ante-rooms. The report of the guardian *ad litem*, although confidential, may also be read out in court. In Scotland, in most cases, the parties to an adoption petition are not required to appear before the sheriff.

The guardian *ad litem* in England was appointed specifically 'to investigate as fully as possible all circumstances relevant to the proposed adoption with a view to safeguarding the interests of the infant before the court'.[66] He must make enquiries into all statements and verify these and interview all persons concerned. He might appoint an agent to do such interviewing. Under the 1949 and 1950 Rules (Second Schedule) are specified: 'Additional matters subject to investigation and report by the Guardian *ad Litem*.' These relate to specific factual information first about the applicants, secondly about the infant, and, if the infant is old enough to understand, whether he wants to be adopted, and finally about the consents of the biological parents or guardian. In Scotland similar functions were performed under the 1950 Act by the curator *ad litem*, but his functions were more limited and less clearly defined[67] than under the Rules for English Courts.

The Adoption Act 1950 was in operation until 1st April 1959 when it was superseded by the Adoption Act 1958. This Act was introduced following the report of the Hurst Committee.[68] In the amendments to the 1950 Act, there was again evidence of a further slight shift away from emphasis on the rights of the natural parents. To the powers given to the Court to dispense with the consent of the natural parents was added the power to dispense with such consent 'if the Court is satisfied that any person whose consent is required . . . has persistently failed without reasonable cause to discharge the obligations of a parent or guardian. . . .'[69] Under this Act, as already mentioned, the position of local authorities was clarified and they were given 'power to make and participate in arrange-

Introduction

ments for the adoption of children'.[70] In making such arrangements they now are regulated as far as procedure is concerned in the same way[71] as are registered adoption societies. Provisions too are made in the Act to facilitate the adoption of children by British subjects and others resident abroad. For the first time also, on the recommendation of the Hurst Report, a medical certificate as to the health of each applicant is required to be presented in court, except that no such certificate need be presented if the applicant, or one of the applicants, is mother or father of the child.[72]

Adoption Societies prior to this had insisted on such a medical certificate. What was previously specified by law however in England was that the guardian *ad litem* should investigate whether the applicant for an adoption order . . . 'suffers or has suffered from any serious illness, and whether there is any history of tuberculosis, epilepsy or mental illness in his or her family'.[73] In Scotland no such specific information about health was required.

The Court Rules in England also specify, except in cases where the applicant is the mother or father of the infant, that as the Court may require up-to-date medical information about the health of the infant, a medical report on the child should be attached to each application. Since 1943[74] such a medical report has been required in the case only of children about to be placed by an adoption society and not subsequently before legalisation. In Scotland this more limited requirement still applies, but also now included are all placements by the Children's Departments of local authorities. The function of the guardian *ad litem* and curator *ad litem* under the 1959 Court rules for England and an Act of Sederunt of the same year for Scotland, are similar to those specified in 1949 and 1950. The specific areas of enquiries, however, for the curator *ad litem* in Scotland are still somewhat more circumscribed than those of the English guardian *ad litem*.

A further point of interest, particularly for this present research study, is the difference which still exists between English and Scottish law on the question of whether a legally adopted person should be able to obtain information about his or her biological parentage through the official records. The Hurst Committee in 1953 took evidence on this point. 'A

Introduction

number of witnesses in England thought that the adopted person has a right to this information, and expressed the view that it is not in the interests of adopted children to be permanently precluded from satisfying their natural curiosity.'[75] The Committee however considered that there would be practical difficulties in introducing such a provision in England, and recommended that by statute it should be possible for an adopted child on reaching the age of 21 to apply to the court which made the original adoption order for a full copy of the adoption order which would give as much information as would be available from the records of the Registrar-General. For Scotland the Committee recommended that there should be no alteration in the procedure whereby an adopted child could apply to Register House, but they recommended that the age should be raised to twenty-one. Under the Adoption Act 1958, a court order is still required before such information will be made available in England and the age of enquiry in Scotland remains at seventeen.[76]

This historical review of adoption legislation in Great Britain shows how over the years the State through legal protections has come to play an increasingly active part as guardian, as it were, of the children in the community. Another change has been towards requiring that more and more enquiries be made, not only about the child and its background, but also about the adopters. This is evidenced in the particulars required to be obtained by adoption societies in 1943, the continual clarification of the rôle of the guardian and curator *ad litem* and in the most recent legal provision that a medical certificate on the health of the adopters should be presented in Court with an adoption petition. This suggests a more discriminating attitude towards those who apply to become adoptive parents than that of the Hopkinson Committee in 1921, which assumed that the very desire for parenthood was the best guarantee for the welfare of the child.

The evolution of legislation shows also a change in emphasis away from stressing the rights of natural parents to favouring adoption. Adoption, too, has greatly increased in popularity until now it has become acceptable and desired in all social classes and it is reported[77] that there are possibly ten potential adopters for every child available for adoption. This indicates

Introduction

a complete reversal of the position as described in the Tomlin Report.

There has been, furthermore, a continual process at work which has sought to emphasise and consider primarily the welfare of each child. The Horsburgh Committee were the first to state clearly that in all cases it was necessary to consider first and foremost the needs of the child and to give secondary consideration to the craving of childless couples for parenthood. This emphasis, however, is not always maintained and policies designed primarily to satisfy the needs of childless couples are still prevalent in adoption work today. The administrative provisions and regulations which have been introduced, have aimed, however, to protect all parties to an adoption placement, the biological parent, the child and the adopters. A current opinion on these provisions is that:

> although in the last resort a great deal depends on the knowledge and insight of the guardian *ad litem*, the provisions of the Adoption Acts and the Statutory Instruments accompanying them go a long way towards ensuring that only those who really want to bring up another person's child as their own and who are competent to undertake this delicate and difficult task will be given the opportunity of doing so.[78]

The same writer also states that the guardian *ad litem* in making his investigations . . . 'should take into account motivation and emotional attitudes as well as material conditions, such as health and financial circumstances. . . .' The information, however, required by statute relates primarily to material conditions.

Those who can now arrange the adoption of children in this country are adoption societies, local authority Children's Departments and third parties. No way has been found to control the latter, and in fact there is divergence of opinion as to whether they should be controlled. Some control has been established over the operation of adoption societies, and of local authority placements. The effectiveness of this legislative provision and control depends ultimately however on the skill of those making the assessments and the placements, and in the case of third party placements, on the skill of the local authority visitor who supervises during the three months'

Introduction

probationary period before legalisation. In the last resort, however, the crux of adoption legislation appears to lie ultimately in the quality of the investigation by the guardian *ad litem* and curator *ad litem*. In England this would almost always be done by a social worker. In Scotland, it would frequently be done by a lawyer.

Although it is true that the kind of placements described by the Horsburgh Committee would not now occur, unfortunately there has been no established body of knowledge on which to draw in order to make possible the objective assessment of motivation and emotional attitudes which would ensure that only '. . . those who are competent to undertake this delicate and difficult task (of bringing up another person's child as their own) will be given the opportunity of so doing'.[79] There is also a further weakness in adoption legislation itself. Failure to obtain an adoption order in respect of a child placed by an adoption society or a local authority, means that the child must be returned to the society or local authority within seven days.[80] In third party placements, however, where a child may have been placed in a casually chosen home, failure to obtain an order does not lead to the removal of the child. On the contrary, it may not be removed unless neglect or other grossly unsatisfactory circumstances can be established. Also the problem of finding alternative provision for a child sometimes means that a court will legalise an adoption placement not otherwise desirable.

The Need for Research in Child Adoption

This historical review of changing attitudes and of the legislative provision in Great Britain for child adoption shows how far removed we now are from adoption being a chance affair arrived at after finding a child on a mountainside or in the bulrushes, or the twentieth-century equivalent.

A policy of arranging adoptions for children has now been given official sanction and encouragement by government legislation following the contention of the Curtis Report (1946) that if it was successful it was 'the most completely satisfactory method of providing a substitute home'.[81] Internationally there is evidence of the same attitude. Mental health

Introduction

experts meeting in Geneva in 1953, stated in their report, 'Adoption is regarded as the most complete means whereby family relationships and family life are restored to a child in need of a family. When constituted of mother, father and children, the family shows itself to be the normal and enduring setting for the upbringing of the child.'[82] It is thus accepted that human intervention can assume the full responsibility for selecting a particular child for particular parents, a responsibility usually left to nature. This being so, it would be expected that there would be, first, a well-defined policy for adoption placements, and secondly, an indication of how successful adoptions are on the whole, and, where they are not successful, why this is so. One finds, however, neither of these things and in fact in this country there has been comparatively little written on the subject and what has been written has often been statements of subjective opinions rather than descriptions based on objective observation or proved fact. The Curtis Report, for example, gave its opinion here as follows: 'There is no statistical evidence of the percentage of happy results, but in the absence of evidence to the contrary it is reasonable to suppose that in the large majority of cases the connection turns out well.'[83] Bowlby, advocating a much more positive approach towards research and also the need for objective appraisal in work with the unmarried mother and the illegitimate and unwanted child, wrote: 'It is urgently necessary in many countries to make studies of what in fact happens to the illegitimate child of today—how many achieve a satisfactory home life with their mothers or immediate relatives, how many eke out their existence in foster-homes or institutions, and how many are adopted and what is the outcome.'[84]

The large number of children legally adopted each year[85] gives further impetus to the need for research. In England and Wales the figure in 1962 was 16,894 and in Scotland 1,621. Of these, it has been variously estimated[86] that only twenty to twenty-five per cent were arranged through adoption societies or local authorities, and over a third[87] were direct or third party placements of children into homes outside their own families. In 1963 the journal *Child Adoption*,[88] however, suggested that adoption societies in England and Wales may now be arranging as many as thirty-five to forty per cent of adoptions

Introduction

into unrelated families. Accurate information here, however, is not available since there is no break-down of official statistics.

The paucity of research studies in any country and the comparative lack of literature on adoption in this country would seem to spring from two causes. First, the subject, like any human problem, is complex and the social sciences have not yet devised tools and techniques for research to the same extent as can be found in the physical sciences. Secondly, and this relates particularly to the paucity of literature in Great Britain, social work in this country has been slow to be fully recognised as a profession which would thus have to be based on an appropriate body of knowledge. This is in marked contrast to the position in the United States of America. In Great Britain, however, social work practice has been often viewed as a vocation rather than a profession. Much of this work grew out of philanthropic and religious ideals and it has adhered to these traditions. This is particularly so in the field of adoption, where many agencies and societies were initially started by one or more individuals with a very definite objective in mind, or in connection with some Church organisation. In the former, policy had roots in the beliefs and attitudes of that one individual; in the latter, policy was that which would be appropriate to the particular denomination. Neither of these starting-off points is likely to lead to an objective appraisal of each human situation. Nor are they conducive to a questioning attitude of mind which could critically analyse the results of such philanthropic actions. This problem is a very real one and it commonly results in the fact that those field-workers who are most experienced in the practical problems of adoption are often those least likely to be able to view their basic assumptions dispassionately. Also preventing an objective appraisal of adoption as a solution for the child born out of wedlock have been the social work attitudes already described when in many organisations adoption has been viewed as the least desirable of the possible solutions for the unmarried mother and her illegitimately born child.

Bowlby, discussing this problem of the attitude of workers, wrote:

> ... Unfortunately, instead of considering objectively what is best for the child and what is best for the mother, workers of all kinds

Introduction

have too often been influenced by punitive and sentimental attitudes towards the errant mother. At one time the punitive attitude took the form of removing the baby from his mother as a punishment for her sins. Nowadays this punitive attitude seems to lead in the opposite direction and to insist that she should take the responsibility of caring for what she has so irresponsibly produced. In a similar way sentimentalism can lead to either conclusion. Only by getting away from these irrational attitudes and preparing to study the problem afresh is a realistic set of working principles likely to be adopted.[89]

Nowhere in Great Britain, then, either from published material or from discussion with those working in the large national adoption societies, or in the more purely Scottish societies, is it possible to find a universally coherent policy in adoption placements. Different adoption societies, all voluntary organisations, pursue somewhat differing policies. The policy of different Children's Officers can be equally divergent. This in itself might be viewed as a sign of health and vigour were it not that the reasons given for certain actions or placements are very often a personal opinion, and as such might have its origin in personal or religious prejudice. An objective appraisal of each situation is often completely lacking. For example, if the child offered for adoption is the second or third illegitimate child born to a woman this would be viewed by some as a bar to adoption because of a 'moral taint', irrespective of why the woman had become an unmarried mother in the first or subsequent instances. At the same time, however, the first illegitimate child of an unstable woman who may have had an affair with an equally unstable man would be accepted for adoption placement without question. No genetic criteria are usually applied. In some cases the criteria regarding second and third illegitimate children is altered depending on how many babies are being offered for adoption. Various ideas associated with the fear of venereal disease influence adoption workers, and the concept of the 'perfect child' makes many adoption societies view as unadoptable the child who has the misfortune to have a visible birth-mark.

In the same way, differing methods and different notions are often associated with the assessment of would-be adopters. Where the applicants are a married couple, adoption societies

Introduction

may require a joint interview with both applicants, although it is not unknown for only one of the spouses to be interviewed. This interview can be quite brief and can consist in simply obtaining factual information about age, marriage, occupation and so on, as required under the fourth schedule of the Adoption Agencies Regulations, 1959, for England and Scotland. How brief such an interview may be has been illustrated by the findings of a recent study[90] of the practice of adoption agencies. Here it was found that one society which had 2,000 applications in a year employed only one worker to deal with these. In other cases the interviewers state that they aim to assess the marriage relationship of the adopters and their motivation in applying to become adoptive parents. Some obtain details about the couple's inability to have children of their own, but others feel that this is too personal and private a matter for discussion. In some societies the interviews are carried out solely by the adoption committee and in some such an interview by the committee supplements a more personal interview. Many adoption workers do not themselves visit the homes of prospective adopters but request others, children's officers, social workers, health visitors, ministers of religion or voluntary workers in the home area to do this. Not all would send a detailed report before requesting such a visit and many would expect simply a report on the accommodation available rather than a detailed assessment of the attitudes in the home.

Most adoption societies have an upper age limit for adopters. Most would not consider adopters much over forty and some insist that wives must be under forty, although they may allow husbands to be somewhat older. Few will consider any applicant over forty-five, nor where there is a great difference of age between husband and wife. Children's Departments, on the whole, may be less strict about this upper age limit.

None of the large adoption societies would place a child in a home where the father was a publican. Most insist on Church membership for all adopters, and it is also common to insist that one of the references required by a society should be from a minister of religion, whether, in fact, the adopters are well known to the minister or not. Many local authority Children's Departments have a less definite policy about Church connection or membership. It is not uncommon for a couple desiring

Introduction

to adopt a child to join a Church specifically for this purpose.

Very generalised details about the health of applicants are required by the schedule. A doctor's certificate is also usually requested but this is frequently not a confidential report sent direct from the doctor to the adoption society. Two references are also required and although these may be obtained by the adoption worker, in other cases the applicants are expected to obtain these themselves. Although most applicants for adoption are married couples, some societies and others will place a child with an unmarried woman, a widow or a divorcee. Some organisations will not place a child where the adopters may have a child of their own or already have a child or children. Some favour family adoption in the sense of placing more than one child with suitable couples; others feel that with so many childless homes, they should 'ration' each couple to one child.

There is now general acceptance of the view that a child should be told of its adoption by its parents at an early age. This is so because it is realised that it is impossible in practice to hide this fact indefinitely and also because it can be very traumatic to a child to learn about its status when it is older. Most adoption workers therefore advise adoptive parents to tell their children of their adopted status. Some judges and magistrates also do so when the petition is heard in court. Differing individuals, however, will give differing advice about how adopters should handle this, some advising a fairy story approach and some an explanation nearer to the facts. Few give any help about whether or how to tell the child about its biological parents or why it was placed for adoption. One adoption society advises all adopters to explain that the child was an orphan, and so to evade any difficulties for the adoptive parents or the child in an explanation of the child's out-of-wedlock birth. Opinions vary, in fact, as to how much the adopting parents should know about the biological parents. On the whole it appears that the policy of most adoption societies is to give only brief details and in some cases to give no details at all. Although the experience in one study[91] was that adopting parents knew more about the background of the children if they were placed by a third party rather than by an adoption society, in such placements too it frequently occurs that little information is made available.

Introduction

The Horsburgh Committee Report recommended that 'an attempt should be made as far as possible to place the right child in the right home'[92] ... and that it should not simply be a question of deciding whether a child is suitable in general for adoption in general. Some adoption societies, children's departments and third parties who may arrange an adoption placement do operate on this principle. Adoption societies on the whole stress that they 'match' the background of the biological and adoptive parents. Others, however, operate on the principle of taking the next adoptive couple on the waiting list for the next baby for whom adoption is requested. It has also not been unknown for adopters to be told to choose a baby for themselves from amongst several babies in a nursery, without reference to respective backgrounds.

Amidst such a plethora of different ideas and methods, the need for research and objective appraisal is evident. After working for several years in a hospital setting as a medical social worker I moved into social work in a voluntary organisation which helped unmarried mothers and made fostering and adoption arrangements. There I realised very forcefully the great inadequacy of social work knowledge when it came to making such decisions, particularly adoption placements. One never knew the really long-term results or outcome. To borrow an analogy from medicine, it was like treating a patient with drugs and assuming that these would do good, but never being quite sure because one lost touch with the patient fairly soon after one had administered the dose. The present research was undertaken in the hope of throwing some light on what happened at the end of the period of treatment as it were. If from such research some information could emerge about the outcome of adoption placements, about the family and other patterns conducive to good or poor adjustment, then it would become possible to replace surmise with something much more concrete. Also from research might emerge some guidance about specific qualities to look for in would-be adopters and also possibly something of their motivation in adopting. This would be helpful to adoption workers, whatever their field of operation, and also to the guardian or curator *ad litem*, in his assessment of any home.

Although there are three parties involved in any adoption

Introduction

placement, the natural parents, the child, and the adoptive parents, I chose to make a study of adoption, not as seen by either set of parents, but as seen by the child after he or she had grown to adulthood. As already mentioned adoption is now being viewed as primarily to ensure the well-being of the child. 'Of secondary importance is the satisfaction of the desire of childless people for children.'[93]

I wished therefore to try to find out how adoption was experienced by the person ultimately most concerned, what problems, if any, did such a person meet, what were the recurring patterns, if any, in the adoption situation, and what particular environmental factors had been conducive to good adjustment and what to poor adjustment. It seemed that only by studying it in this way could one hope to obtain a true picture of the ultimate success of any adoption placement. As already mentioned, the need to tell the child of his or her adoption is referred to frequently by adoption and social workers and by those working in the field of child psychiatry. Discussions about this also often appear in the popular press and many theories are put forward about how this information can be imparted to the child. One wondered what the adopted persons themselves rather than the parents felt about how and when they were told of their adoption and how much information they wanted to have about it and about their biological parents. It will be recalled that the law in England precludes an adopted child from official access to such information although this is not so in Scotland after the child is aged seventeen.

The method used in this research project was to build up retrospective life histories by interviewing a representative group of fifty-eight adult persons, aged 18 and over, who had been adopted as children. I was introduced to this group principally through general medical practitioners in South-East Scotland, in the administrative areas for National Health Service purposes of Edinburgh, the Lothians and Peeblesshire, and the counties of Roxburgh, Berwick and Selkirk. The fifty-eight adults in this study included six who, on a strict definition of adoption, would be viewed as children fostered for reward. Although it had not originally been intended to include foster-children, each of these six was introduced to me as an adopted

Introduction

adult. When they were interviewed, it emerged that the division between the patterns in a fostering arrangement and in an adoption arrangement was not clear-cut. The foster-children met the same basic problems which arose out of the fact that they were being brought up by parents who had not borne them. For this reason it was decided to include this group of six in the total, but for the purposes of certain analyses to view them as a separate group.

After consultation with the medical practitioner who had arranged the introduction, these histories were classified according to the adjustment found at the time of interview. The patterns which emerged in each classification and in the adoption situation itself were then analysed.

Details of Social Provisions Particularly Relevant to the 58 Histories in this Series

This group of 58 adults who had been adopted as children were aged 18 to 60 years when interviewed between April 1954 and August 1956. To understand the individual histories which appear in Chapter Three, it is necessary to elaborate the general details already given about the provision for child adoption in the country as a whole with rather more specific details about provision in South-East Scotland from about 1890 to about 1939.

Only five of the fifty-eight persons interviewed were not brought up primarily in this area, but removed to it later, when their adoptive parents moved into the area, or when they themselves came to the area for work or on marriage. As well as these five, there were a further five where the place of birth and the original placement was made by someone or some organisation outwith the area of South-East Scotland, although in two of these cases the area was still within the borders of Scotland.

In the area of South-East Scotland, the attitudes to the unmarried mother and to child adoption have been similar to those already described for the country as a whole. Thus the area had its Homes of a penitentiary kind, for example, Springwell House, originally called Edinburgh Magdalene Asylum,[94] and its training homes for girls, who were sexual

Introduction

delinquents or in 'moral danger' of some kind, as for example, St Andrew's Home, Joppa, Midlothian.

The first Mother and Baby Home in the area, where the aim was to provide care and guidance for an unmarried mother and where she could stay for a time with her child, was St Luke's Home, later the Lauriston Home. Founded in 1899 by the eminent Edinburgh gynaecologist, Dr Haig Ferguson, the tradition was and still is that the unmarried mother should have hospital care in the Maternity Hospital of the Royal Infirmary of Edinburgh. This Home later became known as the Haig Ferguson Memorial Home. The Salvation Army has run a Mother and Baby Home in Edinburgh from early in the twentieth century and the Edinburgh Home for Mothers and Infants was also founded before the First World War.

It was also common at the end of the nineteenth century and in the early part of the twentieth century for many unmarried mothers to be confined in maternity nursing homes run by midwives. No accurate details, however, can be obtained about the number or adequacy of those in the Edinburgh area since it was only in 1927 that an Act[95] was introduced making it compulsory for maternity nursing homes to be registered with the local authority. Details, however, were obtained about one such midwife on whose premises probably two of the adults in this series were born. Married to an artist, she had a midwifery diploma and since 1908 had laid aside one room in her four-roomed flat as a labour room. A doctor attended all cases. She could take only one patient at a time and she looked after married as well as unmarried mothers.

In 1918, a large private house in Edinburgh was being used as a Home for Babies to meet the needs of those born illegitimately during the First World War. Started by a private individual, this was taken over by a committee in 1920 and became known as the Edinburgh Home for Babies. This Home is still in operation and is now also a school of mothercraft. Between the two world wars there was also a large private nursery run by two trained children's nurses and this was used by those who could afford to pay private fees. Fostering in private homes was also undertaken and babies placed there were supervised by the Public Assistance Department, under the Infant Life Protection Acts. There were also other Child-

Introduction

ren's Homes in the area, under the auspices, for example, of the Church of Scotland and other committees. These were not involved however, in the first part of this century directly in adoption placements. In this present series there were children where it was known that they had been initially cared for in the Edinburgh Home for Babies, in the private nursery and in foster homes.

The principal social work organisations in the area concerned in providing care for the unmarried mother and her child were the Council of Social Service, founded in 1868, The National Vigilance Association (Eastern Division) founded in 1911, and now called the Guild of Service, and the Catholic Enquiry Office founded in 1925. The policy of two of these organisations was to follow the lead of the National Council for the Unmarried Mother and her Child, and on health and moral grounds to encourage unmarried mothers to keep their children. Adoption of the child was viewed as a much less desirable solution.

The first Scottish Adoption Society was founded in 1923 following the initiative of the Medical Officer for Child Welfare in Edinburgh. It became known as the Scottish Association for the Adoption of Children and was stated to be set up to counter the continuing evils of baby farming, and the payment of premiums with babies. Its early experience was similar to that of the national adoption societies already described. It too found a gradual change occurring as child adoption became more popular. This adoption society always stressed the medical supervision available for the babies it placed, with an examination both before placement and again before any final agreements were signed. Its adoption placements, of course, could not be given legal status until after the 1930 Act, but formal undertakings were signed by all parties concerned. It was the only adoption society in Scotland, although some other social work agencies, working with unmarried mothers, arranged a small number of adoptions each year.

The other organisation making adoption placements specifically in the Edinburgh area was the Public Assistance Department. This department also supervised all foster-placements, many of which became permanent and legal adoptions. In

Introduction

country areas such Infant Life Protection Act work was done by the Parish Council Inspector of the Poor. It was not unknown in one area covered in this period for the Infant Life Protection visitor to continue to visit a home after the child had passed the statutory age for such visiting and after adoption had been legalised. There were instances of this occurring in the histories in this series.

Another method of obtaining an adoptive home for a child was for an advertisement to be put in the public press, sometimes anonymously under a box number. Premiums too were sometimes offered in this way. Since 1910, however, there was an arrangement made between the Local Government Board and the principal newspapers in Scotland, that any paper carrying any advertisement of any kind either offering a baby for adoption or offering to care for a baby would give particulars of the advertiser to the appropriate local authority. In this way the Public Assistance Department in Edinburgh was able to provide supervision in the case of any such anonymous advertisement. There were instances in this series of adoption arrangements made in this way.

Adoption placements were also often arranged by so-called third parties, by doctors, midwives, matrons of hospitals and homes, ministers, lawyers and others. Sometimes there was direct contact between the biological parent and the adoptive parents.

Also of relevance for understanding the individual histories is the question of birth certificates and change of name during the period from 1890. With the introduction of the first adoption acts in 1926 in England and 1930 in Scotland, an adopted child now had the equivalent of a birth certificate which gave the child's adopted name, date of birth, and the name, occupation and address of the adopters, but no details about the biological parents' name, address or occupation, as would appear on any original entry in the Registers of Births. Prior to this, although not legally adopted, a child could use the name of its adoptive parents, and this would be accepted and legal in Scotland. In Scotland there is no exact equivalent of a change of name by deed poll as in England but the name could be changed by deed of declaration which at that time could be registered at the Office of the Lord Lyon King of

Introduction

Arms or recorded in the books of Council and Session kept at the General Register House. Sometimes a declaratory statement to this effect was attached to the original birth certificate. The birth certificate itself, however, remained in the form of the original entry and so in the biological name, and details would be given there of the name, occupation and address of the biological mother, or parent registering the birth. Occasionally the birth would be registered in the biological father's name, or his name would also be inserted in the original entry.

Where the child was illegitimately born this was stated in the birth certificate until 1918.[96] After that date it could be implied since the birth certificate would normally give only the name, address and occupation of one parent, usually the natural mother, who registered the birth. A device frequently used before the first adoption act to incorporate the adoptive parents' surname into the birth certificate was for the natural parent, when registering the birth, to use the name of the adopting parents as a middle name for the child. The biological surname was then dropped.

Since 1935, it has been possible in Scotland to obtain a shortened birth certificate of the original entry in the Register of Births. This certificate gives no details of parentage. By an instruction from the Registrar-General in 1936, this was applied also to the Adopted Children Register and not simply to the original entry. In this way it is argued that the fact of adoption and of illegitimate birth can be concealed. Such a shortened birth certificate was not available in England until 1947. These shortened birth certificates are gradually gaining in popularity and in 1957 the General Register Office for England and Wales issued a short certificate of the original birth entry in the cases of under 50% of the total entries, while short certificates issued for adoption entries were over 50% of the total.

Chapter One

PREVIOUS RESEARCH STUDIES IN RELATION TO THE PRESENT RESEARCH PROJECT

TO avoid confusion it seems advisable to make clear what was meant in this research project by adoption. It is defined as follows in the Horsburgh Report of 1937:

> ... the essence of an adoption, whether legalised or *de facto*, seems to us to lie in the creation of an artificial family relationship analogous to that of parent and child, or sonship, which is accepted by all parties as permanent. The child is absorbed into the family of the adopters and is treated as if it were their own natural child.[1]

What I wish to give emphasis to is the type of adoption where, first, the creation of the new family relationship is an artificial one, and secondly, there is intervention by another person to change the natural relationship of the child with its parent to this artificial one. This does not happen to the same extent where a mother or grandmother adopts a child already born and accepted within the immediate family constellation. In such a situation, there is no intervention by an outside party. The point at issue is that adoption, as an active social service provided by social workers and other professional people, is mainly that situation where a child is placed into a family where neither of its adoptive parents is a biological parent and where in most cases they are not in fact biologically related in any way. Research is certainly needed into how successful is the outcome of the cases where biological mothers and their husbands adopt, or where grandparents adopt. Social workers are concerned in this too since they may facilitate such arrangements. That, however, is a subject for research outside the scope of the present study.

Previous Research Studies in Relation to the Present Research Project

An examination of the literature in this field of adoption and in the allied one of fostering yielded a total of six previous relevant research studies, of which three had been carried out in the United States and three in Great Britain. There had been other studies of fostered and adopted children as well as the six quoted here but the aim in these other studies was to assess the relative weights of nature and nurture rather than the success or failure of adoption or fostering, or the problems within the adoption situation itself. These are detailed in notes 17, 18, 19 and 20 to Chapter Two. Since the completion of this study the findings of several other research projects have become available. Any relevant findings or conclusions are referred to in appropriate chapters of this book.[2]

The two early American publications, Theis[3] (1924) and Healy *et al.*[4] (1929) deal mainly with fostering arrangements. In Theis's study, 910 foster-children were followed up when they were aged 18 to 40, and an assessment made of their 'community value' in which objective tests, such as self-support, law observance and response to educational opportunity were used. Although originally it had been planned to make a comparative study with children raised in an institution or with children in general, this proved impossible. Statistics were used to present the results although the assessments were made qualitatively. Of these adopted, 269 of the 910, there was a very high proportion classed as 'capable'. This, combined with the finding of a better adjustment amongst children placed under 5 than amongst those placed over 5, led to the conclusion that adoption, together with early placement, gave better results for the child.

This study also suggested that the relationship between foster-parents and child was more important for the ultimate outcome than the type of foster-home. The assessment of foster-homes into 'types' was done on the basis of social class, work, intelligence, material surroundings, etc. It must be remembered that the date of this study is 1924 and that social work at that time in the United States looked to overt behaviour and adherence to community norms as its criteria. There is, however, already in this study the implication that these are less important for ultimate success than the personal relationship between foster or adoptive parents and the child.

Previous Research Studies in Relation to the Present Research Project

Healy's study of the placement of 501 delinquents in foster-homes revealed, as did that of Theis, a high proportion of successful adjustments. He concluded that delinquency of any kind may cease under good conditions of placement and added the interesting comment that it was as important to understand the foster-parents as to understand the child. There was need he said for more insight into personality make-up.

The most recent systematic study from the United States was by Michaels and Brenner, *A Follow-up Study of Adoptive Families* (1951). It is worth quoting in some length from this study as it dealt, in a way no other research had done, with the intimate inter-personal relationships in the adoption situation, and it emphasised factors which can be paralleled in the results of the present research. The aims of this study were given as three-fold: first, to reassess the families into which this particular Jewish adoption society had placed children, several years after placement, and to see how successfully the child had been 'assimilated'; secondly, to improve the methods of prediction of the child's development (Intelligence tests had been used prior to placement); thirdly, to improve, if possible, the method of home study and of placement. Successful placement was rated with reference to the marital adjustment of the adoptive parents and to the relationship of the parents to the child. Evaluation was made through the parents' attitude and behaviour. The behaviour of the child was excluded. The number of cases studied was 50.

The limitations of the study were given as follows:

First, the sample of 50 was chosen for geographical reasons from 90 cases which were handled by this society from 1941 to 1945. It was not, then, a random sample of all cases. Fifty in itself was considered too small for emphatic conclusions. Secondly, the small number, 6, which were assessed to be unsuccessful meant that analysis and sub-grouping here was of no value. Thirdly, the authors comment that it is easier to assess a situation after the event than to predict in advance how successful a particular adoption placement will be. Fourthly, there had been a change in the agency's policy during the period that these adoption placements were made. It had become customary to ask for more information regarding the sterility of prospective adopters as from about 1942. Fifthly,

Previous Research Studies in Relation to the Present Research Project

the age of the children was mainly pre-school. The oldest was under 7. Finally, the behaviour of the child was, by definition of 'successful', excluded.

A placement was considered successful where it was found that, first, there was a good marriage relationship, and secondly that there were realistic standards and no undue pressure on the child. Together with this an affectionate relationship and an admiring attitude on the part of the parents were further criteria, but these qualities had to be such as were not lacking in judgement. Other indications of success were that the parents were easy and relaxed and for the most part enjoying the child, that they were mild in discipline, and finally that they were giving the child freedom to experiment and to take risks.

With these criteria and with the accepted limitations in mind, there is still much of interest in the main conclusions of this study. A comparison was made of the age of the adoptive parents at placement and the success of placement. No significant connection was found. When length of marriage at placement and success were compared, it was found that couples, no older, but married longer seemed to give a high proportion of the most successful placements. This was also related to the reasons for the couples' inability to have children. The suggestion was that those couples who had been married longer were more able to accept infertility, especially where there was no organic cause. It was found, also, that it was advisable to take time to evaluate a couple who were asking for a baby immediately to replace one they had lost. A comparison of education and outcome of placement led to the impression that it was dangerous to assume that the better educated would provide a richer home emotionally. The same applied with regard to higher income.

With regard to intellectual status, it was found that exact prediction was impossible. The policy had been to consider the possible intellectual capacity of the baby in terms of its background, infant development and infant psychological tests (Catell) and to match this with the adoptive family's background, education, and so on. It was found, however, that prediction based on intelligence testing gave 50 % accuracy on follow-up, whilst assessment by the child's family background also gave 50% accuracy. The individual children, however, accurately assessed by these two methods were different. Michaels and Brenner concluded that, as improvements in prediction are very hypothetical, the implication of this for adoption workers is to choose parents who would not be primarily concerned with the ultimate intellectual status of the child. It was found that it was easier for adoptive parents to relate to the child who was less intelligent if the child were a girl, rather than a boy.

When physical appearance was considered, it was found to be of general advantage for the child to bear some resemblance to its adoptive parents, but this was not stressed. The pathology in each child's background had been assessed by medical and psychiatric consultants before a decision on adoption had been reached. Where adoption was decided upon, the details of any pathology were given to the adoptive parents. It was not found possible to estimate whether the knowledge of such constitutional factors added to the tensions or not.

The question of telling the child that he was adopted was also examined. The agency policy throughout had been to discuss this with the parents and to advise them to tell the child that he was adopted or chosen, and that other parents had borne him. Investigation showed, however, that the adoption workers had tended to over-simplify this situation. They had not realised the emotional problem inherent in it for the adopters. It was found, on follow-up, that eight couples had been unable to mention the fact of adoption to the child. Fifteen had told the child he was adopted or chosen but had given no further elaboration. Twenty-four had told the child he was adopted or chosen but had connected this in some way to the fact that he was born to others. Eleven of these twenty-four had also answered questions as to the child's own parents and what had happened to them.

It was pointed out that the adoption workers, as well as not realising the emotional problem for adopters in telling the child, tend to over-simplify the whole adoption situation. They commonly think of the relationship as exactly like the usual parent-child relationship and without specific problems. The writers commented that there is no body of information from adopted adults to draw from with regard to this.

Previous Research Studies in Relation to the Present Research Project

The studies which have been made in Great Britain are superficial and limited in comparison with the last mentioned. The first was published in 1953 in the *British Journal of Psychiatric Social Work*, a study done by Shaw, 'Following up Adoptions'.[5] This investigation was confined to a special group; those who had announced in the *Quaker Journal* the fact that they had adopted a child. A simple questionnaire was sent to 101 such families. Out of these, 68 were eventually available for follow-up. Of these, 55 were visited, but, because of distance, fuller details were obtained from the remaining 13 by letter.

Shaw admitted that these 68 families were a biased group, and that this was so for the following reasons: all had announced the fact of adoption; all were volunteers, refusals being excluded; the group was homogeneous in so far as social class, economic status and religious faith were concerned. At the time of the study (1951) there were 90 adopted children in these 68 families. The age of the children at follow-up ranged from a few months to 24 years. In the published paper only satisfactory adoptions were discussed, and the main findings were stated tentatively. Some of these are quoted below.

There appeared to be a slight advantage when the child was adopted to complete rather than to create a family. There was evidence that having an adopted child made it possible for some couples to conceive a child of their own. The study showed that those parents who had insight into their own feelings were more able to make a good relationship with the child.

Nearly one third had obtained the children through an adoption society. One third of these were dissatisfied with the arrangements made by the adoption society. Many had found difficulty in getting all the information they wanted from the society about the child's background. By contrast, those who had obtained the children through third party or direct placements had more information given to them about the child's background.

Those children who turned out to be not so intelligent proved in general to be a disappointment to the parents, but this did not necessarily preclude a satisfactory emotional bond between the parents and child. Great emphasis, however, was

Previous Research Studies in Relation to the Present Research Project

laid by adopters on the matching of background to avoid this disappointment. Relatives of the adopters were, on the whole, cooperative. Not quite 19% of the children were legitimate. Telling the child that he was adopted was found to be a problem to the parents. Almost all the parents recognised that the adopted child was always an adopted child. It was felt that this enabled them to forget rather than to deny it.

The second British study, *A Survey based on Adoption Case Records*, was undertaken and published in 1956 by the National Association for Mental Health. This survey was based partly on the records of five adoption societies and partly on the case records of adopted children from two child guidance clinics.

The first section of this study shows how very difficult it is to do other than superficial research from case records which have not been compiled with a view to specific evaluation by a research worker. Often vital information is not recorded. The sample used was admitted to have severe limitations. It was not a random sample, for it included only cases where adoptive parents voluntarily kept in touch with the society, or where they answered a special follow-up letter. In spite of this implied bias, however, the sample was analysed statistically in an attempt to assess significant correlations. When this was done, three factors were found to affect the chances of success significantly. First . . . 'if a child has experienced more than one change of home before being placed, the chances of a successful adoption are reduced'.[6] However, it was realised that since there was a correlation between the age of the child at placement and the number of previous moves, age itself might prove here to be a further factor. Secondly, 'the chances of adoption success are reduced where there is a difference of more than one category between the work status[7] of the child's natural parents and that of the adopters. This factor appears to be operative even where the child was adopted in infancy and therefore the problem does not seem to be merely one of adjustment to different social standards. Nor was there any evidence to suggest that adopters in the higher work status groups produced a greater proportion of the total problem cases than other adopters.'[8] Finally, 'where the adopted child is the only one in the adopters' home the chances of a success-

Previous Research Studies in Relation to the Present Research Project

ful adoption are usually greater than where there are other children'.[9]

The weakness of this study and of using statistical correlation technique is that vital qualitative and intervening factors may be ignored. As Moser wrote 'one can never be certain than an observed statistical association between two variables is not due to . . . uncontrolled (and perhaps even unsuspected) variables'.[10] This weakness was acknowledged by the authors.

Another similar attempt at assessing the proportion of successes and failures in adoption was made by Edwards[11] and published in the journal *Case Conference*. Again the weakness lies in simply choosing two sets of factors, in this case age of child at placement and age of parents at placement, and relating both of these to adjustment. A general conclusion was drawn that the risk of unhappiness in adoption rises more steeply with the age of the child than with the age of the adopters. It seems, however, conceivable that it is the adopters who chose to adopt the child when already past the time-consuming stages of infancy who make the least good parents. Edwards' study in no way gives a total picture of each adoption situation and so such possibly intervening factors are again ignored. Conclusions drawn from such a study may not only be superficial but entirely erroneous.

This survey of the research on adoption previously undertaken indicates some of the methodological problems of research into the efficacy of child care provisions. It also shows that it is a field almost completely uncharted. The three studies quoted from Great Britain illustrate the tendency to view research in this country quantitatively, the aim being to arrive at a statistical assessment of how many adoptions are successful and how many are unsuccessful, and, if possible, but rather incidentally, why some succeed and some fail. The other question which is constantly asked is how does adoption compare with other solutions for the child otherwise deprived of a normal home life. The ideal research project then is often seen as a large scale follow-up survey with matched control groups for comparison of success and failure as between alternative solutions for the child, or as compared with a group of children brought up by their own parents. This is the kind of comparative study which Theis had in mind in 1924 and which

Previous Research Studies in Relation to the Present Research Project

she abandoned as impossible in practice. Quite apart however from the practicability of such a project, it would seem to be inadvisable at this stage in our knowledge. It would be like planning an elaborate laboratory experiment in botany before anyone had done any of the initial collecting or classification of specimens. Also, as discussed further in Chapter Two, since human nature is now viewed as a complex interaction of physical, intellectual, and conscious and unconscious emotional elements, which interaction is itself the result of the interplay of heredity and environment, then any assessment must give regard to the possibility of influence from all these factors and at all these levels. The number of variables then becomes enormous. If one were to embark on matching for a control group, the problem would be that of what factors would one match. Matching by studying uniovular twins is the only way of isolating the factor of heredity. Yet even the twin method is not infallible since it can be argued that the twin situation has its own peculiar and particular features. If one matches by other factors, which would inevitably be more superficial, then one at once excludes these factors from the scope of one's study; and in the present paucity of knowledge we cannot be sure which are the non-vital factors. The use of control groups also implies the use of the statistical method for comparisons. As pointed out by Burgess and Cottrell '. . . present statistical methods deal with averages and probabilities and not with specific dynamic combination of factors'.[12] They are of value for clarification and validation. A project planned with control groups and using statistical correlation technique would indeed ultimately have value in testing hypotheses, but would have no value and could in fact be an encumbrance in an explorative study which aimed at assessing what were the relevant factors in the total situation. From such an assessment it might then be possible to state certain hypotheses.

In order to be able to arrive at meaningful hypotheses it was felt that a study in depth of even a few cases would yield more significant information than a more superficial study of a larger number. A study in depth would attempt to obtain a total picture in each individual case. Comparisons between histories could then be made and various contradictory factors evaluated qualitatively. It seemed that only in this way could

Previous Research Studies in Relation to the Present Research Project

one arrive at an assessment of the relative importance of particular factors in the adoption situation.

As has been shown from the survey of previous research, the most valuable information had come from the study of Michaels and Brenner which was a study in depth carried out by a social caseworker and a clinical psychologist. Here, although a rating scale was used, the assessments were of a qualitative nature. One of the disadvantages of even such a rating scale was pointed out by the psychologist. It meant that in this research the relative importance of different factors could not be assessed. All areas of study, six in all, had to be given the same weight. This study was, of course, of adoption as seen through the attitudes and feelings of the adoptive parents. The present research was concerned to assess adoption as seen by those ultimately most concerned, namely by those who had been adopted. Its aim was to gain as complete a picture of each individual person as possible through direct contact with them, and then to assess, as Theis did, their overt adjustment in the community. It had also to evaluate, as Michaels and Brenner did, first, the interplay of personal relationships within the adoptive family, secondly the adjustment of the adopted person to the adoption situation, and thirdly, what were the patterns, if any, which occurred in this situation.

It was hoped in this way to assess whether this situation, where a child is brought up by parents who did not bear him, is a complicated experiment beset with problems for the child and parent, or whether it is fraught with no more problems than those potentially inherent in any parent–child relationship. Some argue that once a child is adopted he is like every other child in the community;[13] others that he is always different.[14] The basic difference lies, of course, in this question of non-biological parenthood.

This present study hoped to throw light on whether this peculiarity of the adoptive parent–child relationship had its own particular difficulties. One wondered, for example, how the adopted person feels about being told of adoption; what appears to be the best age for this; how much information about the biological parents it was helpful for him to have; how the adoptive parents respond to the growing needs of a child, not biologically their own; and so on. It was realised,

Previous Research Studies in Relation to the Present Research Project

however, that in such exploratory research it was important to have no preconceived ideas of what was important, but to be alert to record all detail for all was of potential relevance. Although keeping in mind the kind of questions which concern and puzzle adoption workers when making a placement, one had to realise that to the adopted person other very different factors might be of vital importance.

Chapter Two

METHOD OF RESEARCH USED IN THIS STUDY

SINCE social workers in Great Britain have only recently undertaken social research and since they have not as yet the established and accepted professional point of view, of, for example, medical practitioners, scientists, psychologists and lawyers, it seems necessary to state specifically the premises from which this research study was undertaken. This description, given in the first part of this chapter, is divided into three, and deals with basic theoretical concepts which throughout influenced the planning and the methods used in this study. First, there will be a discussion of methodology in social research. Secondly, there will be a brief glance at the most important scientific studies which have aimed at an assessment of the relative influence of heredity and environment in human affairs and the conclusions from these will then be related to the present study. Thirdly, there will be a discussion of the principles of social casework. In the second part of this chapter details will be given of the method of referral, and in the third part, there will be a description of the interview technique and the manner of recording and compilation of the individual histories.

I. CONCEPTUAL FRAMEWORK

Methodology in Social Research

Social research, as a discipline, is still in its infancy and many problems of method have still to be solved. Sociologists in their desire to make their study into a science have often taken over directly many of the concepts and tools of the physical

Method of Research used in this Study

scientists. Thus we have a school of thought which insists that all research must follow exactly the same pattern: first, formulation of the problem through observation, secondly, further exploration and formulation of a hypothesis, and finally, a planned project to test the hypothesis.

The sociologist often relies on elaborate statistically planned research for the third phase, tending to leave the first two phases aside, while the research worker with a clinical bias may concentrate on stages one and two and ignore stage three. It seems, however, that until we have adequately solved the problems of the first two phases, we should not feel bound to embark on the third phase. We can find a parallel for this in what has happened in the physical sciences. In the mediæval period, scholasticism held men's mind in its thrall, and men had to learn first to observe before they were able to formulate hypotheses based objectively on facts rather than on *a priori* maxims. The observation and classification preceded by many centuries the planned laboratory experiment. In psychology, as it has developed as a social science, we see a reversal of this process with an early concentration on laboratory techniques almost to the exclusion of other methods of research.

Although men have speculated about the psyche since the time of Aristotle and Plato, it was only in the middle of the nineteenth century that any attempt was made to put this on an observational basis. The beginning of objective psychology, as opposed to subjective psychology or *a priori* philosophy, has often been traced back to Francis Bacon, but it was the development of experiment in the natural sciences in the nineteenth century that really laid its foundations. In the 1890s there was much activity amongst psychologists, so that by 1900 their subject had gained the status of a natural science. Where previously the earlier psychologist had been satisfied with evidence from his memory and ordinary subjective experience, these new psychologists insisted on definite recorded objective data.

Towards the end of the nineteenth century, writings on animal psychology, child psychology and the difference between individuals began to appear. This led to the introduction of tests for measuring individual differences, and from this came the elaboration of intelligence testing. Also very in-

Conceptual Framework

fluential on the thought of psychologists have been the studies of physiologists, notable amongst these being Pavlov (1849–1936). Yet another strand in the picture has been the influence of psychiatry, which, although becoming scientific by the late nineteenth century, was split between those who sought the cause of mental disorders in the purely psychological sphere and those who sought it in brain disturbances or the soma. There have been, however, many advocates of a holistic psychology. A notable early example was Adolf Meyer who in 1897[1] revolted against the body–mind distinction and in 1908[2] advocated the adoption of a psychobiological concept. His point of view has found expression in psychosomatic medicine, a concept now generally accepted and for which there have been many validating studies.[3]

In another way psycho-analysis has had an important and lasting effect on psychology, and the way in which we view human nature. Freud's 'depth psychology', with its emphasis on unconscious motivation and unconscious mental activity has brought a new perspective into psychology which had previously viewed its subject matter as 'states of consciousness'. It has also greatly influenced social work thought and techniques, and has led social workers away from the concept of man as a completely rational being, who could be helped by environmental manipulation to use his own will-power, to a realisation that feelings and emotions are of vital importance in our understanding of man.

Psychology with its particular emphasis on perception, learning, memory and communication, has not yet given us a science of personality. Psychologists, however, for example, Allport and Eysenck, are currently trying out tentative methods of research in this field. Kretschmer and Sheldon in studies of physique and temperament have tried to measure such psychological qualities by relating them to measurable physical attributes. It seems, however, that the descriptive method, despite its lack of exactness in the mathematical sense, may have greater value, and so greater precision, in the sense of arriving at a truer understanding and classification of the problems of personality.

In spite of divergences of view as to emphasis, what is now generally recognised is that psyche and soma should not be

Method of Research used in this Study

viewed as separate entities, but that personality is closely bound up with the central nervous system although the relationship between the two is still obscure. Whereas temperament is largely innate, and probably related to the central nervous system and the endocrine system, '... what we call character is essentially acquired and far more readily modifiable than temperament'.[4] Psychoanalysts argue that the main features of character are laid down in the first two years of life and that the emotional atmosphere at this time is crucial. Although there are no validating research studies of this as such, it is generally accepted that there is enough clinical evidence[5] to show that the early years are formative for the character of the adult.

Although very early environment is not now viewed as exclusively decisive, except by some of the followers of Freud and Klein, the evidence from the clinical studies of Freud that every individual passes through a complex process of emotional development during his or her early years has influenced psychiatrists, psychologists and social workers, all of whom give recognition to the importance of the life history in their assessments of patients or clients. In such a history other factors would also be seen as important: social and cultural factors, general education, moral, ethical and religious influences as well as the child's later relationships with its parents, its peers and others in the community. Bowlby stated, '... Personality growth is the result of an interaction between the growing organism and other human beings'.[6] This emphasis on the need to view each situation in total and each person as a whole in relation to his social and cultural environment is the approach of the social caseworker who is concerned with individual social maladjustment.

Although we can review the changes and advances in the past sixty years in our knowledge of human nature, knowledge which has been acquired through careful observation and research, we cannot make a similar survey of research into social work aims, methods and results, as currently practised, although there has been a considerable amount of research into social and economic conditions, and specific social problems, such as juvenile delinquency. The discipline of social work does not as yet have even a clearly defined body of knowledge and many social workers in viewing their daily

Conceptual Framework

practice have not begun to think along scientific lines. The result is that in many social work fields, particularly in that of child care, we find that, as objective knowledge is lacking, this subject . . . 'has been the source of much speculation and eager investigation by philosophers, psychologists, churchmen and educationists'[7]—all of whom can claim that their dicta are the correct ones. Unfortunately the picture is made even more confused by the fact that such knowledge as we have . . . 'is apt to be a strange mixture of personal experience, memories and prejudices—confused by superstition, folklore and profitless moralising'.[8] Social research then in this field has to rid itself first of these moralising attitudes, just as the physical sciences had in their early years to rid themselves of scholasticism.

Any use of the word 'scientific' in this study is therefore in the above sense, and is used to emphasise the need for objectively acquired knowledge as opposed to a reliance on dogmata or vague generalisations which have often been deduced from experience in an unplanned and purely empirical way. Although social work research must use a scientific method, it also remains an art. This will be seen in the discussion of the method of this particular research project, where the interviewing was done by a social caseworker who was consciously using interviewing and casework techniques, as learned and developed during years as a practising social caseworker.

Too much, however, should not be expected of social research. One cannot hope to evolve immutable laws or exact predictions; nor is it likely that we can aim at acquiring absolute knowledge; nor for that matter is it likely that we shall always be able to follow the fine thread of continuity between cause and effect. These, however, are not problems peculiar to the social sciences.

Some may argue, however, that in the social sciences not only is it not possible to arrive at immutable laws, but that no laws at all are possible in human affairs; that all are different and will act and react in their own individual way. The work of social anthropologists, sociologists, psychologists and psychiatrists, however, has shown that certain patterns of human behaviour can be observed, and it is now accepted that human behaviour does follow certain psychological and social laws

Method of Research used in this Study

and that certain patterns or stages in the developing human being can be observed and charted.

If laws are seen as 'statements of associations of varying degrees of probability',[9] one may ask what happens about the possibility of prediction. It seems likely that prediction in the physical sciences will remain potentially more measurable than in the social sciences, but the differences are of degree and even in the physical sciences absolute prediction is not possible. As one writer said, '... we cannot, and never shall be able to, predict exactly when a particular leaf will fall off a tree or where it will land ...; but this does not prevent us from predicting that most leaves will fall in autumn or that the rate of defoliation will be higher in windy weather'.[10]

The position regarding methodology then from which this research was undertaken could be summarised as follows. As research in the social sciences is still in its infancy, and as this is especially so in the field of operation of social caseworkers, the method employed should be that of observing and classifying. This, although not including a third stage, that of experimenting to validate any hypothesis, can be viewed as scientific, since this term refers to a logic, a method of approach, rather than simply research based on laboratory techniques. Human behaviour, although unique to each individual, also follows certain patterns and stages of development. A search from observed effects to causes, or patterns of possible causes, will lead to the possibility of stating causative trends, which can then have predictive value in indicating tendencies. Absolute and precise knowledge, although still regarded as the ideal, was recognised as unattainable. The aim of this research was to be the servant of the 'social engineer' interested in devising or improving techniques for dealing with particular practical problems.

Heredity and Environment

> Divergence in the viewpoints of different people on the subject of nature and nurture is widespread and of long standing. The attitudes of mind involved are related to religion and politics and are much charged with emotion.[11]

Such attitudes may lead to irrational beliefs quite unsupported by scientific studies, and practitioners in social work have not been immune from such beliefs. It is clear, however, that such a vital question should not be left to individual theorising, but should be decided by reference to factual studies.

A survey of scientific work over the years shows that the evidence[12, 13] at first available suggested that heredity was of prime importance in human affairs. This was followed by evidence [14, 15, 16, 17, 18, 19, 20, 21, 22] which showed the influence of environment however to alter apparent intelligence and to precipitate those potentially liable to psychological disturbance into maladjustment. Mendelian laws though making prediction possible in animals have not proved so widely applicable to man. The consensus of opinion now is that 'the relative weights of nature and nurture are still to be determined . . .' and that '. . . the greatest scientific progress will be made when the interaction of the two can be studied'.[23] It has also been stated that 'in any man or woman we see a body, mind and personality to the construction of which both environment and heredity have contributed their quota. It is impossible to disentangle their effects.'[24]

The importance of the complex interaction of these influences and the extreme adaptability of the human nervous system when compared with that of animals has led to the conclusion[25, 26] that differences in environment lead to greater differences in human behaviour than in animal behaviour. It is argued that the susceptibility of the human nervous system 'obliges us to pay special attention to the effects of environmental agencies in intellectual and emotional development'.[27] On the other hand Kalmus argues that from the study done by Newman, Freeman and Holzinger and from similar studies '. . . it appears that there are certain traits which are fairly independent of environment. These include the character and onset of a few diseases, some psychopathological traits, and special gifts and inclinations.'[28] Also psychiatric studies have shown definitely that genetical causes provide a potentiality for psychosis. Blacker, writing as an exponent of Galton's ideas, states the same conclusions but in a different way. 'The information at present available seems to justify the view that in respect of socially valuable qualities such as athletic skill or artistic genius, nature prescribes a ceiling and nurture determines how near to this ceiling each individual attains.'[29]

The concept of each individual having a particular potential, on which the influence of environment would play, was the standpoint from which the life histories in this present research project were evaluated. These histories were a study of social circumstances and environment and of attitudes and patterns of reactions to such circumstances and environment. The limitations of the study were that genetic factors were inevitably excluded and this was constantly borne in mind in the evaluation and assessment of each individual history. The fact, however, that environment is viewed as of special significance in influencing human behaviour gives theoretical justification for social research confined to environmental factors.

Principles of Social Casework

It is often said that what a person sees or observes in social research depends on the conceptual framework from which he starts. It is necessary therefore, to state the premises from which as a social caseworker, I approached the general question of research in child adoption, and the particular questions of, first, how to obtain access to suitable case histories, and secondly, how the interviews would be conducted and the assessments and evaluations made.

In social casework one is concerned primarily with the individual and only secondarily with society as a whole. In the relationship established between client and caseworker, the client, however, is never viewed as a separate entity but in relation to the context of his whole environment, familial, occupational and social, and to his place in society as a whole.

Social casework has, and has had, many definitions. These have altered with the passage of time and with the growth of knowledge of the social casework process, together with the gradual emergence of social work as a profession. The definition I find most appropriate is that of Swithun Bowers:

> Social casework is an art in which knowledge of the sciences of human relations, and skill in relationship, are used to mobilise capacities in the individual and resources in the community appropriate for better adjustment between the client and all or any part of his environment.[30]

Conceptual Framework

The emphasis in this definition is on 'skill in relationship', which, together with a knowledge of the science of human relations, make the difference between social casework and the giving of commonsense advice. This ability to establish a professional as opposed to a personal relationship with the client is in fact seen as the basic technique of the social caseworker.

Britton has described this professional relationship as providing . . . 'a reliable medium within which people can find themselves, or that bit of themselves, which they are uncertain about'.[31] The caseworker is reliable, first in time, and secondly in place, in that he or she is available at a specific place, social agency, hospital, or the like. He or she is also reliable in being always consistent in his attitude to the client and in retaining a clear idea of the client without confusing him with others. Finally the caseworker is reliable in holding the difficult situation which brought the client to the caseworker, by tolerating it and by not becoming emotionally involved in it as the client is, and by giving support to the client in it, until he either finds a way through it or comes to tolerate it himself. Britton makes the further pertinent point that in such a professional relationship, time is also important in that it sets a limit to the duration of the relationship. It is not a relationship for life, as a personal relationship may be, and so the client or patient is, as she describes it, '. . . more free to make demands on us and express his feelings'.[32] This is very relevant as far as this research is concerned and partly explains why those interviewed were able to give such depth of information and to reveal so frankly their feelings, positive and negative, about the adoption situation, both without embarrassment and in most cases without marked feelings of disloyalty to the people who had brought them up.

Underlying the process of social casework as so defined, there are certain principles and assumptions. First of these is the principle of complete acceptance of the patient or client, acceptance in the sense of lack of judgement or moralising. His actions may not be approved of by the community in which he lives, nor by the client or the patient himself, nor by the caseworker when viewed against the standards she has for herself. This, however, does not affect her complete acceptance of the patient as a person, nor her ability to show that she understands why he may have acted in an anti-social way.

The second principle is that of self-determination for the client; that is, that the conduct of his own affairs, which should include consideration of the rights and needs of others, is ultimately his own responsibility. The caseworker, in letting him talk about his problems, can help him to see the realities of his situation and he can then arrive at his own solution. As stated by Hollis,[33] the assumptions behind this principle of self-determination are as follows: that a person is more likely to act wisely and in the best interests of others when he understands himself and others; and that the strongest, and therefore most permanent, growth comes from within the person himself. He will gain in strength by making his own decisions whereas a decision imposed upon him by another may lessen his ability for independent action. Also linked with this principle of self-determination, is the assertion, first enunciated by Freud, but now generally accepted, 'that human nature can master the most distressing facts and the most appalling calamities if it is helped squarely to face the truth'.[34] This latter assertion together with the principle of self-determination, although apparently not so applicable to research as to social casework in an active setting, proved to be equally applicable in research, and this was illustrated in several of the case histories.

A third principle is the responsibility of social caseworkers to use the scientific findings of other disciplines which also deal with human problems. Thus social casework has incorporated into its basic knowledge the now-accepted findings in the field of psychiatry, psychology, sociology and social anthropology. The acceptance of the existence of psychological and social laws has already been discussed. One of the contributions of psychiatry to casework has been the realisation that feelings are often mixed, or ambivalent. Clients, therefore, may talk and act in contradictory ways. They may show contradictions between what they say they will do and what in fact they do. They may also say one thing at one interview and then give a picture of feeling quite differently about the same thing at another interview. This point had frequently to be borne in mind in the interviews of this research. There is also Freud's

Method of Referral

emphasis on the latent content of what a person said. The social caseworker then must listen, not only to what is said, but to how it is said and in what context, as too to what is not said and to what is implied.

Social casework deals with individual human beings and is based on the 'belief that human life is precious; that the individual has the right to grow and develop and achieve the highest degree of happiness or satisfaction in life of which he is capable. This, in turn, we believe, depends upon his functioning at the height of his own capacities—intellectual, physical, emotional and spiritual.'[35] Also, however, man is seen as a social being and 'we believe... that there are inter-relationships between the well-being of one person and that of another'.[36] His needs then are as much to live as a member of a social group as to develop his own capacities, and his happiness lies in achieving harmony between these two ends, which are in fact complementary.

This idea of a person's potentialities becoming actualities is Aristotelian in conception, whilst the emphasis on man as a social being we can also trace back in our Western thought to Greece. The combination of this idea that man reaches his fullest possible happiness when he can use his potentialities to the full, and yet can also maintain harmonious relationships within himself in his need to be, not an egocentric, but a social being, as well as harmonious relationships or good adjustment with his external environment, is the ideal health towards which medicine in its widest sense strives. It is also the philosophical basis and the ultimate aim or ideal of social casework. It was equally the philosophical basis or value standpoint for the obtaining, compiling and evaluation of the case histories in this present research project.

2. METHOD OF REFERRAL

As already stated, the aim of this research was to meet and to interview adults who had been adopted as children and thus to build up retrospective life histories. A representative group of such people had to be interviewed, representing both happy and unhappy adoptions and also from all classes in society. One of the problems in research into any kind of family

Method of Research used in this Study

relationship is that it is always comparatively easy to get into touch with cases where such relationships have gone awry. They appear at various hospital clinics, courts, social work agencies, and such similar welfare organisations. It is, however, much more difficult to meet the family where parents have sound attitudes to the children's upbringing and where there is no obvious maladjustment. 'The obstacles in the way of making (such a study) seem generally to be regarded as insuperable.'[37]

It was realised, however, that these obstacles had to be overcome. Other surveys and research projects have sometimes used a particular 'population' within the community, for example, Post Office staff, army recruits, students, and so on. This, however, limits the study to this particular 'population'. In such a group it would also have been very difficult to ascertain who had been adopted. It was therefore argued that if a group or several groups of professional workers in the community, who were constantly in touch with people in their everyday lives, could be interested in this research, they could furnish introductions to adults known to them as having been adopted. It was important that the group of people chosen should know the adopted adult for a reason other than adoption, and that they should be in touch with all classes in society.

It was decided to approach general medical practitioners, for since the introduction of the National Health Service Act (1946) which established in 1948 a comprehensive health service for all in the community free of charge, they were now potentially in touch with every member of the community, and as a profession they cover all classes in society. There seemed to be various possible ways in which their knowledge that a person was adopted could arise. This could be because they had known the family for many years or had been in the same district for many years, or because this information had emerged when taking a medical history, or, as they were the family confidant, it had been mentioned to them by the adopted person or the parents. It was also possible that they would learn of adoption because of some upset arising out of it, but it was as likely that they would also know a group of adopted adults where there had been no such upsets and where they had come by the information simply in the course of their

Method of Referral

general medical duties, that is for a reason other than adoption.

The next step in planning this research was to decide how to define 'adult'. This could only be done arbitrarily by age, and it was decided that 18 would be taken as the minimum age. It was hoped thus to avoid in the main the upsets of adolescence, although it was realised there might be advantage in this respect if the minimum age were 20. It was thought, however, that medical practitioners were more likely to know of adopted people in their late teens rather than in the older age groups, so that if the minimum age were raised, it was feared that a large group of potential introductions would be excluded.

It is of interest here to note that Theis[38] also discussed this problem of age. She wondered how much could be deduced about future adjustment from the overt adjustment of those whom she studied from age eighteen to twenty-five. She made a comparison between those aged under twenty-five with those aged over twenty-five. She found that the proportion of those 'capable' and of those 'incapable' was almost the same. This does not prove that individuals will not show different degrees of adjustment at different times depending on the stress of circumstances, but it does indicate that differences in age are by themselves not significant, and this is especially so if evaluation is made against what could be expected as appropriate adjustment at any particular age. In practice in this research it was in fact found that most people interviewed were well over twenty years old.

The question next arose of how to obtain the active co-operation of general medical practitioners in this research. It was thought that there might be some reluctance on the part of doctors to cooperate in such a novel request, that some might be concerned about their patients' reaction to being asked to discuss their personal affairs, and that some might even fear that such interviews would be upsetting to some of their patients. It was realised that it would be necessary for the research worker to become personally known initially to a small group of general practitioners, to interview patients referred by them, and then, by a gradual process, and by using the experience gained by these initial interviews to approach an increasingly wider group. When no refusals were met from patients asked to cooperate and as experience showed that

Method of Research used in this Study

these interviews were not only acceptable to patients but viewed as worthwhile, it became possible to gain the co-operation of an ever increasing number of family doctors.

Ultimately with the active cooperation of the Local Medical Committees, their officials, and the South-East Scotland Faculty of the College of General Practitioners, all family doctors in the administrative areas of Edinburgh, the Lothians and Peeblesshire and the Counties of Roxburgh, Berwick and Selkirk were approached. This involved personal letters to 403 general practitioners or groups of general practitioners.

It must be stressed throughout that it was the willing co-operation of many general practitioners which made this research possible. Some not only arranged introductions but also talked to their colleagues and persuaded them to help. The effect of this widespread goodwill was cumulative and as time went on, referrals continued to come in. One doctor, for example, referred a case eight months after receiving an initial letter about the research. The patient had been ill in the interval. Another did likewise after a delay of one year and only after hearing that patients approached about this by their family doctors cooperated willingly. Others came across adopted adults in their practice whom they had not known to be adopted when initially contacted. The result of this was that when the project was finally given a closing date for referral, it was found that the total number of persons interviewed was 62. Of these 4 have not been included in this study; two were outside the area, and two did not come within the definition of adoption ultimately used.

Of the fifty-eight included in this study, 37 were referred through medical practitioners in the Edinburgh area, and the remaining 21 were from the county areas. The source of referral in all but 7 of these cases were the patients' own general practitioner. There were 2 cases referred directly to the worker by hospital medical staff who had heard from general practitioners about this research, and one case was referred by a health visitor who had similarly heard of the research. There were 2 cases where medical practitioners knew adults who had been adopted as children and who though not his patients in general discussion with the medical practitioner agreed to meet the worker. Finally, there were 2

Method of Referral

adopted adults referred by a general practitioner especially interested in this research who was not their family doctor, but where the knowledge of their adoption was community knowledge.

How the general medical practitioners and the hospital staff came to know that these particular patients were adopted was seen as important since this determined how far the group of adults interviewed could be viewed as a representative group —not a random group in the statistical sense. It was argued earlier in this chapter that general practitioners were likely to know of such adults for a reason other than adoption and that, provided their knowledge of the fact of adoption did not arise directly out of a problem or upset in the adoption situation, then it would be fair to assume that I had been introduced to a cross-section of adopted people with no particular bias towards happy or unhappy adoptions.

The following details show how the fact of adoption emerged. First, in 4 cases, the general practitioner or his predecessor had been the family doctor at the time of the adoption, 20 or more years earlier. In 3 cases, the fact of adoption was mentioned by adoptive parents when they first came on to a general practitioner's list and he had been getting to know them. Secondly, in 18 cases the general practitioner had been attending the adoptive parents or some other member of the family, other than the adopted person, when they were ill. In some cases the information about the fact of adoption emerged because of general discussion about family affairs, arrangements for the sick person, and so forth. In 4 cases, it emerged when the doctor asked specifically for a gynaecological history of the adoptive mother, and in one case when asking for a family health history because of an unusual medical condition from which the adopted person's son was suffering. Although the reason for the contact of the general practitioner with the family in all 18 cases was for a reason other than adoption, there were 4 cases where it might be argued that the fact of adoption might not have emerged unless there had been a family upset coinciding with the illness. For example, two adopted people mentioned their adoption when an adoptive parent had died, in one case confiding that she was not getting on well with the other adoptive parent, and in the other case,

Method of Research used in this Study

confiding in the general practitioner about how hurtfully he had been told of adoption by the dead adoptive parent. In two cases the adopted person's wife confided in the general practitioner at a time when the adoptive mother was being very importunate, but in both these cases what took them to the general practitioner was an illness unconnected with the adoption situation. In a fifth case there was the situation of a general practitioner being the family doctor to two families, and being brought in when a dispute occurred over the engagement of the respective son and daughter of these families. It was during this time that the fact that one of them was adopted emerged.

The third group, 10 in number, were those where the fact of adoption became known to the general practitioner when the adopted person consulted him about some medical condition. In two instances, this was when the patient was pregnant and in one of these cases it was the adopted person who mentioned adoption and in the other the adoptive mother when discussing the general care of the other children. In one case, a married woman, the reason for consulting the general practitioner was inability to have further children and a desire to become an adoptive parent herself. In another case the adoptive mother was asked about the family health record because the adopted person had developed pulmonary tuberculosis. In the remaining 6 cases, the medical condition causing the adopted person to consult his or her general practitioner could be viewed as partly psychosomatic and was in fact so viewed by the respective general practitioners. Thus, two were suffering from migrainous headaches, one from dermatitis, one from thyrotoxicosis which was not responding to chemotherapy, and two were viewed as hypochondriacal. When asked about their family history and about any anxieties, the fact that they were adopted emerged. In all these 6 cases the individual had had considerable difficulties in relation to his or her adoption situation.

In a fourth group, 6 in number, the information that the person was adopted had emerged when a history was being taken on admission to hospital. In 5 cases the adopted person was the patient and in one case the patient was a daughter. Three were admitted for gynaecological conditions and one

Method of Referral

for a pregnancy. The daughter was suffering from glandular fever. The sixth case was of a man suffering from severe asthma and the medical opinion was that there was a large psychological element in this related to his early history.

There was a fifth group, 10 in number, where information that the person was adopted came to the general practitioners through others working with him and with whom he had discussed this research project; for example, secretary, health visitor, midwife, and so on. There was one general practitioner in a small country town who was particularly helpful in this way and in fact 8 adopted adults were referred in all from this practice. In five of these cases, the secretary knew that these adults were adopted when the general practitioner had not done so, since they were so completely absorbed into the community, and in two cases she reminded him of adults amongst his patients who had been adopted. He then made a confidential approach to them all and secured their cooperation. In two cases health visitors were told by patients of their adoption when visiting them in connection with the birth and care of their own babies. In one case a health visitor, asked by a general practitioner if she knew of any adopted adults in the practice, indicated that she herself had been adopted.

Finally in the remaining 7 cases the information that these people were adopted arose in a variety of ways. In two cases this was very much community knowledge in a fairly small, close-knit community where both were fairly well known; in one case the information was volunteered to the general practitioner after he himself had adopted children; and in one case the general practitioner was also the adopted person's employer and had learned informally about her early history. One adopted adult was a doctor himself and in two cases the knowledge came to medical practitioners through more general social contact and through discussing this particular project.

In these six groups then, it is possible to see that by far the greatest majority were known to medical practitioners for a reason other than adoption and not as a result of an upset in the adoption situation. Although none were known as a direct result of an upset in an adoptive family, the case where the general practitioner became involved in the engagement dispute was fairly near this situation, as too, it could be argued, were the six who consulted their family doctor and the one who was admitted to hospital because of psychosomatic conditions. To counterbalance these eight where some bias might be seen, there are however the other fifty where the referral and knowledge of adoption arose in a way quite unconnected with adoption. It must be remembered too that this study did not aim at a random sample in the statistical sense. This study also did not set out to cover all the possible variations in the adoption situation, and in fact it was not known what all these potentially were. It was a purely exploratory study and it aimed at describing the life histories of a group of adopted adults, some of whom had been happy and some unhappy in their adoption situation.

As the interviewing progressed an unexpected problem arose as to which histories to include under the original label of adopted adults. It has been assumed that it would be easy to establish who had been adopted. In practice, however, it was found that there was a wide variation in the adoption situation and a great number of factors which could enter into this situation. Also it was not so easy to differentiate between the fostering arrangement and the adoption arrangement as it had been anticipated. The dividing line was not clear-cut and for those near the borderline it was often a question of differences of degree.

Arising out of the definition of adoption given at the beginning of Chapter One, the definition used when planning this research, there are then three points which should be made in relation to this group of 58 retrospective life-histories. First, from the definition it is clear that the Horsburgh Committee did not define adoption in legal terms. As the aim of this research was to study the inter-personal relationships and adjustments within the adoption situation, the legality or otherwise of the adoption was viewed as relatively unimportant. As adoption was only made legal in England in 1926 and in Scotland in 1930, anyone over twenty-five who was interviewed was not likely to have been legally adopted—certainly not as an infant. Statistics[39] show that the total number of persons legally adopted who were likely in 1954 to be in the adult age group (over 18) was 3268, assuming that the legalisation of adoption was carried out when the child was under a year old.

Method of Referral

There may, of course, be many where a *de facto* adoption had been given legal status when the adopted person was well past early childhood. There are eight instances of this amongst those interviewed.[40]

Both *de facto* and legal adoptions are included then in this study. Of the 58 cases interviewed 33 were *de facto* and 24 were legal adoptions. It might be argued that as the majority of planned adoptions are now made legal the inclusion of such a large number of *de facto* adoptions reduced the validity of this study as relevant for current practice. In fact, what has emerged very forcefully is that what is important in adoption is the emotional climate in which the child is reared. This in essence is not affected by the legalisation of adoption although there are some instances in the histories where particular difficulties and situations might not have arisen if the adoption had been legalised. These differences, however, are of degree and not of kind and are referred to and taken into account in the individual assessments.

Secondly, mention has already been made of the fact that the arranging of adoptions has now become no chance affair but a consciously planned policy. It might then be argued that no adoptions arranged by chance should be studied but only those arranged by adoption societies. In fact, however, it is calculated[41] that adoption societies even now may arrange only 35% to 40% of adoptions into unrelated families and until recently this figure was thought to be in the region of 20% to 25%. Many are still arranged by third parties. It is often argued that these are less satisfactory than those arranged by adoption societies, but there is no proof of this as far as ultimate outcome is concerned since full studies have not been done. Also as the aim of this research was to study the problems within the adoption situation, these were not likely to be different in kind in adoptions arranged by adoption societies or those arranged by other parties.

Thirdly, of the total 58, there were 6 where it was clear that at least part of the motive of the parents in taking these children had been that they were fostered for payment, and in at least two of these cases it was known that payment was made by a local authority and had continued until the child was 16 years old. In two other cases it was likely that payment had been made by the family of one of the biological parents but little was known about this by the adopted person, even when an adult, and in one case they had been quite unaware of it as a child. They used the adoptive family name and were brought up as if they were one of the family. In the remaining two cases payment had initially been made but it ceased in one case possibly quite soon after placement and in the other when the child was 9. All these 6 children continued to live with the adoptive family.

Initially it had not been intended to include in this study foster-children where payment was made but these six were introduced to me as 'adopted adults'. They looked on themselves as adopted and in fact it emerged that they could fall within the definition of adoption used in this study, i.e. they were brought up overtly as if they were the adoptive parents' children. In four cases they always used the surname of the adoptive parents, and the adoptive parents were the only ones they knew as parents. A more typical fostering arrangement, by contrast, is where the foster-parents are purely substitute parents, where biological parents may keep in touch, and the child continues to use his biological name. Only in two of these 6 cases was there some contact with biological parents but this was only superficial and infrequent. In the two cases where a local authority paid for fostering their inclusion in this study may seem to be stretching the definition of adoption rather far, for payment here was not made secretly. In analysing their histories, however, it was found that in some ways they faced the same kind of basic problems, although different in particular details, as did the child who had been adopted in the more generally accepted sense of the word. They were being brought up by parents who had not borne them, and yet whom they looked on as mother and father. They had no contact with their biological parents and so there arose for them too the question of how much they felt able to talk of their adoption; how much they wanted to know about their biological parents, and so on. It was therefore decided that, although for certain comparisons and classifications these six should be viewed as a separate group, when other patterns were being examined, they could be included with the other fifty-two.

Method of Referral

Fourthly, as this study progressed, there was one further slight change made in the original interpretation of the definition of adoption. Originally it had been intended to interview only adopted adults who had been brought up in an unrelated family as this was the type of adoption usually arranged by adoption societies and other professional social workers. Introductions, however, were arranged with eight people who it was found on interview, either with themselves or with their adoptive mother, had been adopted by a relative. In six cases one or other of the adoptive couple was a sibling of one of the biological parents. In five of these cases the adoptive couples were childless. There was little or no contact maintained with the biological parents and certainly none as parents, and the children were all brought up as if they were the son or daughter of the adoptive couple. In the sixth case, the adopting couple had other children and although they told the child of adoption they gave no indication that they were biologically related. In the other two cases, the relationship was with an older generation, that is, the adoptive parents had the relationship of uncle or aunt to the biological mother. These adoptive parents were not childless but they brought the child up as if it was one of their family. Again there was no significant contact with the biological parents. Here too it was found, on analysis of the histories, that these eight children had met many of the same kind of problems as those who had been adopted into an unrelated family. It was decided, therefore, that these histories could be included when such comparisons were being made and that where the fact of being related produced a particular nuance this would be noted and stated as a possibly modifying factor.

It will be remembered that it was hoped that introductions from general medical practitioners would put me in touch with people from all social classes and who in age were past adolescence. To illustrate the social grouping of those interviewed, an analysis was made of the occupational status at the time of placement of the adoptive father, or of the adoptive mother if she were not married. When the adoptive mother was a widow, the occupational status of her late husband was used. The analysis here was done from the Classification of Occupations[42] compiled for the 1951 Census. The groupings there used are

Method of Research used in this Study

described in subsequent annual reports of the Registrar-General for Scotland as follows: 'The five social classes are those into which occupations have previously been grouped in vital statistical investigations. Class I represents the professional and financially independent section of the population, Class III represents the skilled artisan and analogous workers, Class V labourers and workers in other unskilled callings. Classes II and IV are intermediate, comprising occupations of mixed types, or types not readily assignable to the class on either side.'[43] When classified in this way, of the 52 adopted adults, 4 had been brought up by parents in Class I, 7 by parents in Class II, 25 by parents in Class III, 14 by parents in Class IV and 2 by parents in Class V. Of the 6 who were being brought up originally as foster-children, there were none in the first two Classes; 2 in Class III, one in Class IV and 3 in Class V.

These figures for the group of 52 are of interest especially when they are related to the figures given by the Registrar-General for Scotland of live legitimate births in relation to social class. Stated in percentages of the total live legitimate births, in 1955, those in Class I (to the nearest whole number) were 4%, in Class II were 11%, in Class III were 56%, in Class IV were 16% and in Class V 13%. In the group of adopted adults interviewed equivalent percentages of the total were 8%, 13%, 48%, 27%, and 4%. These figures are roughly comparable, particularly so if Class I and II, and Class III and IV are taken together, a justifiable amalgamation when the series in this study is so small. When this is done the percentages of live legitimate births become respectively 15%, 72%, and 13%. In the series of adopted persons the percentages become 21%, 75%, and 4%. Thus there is a slight shift towards the higher occupational groups in the adopted series but in the largest group of the population, skilled artisan and semi-skilled, the percentages are almost identical.

It is not suggested that these figures are truly comparable since they refer to different years, do not include still-births and since a very high proportion of the adopted adults interviewed were reared as only children—possibly a higher proportion than in families of biological children, although there are no figures for this. Also the live birth figures are likely

Method of Referral

to be influenced by the differential fertility rate between different social classes, whereas the figures for adopted children will have been influenced by the different attitudes to adoption of the different social classes 20 and more years ago. These influences, however, will not necessarily affect the figures in the same direction.

In spite, however, of all these qualifications, the percentages indicate that this group of adopted adults followed fairly closely the pattern of distribution by social class of live legitimate births in Scotland for the year 1955, and so it can be argued that they are a reasonably representative group from the point of view of social class.

As far as age distribution is concerned, of the group of 52, 3 were under 20, 14 were aged between 20 and 24 inclusive, 10 between 25 and 29, 10 between 30 and 34, 6 between 35 and 39, 3 between 40 and 44, 1 between 45 and 49, and 5 were 50 and over. Of the group of 6 foster-children all were in older age groups: 1 was aged between 35 and 39, 3 between 40 and 44, and 2 between 45 and 49.

Finally when sex distribution is considered, it emerged that of the total 58, 14 were men and 44 were women. One can only surmise as to why this should be so. First it is possible that general practitioners were more likely to know of women who had been adopted as children rather than of men since daughters tend to remain nearer their parents than sons. There were in fact several instances of general practitioners indicating to the worker that they had known of adopted adults who were men, but who now were away from home. There was also a group of women referred where the knowledge of adoption emerged when they were having medical help with regard to their own pregnancies. There were nine women in this group and naturally there was no equivalent group of men referred. Thirdly, it is well known that amongst couples wanting to adopt children, a much higher proportion apply to adopt girls than boys.[44]

This group of histories then can be seen as fulfilling the conditions originally aimed at. They are not, however, the total number of adopted adults known to general practitioners in the three areas covered. For various reasons approximately fourteen potential introductions did not materialise. Two were in

Method of Research used in this Study

mental deficiency institutions and were of very poor intelligence. They would not have been fully able to cooperate in interviews. Three men were currently serving in the armed forces. In seven cases, three men and four women, it did not prove possible to obtain the person's cooperation. In one of these the general practitioner in error made contact first with the adoptive mother and it then became difficult to establish contact with the adopted adult. In one case, the adopted adult was willing to meet me but one of the adoptive parents objected. In only five cases did the adopted adult when approached directly about this by their own family doctor decline to meet me. In two of these cases the patient simply stated that they would prefer not to, and in a third case the doctor found it impossible to establish any kind of contact with this patient because of her withdrawn type of personality. Two others, both women, after initially agreeing to meet me, failed to keep their appointments.

From the details available about those whom it was not possible to meet, there seems however no reason to assume that they formed any kind of homogeneous group as far as adoption is concerned, with features any different from these presented by those whom it was possible to meet. The only possible exceptions to this are two. First, there is the group of five who declined to meet me. Even here, however, it is not certain that they declined because of some special aspect in their adoption situation. It may equally well have been that they did not know their general practitioner well or that they felt that he was too closely identified with their adoptive parents; or they may simply have been busy or shy or have preferred to spend their leisure time in other ways. Secondly, there are the two certified as mental defectives. The problem of mental defect and its implications for adoption placement policy is, however, a subject which requires a study of its own.

From the details already given, it will be seen that, although a great deal of time had initially to be spent in contacting and interesting general practitioners, this ultimately put me in touch with a group of adopted adults such as I had anticipated. To obtain these 58 histories it had been necessary to contact over 420 general practitioners. Although this may seem a large number of general practitioners, many such prac-

Details of the Interview Technique. Manner of History Recording

titioners were in fact surprised that so many introductions had been obtained. Many were also personally surprised at the willing cooperation of their patients when they contacted them about this. Each individual general practitioner effected these introductions in his or her own individual way. Some talked of me as a friend, others as someone writing a book, whilst others again gave more formal details about the research. They all stressed the strict anonymity for the patient and asked them personally or their parents for their cooperation.

3. DETAILS OF THE INTERVIEW TECHNIQUE
MANNER OF HISTORY RECORDING

In the initial planning of this research it was necessary to consider the various methods used to obtain information in social and psychological research. Various tests have been devised to assess particular aspects of total personality: intelligence tests, Rorschach tests, personality inventories, social maturity tests, and many others. None of these tests, however, give a total picture and most of them are now recognised as only aids to certain aspects of diagnosis. As this present study aimed to gain as complete and total a picture as possible of each individual person and their background, it was clear that no single test would give this. The idea of a battery of tests, even if this had been practicable, was also rejected, for these could have assessed only what had already been decided as important for the tests. Although, for example, it was aimed to evaluate a person's adjustment and social maturity, a test to measure actual social maturity would have little value for exploratory research where the aim was to indicate the causes or possible factors which had influenced the particular adopted person's adjustment or brought about his or her particular level of social maturity. Furthermore no test has been standardised in relation to the adoption situation. It was decided, therefore, to use solely a clinical approach based on personal interviews. Subsequent research studies[45] which have relied heavily on development and projection tests have shown the inevitable limitations of these for research in the field of adoption and have illustrated further the need for exploratory research to find out first what are the relevant factors in this field. It was realised, however, that in some cases where there was, for example, the possibility of poor intellectual achievement due to maladjustment, it might be difficult to assess accurately from interviews a person's potential intelligence. The practical difficulties, however, for obtaining the cooperation of adopted adults in order that a psychologist might test them intellectually proved at the time to be insurmountable. Also from detailed interviews it would be possible to assess if there were problems where poor intellectual achievement might be related to maladjustment. In the section giving details of the individual histories, it will be seen that problems of this specific kind did occur in two cases and it would have been helpful in order to complete the picture to have had an intellectual assessment by a psychologist.

In so far as the interview itself was concerned there were three possibilities. At one extreme there was the completely unstructured non-directive interview which is used in psychoanalysis and often in counselling work. All interviewing of this kind stems ultimately from Sigmund Freud and from his recognition of the underlying importance of unconscious motivation in influencing a person's behaviour and attitudes.

This kind of unstructured and completely non-directive interview would, however, for research purposes have proved very time-consuming as well as being confusing and embarrassing for the persons interviewed. The latter did not come with a problem which they hoped they would be helped to solve. They came hoping to solve some of my problems as a research worker and so expected me to have definite topics which I wanted them to talk about, or even questions I wanted to ask them. Also with no direction specific relevant information might not have emerged.

At the other extreme there is the rigidly structured interview, often based on a questionnaire. This has been used a great deal in social research and in mass surveys. In fact . . . 'the major effort in the design of interviews, throughout the world, has gone into the devising of means whereby interviewing can be transformed into a routine task, to be carried out by highly trained but not necessarily creative workers. For some purposes it can be fully mechanised, and is then known as a questionnaire'.[46] A choice, however, has to be made between richness

Details of the Interview Technique. Manner of History Recording

or depth of data and quantity of data. The questionnaire method has value for the latter, but it has very severe limitations and dangers for the former. It is inevitably limited to facts and it cannot assess subtle opinions or attitudes, or the complex interactions of family relationships.

A form of interview between the two extremes described was seen as desirable. It is called in sociological books the 'guided' or the 'focused interview'.[47, 48] This in fact is basically similar to the type of interview generally advocated in social casework, but modified or structured to suit research purposes. In brief, this meant that in such interviews I encouraged the persons interviewed to talk about their adoption situation, early life, and so on, in their own way, but I had in mind various areas which I wished to cover with them and so, where necessary, I would guide the interview to keep it relevant. I aimed to have at least two interviews with each person and any areas not covered in one interview could be introduced in a second or subsequent interview. A tentative 'interview guide' was drawn up to cover the areas of enquiry which my previous experience of adoption had led me to surmise would be significant. No definite hypotheses, however, were made about this since there was no previous research or knowledge on which to base these. As the interviewing proceeded new areas were added to this guide. These were to cover aspects of the adoption situation which emerged as important to the individual adopted person but which had not originally been conceived as important.

Guidance and direction in the interview were, however, at a minimum, since non-direction 'gives the subject an opportunity to express himself about matters of central significance to him rather than those presumed to be important by the interviewer'. 'Furthermore it permits subjects' responses to be placed in their proper context rather than forced into the framework which the interviewer considers appropriate.'[49] In this way the latent content of what is said and the possible substitution of one thing for another, as discussed earlier in this chapter, can be evaluated. Experience too has shown that ordinarily an informant is much more articulate and expressive in a non-directive interview than in an extremely directive one. The focused interview, with its interview guide in the background, has also great advantage over a completely un-

Method of Research used in this Study

structured interview, in that the interview can be kept within the bounds of relevance and prevented from wandering into unproductive digressions.

Although non-direction was the guiding principle, this does not mean that no questions were used. Garrett writing on this said: 'Perhaps the central method of interviewing is the fine art of questioning.'[50] The method in casework, she argued, is that of friendliness, of asking questions in order to understand and to be of assistance. The same method was used in this research. The questions were asked in such a way as to indicate that there was concern fully to understand the adopted person.

The type of question used is of great importance in all history taking and it is especially important in research where an accurate and precise picture must be obtained. Merton and Kendall advocated the 'unstructured' question. Sociologists and others involved in interviewing would call this 'the open question'.[51] This means that questions are framed in such a way that they invite comments from the subject on any aspect of the particular situation being examined. Thus they give the subject the opening to reply, not simply in the affirmative or negative, but in any number of possible ways ranged between these. Questioning must also be framed in such a way as to be completely non-committal as to the interviewer's own attitude. In this way any possibility is avoided that the subject will give an answer which he or she feels would please the interviewer or be what the latter was expecting to hear.

When more specific detail about any particular aspect was desired and such an open question did not elicit further information, there were several alternatives available. First, that area could be left aside for the time being and later, either in the same interview, or in a subsequent one, the subject's responses, as far as they had emerged could be represented to him. This in itself often encouraged further detail and comment, without any further questions being asked. Secondly, another method of arriving at more specific detail was to frame questions in such a way as to give a wide range of alternatives. Thirdly, a 'provocative statement' could be used. This usually took the form of a statement of what someone else who had been interviewed had said about a particular

Details of the Interview Technique. Manner of History Recording
aspect of the adoption situation. This was then followed with: 'What would you think or feel about this?' or 'What would you advise?' Whichever method was used depended on the interviewer's assessment of the interview at the time, and how the person being interviewed was responding. The interviewer was always on the alert not to force the pace of the interview, that is to say not to force the subject into giving detail which he was not ready to give at that particular stage in his relationship with the interviewer.

Occasionally the person interviewed reversed the rôles and would ask: 'What do you feel about this?' or 'What would you do?' This could indicate that this was an area highly charged with emotion for them and the interviewer then had to assess whether they were ready to go on talking about this, or whether this was an area to return to at some future date. Where direct advice was asked for, this was initially referred back as a question to the client. Where however it became clear that there was in fact a problem underlying such a question this was discussed with the general medical practitioner.

In the same way, silence, the refusal to pick up questions put by the interviewer, or a sudden change of topic, could all equally well indicate the presence of an emotional blockage. Here again an assessment had to be made of why the person had fallen silent or changed the subject, whether there was a straightforward reason for this, or whether it indicated reluctance to pursue discussion in that area.

In all such interviewing, starting from the premise that human individuality is to be respected, one always had to keep in mind that, although one was seeking information and guidance to avoid potential problems in the future, this information must never be obtained at the expense of damaging anyone with whom one was in contact. It was thus accepted that there might be areas in particular cases where one would have to be content with clues from what was said or from what was not said, rather than insist on complete details.

In building up a retrospective life history, not only were details needed of what the subject remembered as happening in the past, but also how he felt at the time. To gain a picture of this often required that he be given considerable opportunity to talk around this subject and that the interviewer be

Method of Research used in this Study

alert to note possible allusions to it in other contexts. There was also in the retrospective introspection of many of the subjects considerable evidence of ambivalence. Contradictory pictures then were given at different interviews. These contradictions were recorded and ultimately an evaluation of them was made. Such contradictions emerged principally in areas highly charged with emotion, for example, the relationships within the adoptive home, the personality of the adoptive parents and the adopted person's feelings about having been adopted, and about illegitimacy. Here the technique was to get the adopted person to talk about various areas of relationships within the home, and gradually piece together the evidence, requiring proof from several sub-areas before arriving at any conclusion about the whole. It also became very clear that how a person had responded to a particular situation could be influenced by their previous experience. Thus it was not just necessary to find out, for example, how a person had felt when told of adoption in a certain way and at a certain time, but also what his previous experience or his preconceived ideas of adoption had been.

To obtain this kind of specificity, the techniques already discussed were used, the unstructured question, the representation of data, the provocative statement. The questions were framed in such a way as to make it clear what aspects of the total situation the interviewer was interested in, yet they were left 'general enough to avoid having the interviewer structure it'.[52] In this respect it was found helpful in obtaining specificity and in maintaining a good relationship to explain to the subject why it was important to have particular details. This was often done by telling him how these details related to the kind of problems which faced adoption workers or seemed to face adoptive parents.

From the foregoing details it will be clear that the kind of interviews employed in this research was of a very fluid and fluctuating nature where there could be considerable movement backwards and forwards from one area of enquiry to another. It was important constantly to evaluate the situation and pursue, or not pursue, cues and clues, as seemed appropriate, both with regard to their relevance and with regard to maintaining a warm and comfortable relationship between the subject and the interviewer. In this respect it is important to

Details of the Interview Technique. Manner of History Recording

emphasise, as did Sullivan that there is '... a certain important ingredient of successful interviewing which is frequently more adequately conveyed by gesture and tone of voice than by words. This quality or ingredient is shown by the interviewer's being keenly responsive to the needs of the interviewee, and doing nothing to lower that one's self-esteem.'[53]

These then were the general principles on which the interviewing was based. It remains to give details of how this worked out in practice. An interview has been defined as a process of human interaction with two characteristics. First it is between a client and an expert; secondly it is based on the conception of two equal human beings entering into a contract. In a clinical interview someone in distress or with a problem comes to the expert. The interview is both diagnostic and therapeutic. There is a two-way flow between client and expert. It is often argued that in a research interview, the flow is all from the side of the client. Bowlby[54] and others contend however that in research to arrive at relevant data an interview must be potentially therapeutic. The experience of this research indicates that this need not necessarily be so, for it was not simply interviewees who had met problems in the adoption situation who were willing to cooperate, nor was it only in interviews with such people that relevant depth of detail was obtained. One can only assume that, on the whole, when asked for their advice or to make a worthwhile contribution, people are very willing to do this. This was borne out by the comments of those interviewed. In two cases it was clear that the interview, aimed as it was purely at research, did in fact have a therapeutic value for the interviewee. This, together with the fact that only 3 out of the 58 declined or failed to keep an appointment for a subsequent interview, and in all 3 cases there was enough reason[55] for this failure quite apart from the interviewing process itself, indicates that research interviewing along the lines already described can also be 'a contract between equals', where the interviewed feels that the experience is at least a positive one for him.

The first practical step in the interviewing part of this research was to draw up the interview guide, already mentioned. The main areas covered were as follows. First, about the subject himself, his early history up to age five, school record, work record, health record, social relationships and interests, details of marriage and of children. Secondly, about the adoptive parents, their early history, education, work, health, religious denomination, personality and interests, age at marriage, and when they adopted, together with any information available about their inability to bear children. Thirdly, about the relationships within the adoptive home, between the two parents, between the parents and the adopted child, and other siblings. Fourthly, about the adoption situation itself, the adoptive parents' reasons for adopting, when and how the child was told, or found out, about its adoption, how much information the child wanted to have, attitudes to and details of biological parents, attitude to discussion of adoption with others, and any relevant information about the legalisation of adoption.

Various factors which emerged as important for individual adopted adults were added to this list. Thus it became necessary to include details of relatives and their attitudes to the adopted person. The inability of some adoptive mothers to admit even in some cases to themselves that they had not given birth to the child led back to a more detailed study of the personality of these mothers. After an analysis of the first ten histories and again after an analysis of twenty histories, other areas emerged as important. An example of this was the apparent inability of children to ask their adoptive parents for details about their adoption even if they wanted these. This led to a more detailed examination of the adoptive parents' attitude to talking about the biological parents. The adopted person's knowledge of adoption and illegitimacy prior to knowing that they themselves were adopted, emerged as very important and so this too was added.

It must be remembered here that, although it was possible to maintain contact with these adopted adults over a period of a few months, when viewed against their total life histories, this research was a study of their adoption situation at one point in time. Thus details of their early history could be obtained only in so far as they remembered these or had been told of them. In the same way it was not always possible to obtain details of the adoptive parents' early history, their motives in adopting, the reasons for the lack of biological

Details of the Interview Technique. Manner of History Recording

children, and other information of a very intimate nature. Much, however, could be gleaned about these from the details given about parental attitudes in general, and it was also possible here, in some instances, to obtain confirmation of specific impressions from the family doctor. In 7 cases too it was possible to meet the adoptive mother, in 2 both father and mother, and in 1 an older adoptive sister. In this way some further details were added and some interesting information emerged on the question of telling the child of its adoption.

A further point about this research, as a study at a point in time, was that, although details frequently emerged about biological parents and about how the adoption was arranged, these details were not followed up nor was an attempt made to obtain further information from official records and the like. The reasons for this were threefold. First, the scope of this research had been defined as adoption as viewed by those who were adopted, and the limit had been set of studying principally environmental factors. Although some relevant information might have emerged in individual cases, it was unlikely that enough would have emerged to make an assessment possible of familial level of achievement, social circumstances and so forth. Secondly, even if it had been decided to extend the scope of this study, by attempting to obtain some information from official sources there would still have been a group of 11 where no such information could have been obtained, since the adopted adults themselves had no factual information about their biological parents or how their adoption had been arranged. Finally and most importantly, such enquiries could only have been made with the adopted persons' full permission and to suggest making such enquiries might have been disturbing to many of them. This indicates clearly how social research, because it studies fellow human beings, must inevitably have ethical standards in a way not implicit in the actual gathering of data in the physical sciences.

The length of interviews varied greatly. These lasted anything from forty minutes or an hour to 3 hours, depending, first, on how complicated were the details of the adoption situation, and secondly, on how long it took to establish a sufficiently confident relationship with the interviewee to enable them to give depth of detail. It was generally found better, where there was

Method of Research used in this Study

very great detail, not to allow the interview to go on for longer than an hour and a half to two hours, but to suggest, at a suitable moment, that a further meeting should be arranged soon. In this way sometimes three initial interviews were held.

This leads to the question of note-taking during the interview. Some writers, for example, Madge,[56] consider that in taking notes at the time there is at least the advantage of speed and accuracy. Sullivan, as a clinician, however wrote that the interviewer, in his case the psychiatrist, is too busy concentrating on the flow of the interview to be able at the same time to take notes. He also thought that '. . . patients, like the rest of us, can usually talk with relative freedom if only their own and the other fellow's memories are later to be consulted as to what was said'.[57] He further made the point that in any case verbatim verbal reports do not give a true picture. One has to add the impression and expression that went with different statements, explaining why things were expressed in a particular way. There was no fixed policy in this study about note-taking. Where this could be achieved without upsetting the spontaneous flow of the interview it was done, but, without exception, this was towards the end of the interview. An explanation was given to the interviewee that it was an aid to the interviewer's memory to have a note of some of the salient dates, and ages, when particular things had occurred, and that these were important for accurate comparisons. In this way, the social data and the salient points could be recapitulated with the interviewee. This in itself sometimes led to further elaboration by the interviewee.

Immediately after the interview, the skeleton factual details were supplemented with notes on attitudes, reactions and the kind of detail mentioned by Sullivan. Where appropriate the actual words used by the subject to describe how he had felt were recorded, as too his behaviour and expression when discussing particular aspects. This total picture was then written up as a permanent record with the information grouped as far as possible under the various headings mentioned in the interview guides. There was, of course, inevitably overlapping between these areas. Any queries, ambiguities or contradictions were also recorded. A second and if necessary a third interview with each adopted person was usually arranged with-

Details of the Interview Technique. Manner of History Recording

in two or three weeks. A total of 136 interviews with adopted adults took place. In 3 cases, as already mentioned, only one interview was possible, in 19 cases three proved necessary and in 2 cases four interviews took place. In all other cases an adequate social history emerged as the result of two interviews. Where only one interview was possible the family doctor was in all cases able to supplement and clarify the background information.

From these two or three interviews, a detailed social history was compiled, grouping the material under the same headings as used in the interview guide. An assessment was made of the adopted person's adjustment to all aspects of his or her total current situation, including the adoption situation. In making assessments, proof was first needed from several sub-areas. For example, for assessing the relationship between a parent and an adopted child, it was necessary to know the parent's general attitude to the child at home, what kind of behaviour was expected of it, whether the parent was accepting, critical or demanding of the child, and what were the parent's attitudes to schooling, choice of occupation, friends of both sexes, interests and activities. Again proof was required from specific incidents or from discussion of everyday life before statements were made about the attitudes of others in the family and of relatives to the adopted person. About the relationship between the adoptive parents, an assessment of this was made only after there had been evidence to support it from various other areas, for example, the atmosphere between the parents at home, any quarrels, and about what and for how long, the ambitions, friends and activities of each parent and whether these complemented each other or were opposed and so gave rise to tension. If one partner was dominant at home, which one it was, and whether the other had accepted this, which parent had played the major rôle in the upbringing of the child, and whether both parents had the same ideas about bringing up children.

In assessing this and in assessing the personalities and adjustments of the adoptive parents, the details of their early histories frequently gave clues and corroborating evidence. Thus the mother who wanted a very close relationship with her adopted daughter and did not want her to have friends of her

Method of Research used in this Study

own age and grow away from the home in adolescence, frequently had had a very close and dependent relationship with her own mother. She became irritated and angry with her adopted daughter if the pattern did not repeat itself. The parents who were very strict about behaviour in the home often had had very strict and rigid parents themselves.

When such a detailed social history had been compiled, it was then sent in confidence to the respective general medical practitioner, and he was asked to comment on it and to confirm or otherwise the impression gained. He was asked specifically for details about the adoptive parents, if he knew them, their health records, occupation and personalities, about their inability to have children, if appropriate, and for his impression of the relationships in or with the adoptive home. He was also asked about the adopted person's health record and adjustment, about his or her acceptance and standing in the community, and, where this was not known to me, about the possible attitudes to adoption in the particular community in which the adopted person had been reared. It was also ascertained from the general practitioner at this stage how they had learned that the person interviewed was adopted, and also how long they had known the adopted person individually, or the adoptive family. Of the 58 interviewed, it was possible in 55 cases to consult with the family doctor or referring doctor about the accuracy of the assessment made. In the remaining 3 cases, this was not possible because of the original method of referral. In 44 out of the 55 this consultation took the form of going to see the family doctor for a discussion. In the remaining 14 cases, the general practitioner sent his comments by letter and where necessary, these were supplemented with a telephone conversation. In 11 instances there were two or more discussions with family doctors because of the need to have confirmation of additional information and in 9 cases the initial discussion was supplemented later by a letter or telephone conversation to obtain some straightforward, factual information.

The amount and depth of information known by general practitioners about individual adopted persons and their families varied considerably. This depended first, on how long they had known the family, and secondly, on how much illness there had been in the family. In only 3 cases, however, did the doctor say that he knew the person so little that he could not really confirm the detailed assessment sent to him. Even in such cases, however, he could confirm the health record of the adopted person, occupational status and community standing. It is interesting to record that there was no instance of a family doctor finding that the social history, together with an outline of the health record, as reported by the adopted person, did not correspond with his impression of the family and what he knew of them. In all cases the history was of course in much greater detail than that which would normally be taken by a family doctor but the end result corresponded to the doctor's general impressions. In 15 cases, valuable additional information was supplied by the doctor, particularly details of complicated health problems which could inevitably not have been given by the person interviewed. In the 37 cases where general practitioners knew the whole family, there were 13 where there were few problems in the adoptive home and the relationships between adoptive parents and adopted person were good. General practitioners here found they agreed with the impression obtained of the adoptive parents, and this was also true in 19 cases, where the relationship was strained. In 5 however, of these latter cases, the general practitioner felt that the adopted person, far from exaggerating the lack of understanding and warmth on the part of the adoptive parents, had made this appear less than in fact it was, out of a feeling of loyalty to their adoptive parents. The general practitioner's comments therefore high-lighted aspects in these particular adoptive homes which could only otherwise have been inferred. Now they could be stated confidently as facts.

This consultation with general practitioners as well as being a clarification and an additional source of information, had two further values in so far as this research was concerned. In the interviewing part of this research great care had to be taken to reduce the influence of the participant observer, and thus questions were framed to avoid implied bias, and evidence was collected from many areas before an assessment was made. With all this, however, these histories were compiled from retrospective introspection and so inevitably they were in part subjective impressions. Also although the interviewer had been

Method of Research used in this Study

objective in approach and had insisted on evidence for every statement, a certain amount of subjective understanding of people and human situations albeit based on training and experience had been used to make the assessments and interpretations. The discussion with the general practitioner, however, served to show that retrospective introspection, carefully recorded and viewed against the total current situation, can be valuable, factual and reliable. The discussions with the general practitioners also validated the worker's assessments.

Once the comments of the general practitioners had been incorporated into the social histories, these were then ready for analysis. How this was done in relation to the interview guide is discussed in the following chapter.

Chapter Three

DESCRIPTION OF HISTORIES

THIS chapter is concerned with giving a picture of the 58 histories in this series. First some general factual information will be given about the whole series and about the adjustment classifications used. This will be followed by a selection of actual histories to illustrate the adjustment classifications and the complex interaction of factors found.

As already mentioned, of the total 58, 14 were men and 44 were women, the sex distribution being exactly equal among the sub-group of six who are viewed as foster-children. Of the 14 men, 10 were married, one being a widower, and those unmarried were in the younger age groups, ranging in age from 18 to 24. Of the 44 women, 27 were married, and of the 17 who were unmarried, 11 were under 25 years old with an older unmarried group of 6 whose age range was from 34 to 60. Of those married, one man had been divorced and had re-married, whilst one woman was currently seeking divorce and was planning to re-marry. The former had had children by his first marriage, but none by the second. Of the remaining 35 married, 32 had children. In three of these families the children were adopted. In one case this was in itself quite unrelated to the adoption situation but in two cases there was no known organic reason why children should not have been born and in fact in one case a child was born exactly one year after the placement of the adopted child. In two other cases although children had been born to the marriage it was planned to add further children by adoption. This in one case was because of diabetes in the adopted person, but in the other case there were many neurotic features in the situation and at least part of this mother's apparent motivation was to repeat the pattern of her own adoption.

There were two adopted adults, married, but only for one

Description of Histories

to two years, who as yet had had no children. There was one adopted adult who had married only on condition that there should be no children, and this related to his own very unhappy experience as a child.

Of the total 58, there were two where it was known that, though not particularly promiscuous, they could by their behaviour have themselves become unmarried parents, and there were a further two who, it could be assumed, were likely to have thus deviated. All four, however, were brought up in adoptive homes where there was a great deal of tension and unhappiness for them.

The adopted person's occupation was classified according to the Classification of Occupations.[1] This showed the following distribution:—

TABLE I. OCCUPATIONAL CLASSIFICATION OF THE ADOPTED PERSON

Occupational Status	Adopted Adults	Fostered Adults
Class I Professional etc. Occupations	1	
Class II Intermediate Occupations	10	
Class III Skilled Occupations	36	3
Class IV Partly skilled Occupations	4	1
Class V Unskilled Occupations	1	2

Of the 58 interviewed, 46 had been born out of wedlock and the remaining 12 were legitimately born. This gives a proportion of 79·3% to 20·7%. Official figures from the Registrar-General for Scotland[2] show that over the years 1946 to 1953, the proportion of illegitimate children whose adoption was legalised in these years ranged from 80·9% to 76·2% for illegitimate and 15·7% to 11·7% for legitimate children with a small percentage where the status was unknown (8·8% to 2·8%). Of the twelve legitimately born, six were adopted because of the death of the biological mother. In four cases

Description of Histories

this was at childbirth, in one case when the child was 5 months old and in another when aged 2 years. Of the remaining six, two were adopted when the biological parents separated, and although in one case the parents returned to live together in later years, the child remained with its adoptive parents, since the biological parents had also neglected it. In one case, the biological parents were not caring well for the child, first because there were other siblings very near in age, and secondly because of poverty. In another case the biological father had died a few months before the birth of the child. In two cases it was not known why the parents had placed the child for adoption. In two of these twelve cases where legitimate children were placed for adoption it was known that the parents had been married for only four and six months before the child was born. This circumstance might account in part for the decision to place these children for adoption rather than that some other member of the biological family should undertake to care for them. A marriage contracted because of a coming child does not always have the support of the whole family.

There is also the question of how the introduction of the adoptive parents to the child and vice versa was arranged. Of the 52, there were 15 where it was known that the contact was made through some official body, adoption society, social work agency, children's home, hospital or Public Assistance Department. In two of these cases, the biological parent had advertised in the press that there was a baby for adoption—a practice at that time possible, though in the Edinburgh area controlled to a certain extent through the Public Assistance Department. There were 7 cases where the contact was made through some interested third party, one where a midwife made the arrangements and one where the contact was simply through an advertisement in the press, although in fact this adoption was made official by legalisation within two months. There was also a group of 18 where there had been some contact between the biological mother or her family and the adoptive parents or their family. Included in this 18 are the 8 cases where the child was adopted by a relative. In the remaining 10 cases it was not known how the adoption was arranged. Of the six foster-children two were boarded out through a local authority, and in three cases there had been a direct contact between biological and adoptive families, whilst in the sixth case it was not known how the contact had been made.

Regarding the age of the child at placement, there was a wide range from a few days to 4 years old. Of the 52 adopted children, 16 were aged 10 days and under when they were placed in their adoptive homes, 13 were aged 2 to 8 weeks, 6 were aged 3 months to 6 months, and 9 were aged 6 months to 1 year. One was 16 months old, one 18 months, one 2 years, one $2\frac{1}{2}$, and 2 were aged 4 at placement. There were 2 where it was not known exactly how old they had been, but from what was known it was likely that they were well under 8 weeks when placed and so this group could be viewed as 15 rather than 13. Of the 6 foster-children 2 were placed within 10 days of birth, one at 3 weeks, one at 2 years and 2 at 4 years.

An analysis of the family pattern showed that by far the largest majority were brought up by two parents and as only children. 45 of the 52 had two adoptive parents throughout their childhood, although in 7 cases one parent died while the adopted person was still in his or her teens, and in one case there was a change of father-figure at age 6 because of the divorce of the adoptive parents. In 4 cases one of the adoptive parents died when the child was under 10. In 3 cases this was the father and in one it was the adoptive mother, the child in this case being one year old. In this last case and in one other the child later gained a substitute mother- or father-figure through re-marriage or the amalgamation of two families. There were 3 cases where there was only one parent involved in the adoption situation. Two were widows. One had had one child of her marriage but had been a widow for 22 years, and the other had two young children of her marriage and had been widowed for only a few months when she took on the care of a year-old baby. One was a single woman in her early thirties who remained unmarried.

When other siblings in the family were considered it was found that the 52 could be divided into 4 groups. First there was a group of 29 brought up as only children. Secondly there was a group of 4 where the person interviewed was one of an 'adopted' family; in 2 cases the older of two adopted children, in one case the eldest of three, and in one case the younger of two. In all other 19 cases the family was a mixed one, in the

Description of Histories

sense that there were also children born to the adoptive parents. These have been divided into two groups. First, there was a group of 13 where the adopted child was the youngest in a family of other children who had been born to the adoptive couple. There were here, however, two instances where in the family there were also other adopted or fostered children. The adopted child in this group of families was anything from 23 to 4 years younger than the others in the family. Where there was a wide age gap the adopted child was in some instances brought up virtually as an only child. This was so in 4 cases. In one other case the adopted child was virtually an only child and this was where the other child in the original adoption situation had been a child of the adoptive father by a previous marriage. A divorce separated the adopted child from this sibling. For analysis purposes this child has been grouped with the only children. Secondly, the remaining 6 cases form a separate group, since they were either older than the children born to the adoptive parents, or they were in the middle of the family. Thus there was one adopted when the adoptive parents' first child was stillborn and they subsequently had two further live children. There was one adopted, where the parents thought they were not to be able to have any children and subsequently, 10 months later, a child was born to them. There were three cases where the adopted child was second or third in a family of three or four, and there was one case where a child was adopted because the parents had been medically advised that they could have no further children, having had three, and one year after they had adopted, a further child was born to them.

Amongst the six foster-children, 3 were placed at three weeks or under, one at 2 years and two at 4 years. In two cases the child was brought up by one adoptive parent, one a widow and the other a married woman separated from her husband. One was brought up as an only child until 7 when she became the youngest by 11 years in a family of four. One was the youngest of three adopted or fostered children and the others were the youngest or second youngest in families where there were children to the adoptive parents, aged 7 to 19 years older than the foster-child.

The actual analysis of the histories and the assessment of the

Description of Histories

degree of adjustment of the adults interviewed were done by breaking down the total information contained in each social history. Headings sub-dividing the original areas of enquiry were used for this. Thus on sub-division the area in the interview guide called 'Early History' became age at placement, previous experience, separations and changes of parent-figure, reasons for adoption, and how the adoption was arranged. The area in the guide termed 'Relationships in the Adoptive Home' was sub-divided into four: first, the relationships between the parents, secondly, the relationship between the father and the child, thirdly, between the mother and the child, and fourthly, with siblings, and others in the immediate family.

This was then further assessed, first in relation to the basic security and happiness of the marriage of the adoptive parents, and secondly with regard to how adequately the emotional needs of the adopted child growing up in such a situation were satisfied.

The area termed, 'the Adoption Situation', left purposefully not predetermined at the planning stage of this research, as it was important to have no preconceived ideas of what to include or exclude here, was broken down into 15 groupings. Thus under 'Factual Details', information was grouped under headings, such as, 'Reason for Adoption', *de facto* or legal adoption, contact with biological parents by adoptive parents and child at an age when the child could remember, official visits by welfare officers as they were recalled by the child, and whether the child was related. Under the wide umbrella of 'Attitudes in the Adoption Situation', there were sub-divisions for chronological details of how the adopted person was told or learned of adoption and his or her reactions to this, and for the attitudes to talking of adoption, first of the adoptive parents to the adopted person and to outsiders, secondly, of siblings, and thirdly of the adopted person himself within the family, to relatives and close family connections. There was a sub-division which gave details of the attitude of the adopted person to discussions about his adoption, first by himself to friends, secondly to strangers, thirdly to his or her own children, fourthly by parents within the family and fifthly by parents to strangers. Three further sub-divisions gave details of the adoptee's attitudes to the biological parents and the informa-

Description of Histories

tion wanted about them, of the adoptive parents' attitude first to the biological parents, to unmarried mothers, and to illegitimacy, and, secondly to discussion of sex, and to the adopted person in adolescence. Similarity or otherwise in physical characteristics and temperament between the child and the adoptive family formed a further sub-division. The adoptees' knowledge or experience of adoption before they knew themselves were adopted, their attitude to their adoptive parents and their comments about adoption in general were three further sub-divisions.

Finally, the evidence of how the person had adjusted, or the use they had been able to make of their respective potential abilities was tabulated under the following headings;—school and education, work record, health record, social relationships and interests, chronological history since adolescence and details of marriage and of children, and finally any deviations from the socially accepted norms of behaviour.

Of the 52 adopted adults, there were 15 who had a good adjustment in all areas at the time of interview and who had not experienced major problems as they grew up, either in their relationships in their adoptive home or in their adjustment to the adoption situation itself. At the other extreme there were 10 whose adjustment was poor or abnormal in many areas at the time of interview and where there was evidence to suggest that their particular degree of poor adjustment was of a permanent nature, and, from what was known of their total situation, not likely to improve in the future. They all had had problems with regard to relationships in their adoptive homes and with regard to the adoption situation itself.

There were a further 21 who had had or were having severe problems in their upbringing, related in some way to the adoption situation. Of these, two could be viewed as being emotionally free of these problems at the time of the initial interviews, and 8 others were at the stage of becoming partially free or more free as they gained in confidence and independence through living away from home, through marriage, or through the death of one or other of their adoptive parents. Contact two years later with two of these adults proved that this assessment of their being in a state of transition was correct. The remaining 11, however, were still tied in one way or another to

Description of Histories

the problems of their adoption or their upbringing, and it was not possible from what was known of their total situation to forecast with any certainty that with the passage of time they would become less tied. In fact in 7 cases it seemed unlikely that any change would occur. These 21 cases have been separated from the 10 others since although they had problems, these had not prevented a reasonable adjustment in at least some of the fundamental areas of their lives—their work, marriage, the rearing of children, and relationships with others.

There was a further group of 6 who came nearer to those who had no problems. There were 5 here who had dominating and possessive adoptive mothers, but who had asserted their independence and had coped with the situation without becoming guilty and uneasy about it. There was one whose personality was somewhat inadequate but this was comparable to her adoptive father.

To illustrate how the total 52 histories were classified according to adjustment, detailed case histories are given, in the ratio of approximately one third to each group. Thus 5 histories illustrate the group with good adjustments, 4 those with a very poor or abnormal adjustment, 7 the third or intermediate group, and 2 the group with a fairly good adjustment. These could well have been selected in a random way by taking every third history when arranged in alphabetical order. It seemed more valuable, however, for qualitative presentation and in order to offer clear illustrations, for a selection to be made of cases which would represent sub-groups within these main groups. Thus in the group of fifteen who had a good adjustment, 2 being men and 13 women, it would obviously have value for prediction if the history of at least one man was given and among the women if there were histories showing the adjustment of a married woman with children and that of a single girl. On examination it was found that there were 6 women, married and with children, 5 of whom had no problems in relation to the upbringing of their children, whereas, there was one who was meeting some problems and these related to the adoption situation. The decision then was to choose one history which illustrated the first group well and the one which illustrated the second. Of the single girls, 5 showed no problems of adjustment, whereas 2 showed some

Description of Histories

slight insecurity or tension. One history from each of these sub-groups could illustrate these slight differences.

In the second group, 10 in number, all with poor adjustment, 2 were men and 8 were women. The adjustment of the two men had many similarities and so one history is given. Amongst the women, there were 3 sub-groups; first there were 2 women whose whole life situation and capacity to lead a full normal life had been dominated by their adoption situation, and, although they themselves had remained relatively stable, they had never been able to develop their capacity for full normal living. Secondly, there were 3 unmarried women equally dominated by their adoption situation who showed obvious signs of maladjustment of one kind or another. There was a third sub-group whose maladjustment was apparent in their marriage and in the care of their children. One history is given in detail to illustrate each of these 3 sub-groups among the women.

In the third group, those with an intermediate level of adjustment, for the purposes of illustration, three sub-groups could be described. First there were 2 adults who were now free emotionally of the problems they had experienced and one history is given here. Secondly, there were 8 whose adjustment was apparently improving. Of the two men here, one is quoted. Of the 6 women, one is given in full from amongst four whose adjustment was being improved through the understanding and help of husband or fiancé, and one from the remaining two whose adjustment was apparently improving as they grew older, as they found confidence in their own abilities, and as they were able to move away from dependence on their adoptive homes.

Of the remainder of 11 adults, all of whom were still tied to or involved in the adoption situation, three histories are given, one to illustrate the situation of two men, both married, one to illustrate that of seven women, also married, and one to illustrate the situation of two unmarried adolescent girls.

In the final group of 6 (those fairly well adjusted), 2 histories are given to illustrate how a good adjustment was possible in spite of difficulties in the adoption situation, in most cases associated with a dominating adoptive mother.

Although the histories are thus divided into four groups,

Description of Histories

these are in no way to be regarded as water-tight compartments. The sub-groups too are only devices to group together certain similarities. The whole range of fifty-two histories should not be viewed as divisible in any quantitative way. They should be viewed rather as being on a sliding scale with the differences those of graduated degree. Some grouping of a mass of qualitative detail, however, is of inevitable value for presentation, although each history retains its essential individuality, and showed the complicated interplay between the various areas of the individual's total life situation and the great variation found to be possible within the adoption situation itself. Because of the need for anonymity, different initials from the original ones have been used in presenting the histories and later in the text they are simply referred to by number. Wherever possible details have been given in such a way as to avoid any identification of the individuals concerned.

Although these histories are viewed on a graduated scale running from good adjustment, to fairly good adjustment and so through intermediate adjustment to poor or abnormal adjustment, yet for clarity in presentation, it was found advisable to adhere to the order originally used in describing these different groups.

Thus those who were well adjusted (Group A—GOOD ADJUSTMENT) are described first, and those at the opposite end of the scale are considered second (Group D—POOR ADJUSTMENT), thus demonstrating the wide degree of difference in adjustment that was found to be possible. The third group presented are those in Group C regarded as showing 'INTERMEDIATE ADJUSTMENT', where the adjustment is understandably classified in a different group only when this is compared with the group who had a poor or abnormal adjustment. In the same way those cases described as having a 'FAIRLY GOOD ADJUSTMENT' (Group B) can be seen as falling into a separate group when they are compared with those who had a good adjustment.

The six fostered children are presented in a group by themselves (Group E—ADJUSTMENT OF FOSTER-CHILDREN). Of these six children, only one viewed himself as having had a happy adoptive home and even here his adjustment seems to have been a good one because he was very

Group A—Good Adjustment

accepting of any situation. The other five had had very unfortunate early experiences and in all cases their adjustment had been affected by these. To illustrate this group 2 histories are given.

GROUP A—GOOD ADJUSTMENT

Of the 15 who were well adjusted, two were men and 13 were women, and the age range was 55 to 20. Two were legitimately born and 13 illegitimately. Those who were married had stable marriages, and those with children were making mature and loving parents. They all had good relationships in their adoptive homes and with others in the community. They were competent at their work and happy in the occupation they were following or had followed before marriage, although it was evident that six might have achieved more in slightly different circumstances. Thus five passed examinations to go to Senior Secondary Schools but three did not take advantage of this and two did not complete the course. In one case the adoptive mother could not afford the extra expense involved, in another the girl had to leave school at 14, partly for economic reasons, and in a further case, the child was off school for about one year at the beginning of her Senior Secondary School education. Two others preferred to remain with their friends at Junior Secondary School. In a sixth case, inadequate advice led a girl of high intelligence to assume that she could not follow her particular ambition in a university degree course and she took instead a course at a teacher's training college. None of these six, however, had regrets about their educational achievements or were other than happy in the occupations they ultimately chose. Of the women, two were factory workers, 5 were shop assistants, one was a hairdresser, one was a clerical worker, 3 were shorthand-typists and one was a school teacher. Both the men were apprenticed joiners, one having also studied at evening classes. As far as health records were concerned, there were some problems of ill-health, but only two would be generally viewed to be associated with psychological factors. Thus one had had dermatitis when aged 12 and one reported that she was unable to have children without any demonstrable organic cause.

Description of Histories

The detailed history to illustrate the first sub-group, that of two well-adjusted men, is that of B.B., No. 43. Aged 31 and recently happily married, he was a competent and ambitious skilled tradesman, anxious to study for further qualifications. He had many friends and his interests were photography and music. He was a Church organist and played in a dance band.

Illegitimately born, he was adopted at the age of 8 months through an adoption society by a married couple of 29 and 37 who had been married for 5 years. The adoption was legalised formally when B. was 16.

The adoptive father had had little education but he had regular and skilled work as a greenkeeper on a famous golf course, and he had many friends as he himself was an expert golfer. His ambition, unrealised, was to become a professional golfer. He was very conscientious, thrifty and good-natured.

The adoptive mother, older than the adoptive father by 8 years, and whose previous occupation had been as a factory worker and assistant nurse, had been married before but her first husband and the one child of the first marriage had died. She was unable to have further children. She was a competent housewife and a warm, mature, easy-going and sociable person, being an active worker in her Church (Church of Scotland), and in the Women's Rural Institute. She was also an enthusiastic whist player and swimmer.

Neither of the adoptive parents had had health problems until the adoptive mother died when B. was 18, after an illness of 2 weeks, and until the adoptive father developed pulmonary tuberculosis when he was 51. He was unable to work from then until his death at 58 which occurred during the time of the interviews.

Finances were adequate when B. was a child although strained for him when his father was unable to work. The family lived at four different addresses but they were all within the area of the same country town.

The relationship between the adoptive father and mother was an affectionate and happy one. Each had their own interests but many mutual friends and relatives visited their home. Their general attitude was that life was something to enjoy and they wanted B. also to enjoy life. They were both loyal members of the Church of Scotland, but with no particularly rigid religious ideas.

B. was given emotional security and guidance by his parents but he was also given freedom to experiment and to develop along his own individual lines. He was encouraged at school, but

Group A—Good Adjustment

no pressure was put on him. His parents wanted him to have a trade, but he chose this himself. His friends were welcomed about the house, and his mother arranged many outings for him and his cousins and in the company of others of his own age. He was encouraged in his interests, for example, playing musical instruments. When in his teens he mixed easily socially, and was president of a youth group. When he chose to follow a different religious denomination from his adoptive parents, they protested at first but then accepted this.

His mother without embarrassment had given him details about her other son, born to her, but she did not talk about him in general conversation, nor were there photographs of him displayed in the house. There was no question then of the adopted son being compared with a biological son. All relatives treated him as if he were the son of his adoptive parents, and no comments about adoption were ever made by them. Although everyone in his home area would know that he was adopted, there were again no comments.

When he was 9 or 10, his mother, with his father present, told him quietly and without embarrassment, that he had been someone else's child and that she had been unable to have children. Though he had been someone else's child, they looked on him and loved him as if he were their own. 'I was her own little boy'. B.'s reaction to this information was to become quiet and to say nothing. He reported that it was not a shock. What struck him however was that the home atmosphere was exactly the same after he was told of his adoption as it had been before. It made no difference. He also remembered particularly and with pleasure his mother's final comment. His adoption was never discussed again with his parents until the request for B.'s cooperation in the research. His adoptive father had been anxious that he should cooperate. His adoption was never at any time mentioned to outsiders.

When aged 25, B. saw the documents about his adoption for the first time when his father, ill in hospital, had requested B. to bring a particular file to him. When B. was aged 26, a girl whom he had known for only a short time, and who came from another town, mentioned adoption to him. This gave him a surprise. He commented that he found it interesting to realise how easily such information spread, and that to have heard about his adoption for the first time at that age and in that way would have been a shock to him.

After this incident, it occurred to him to be curious about his adoption, but he would never have asked his adoptive father,

Description of Histories

since 'it would have hurt him'. If he had been really curious he felt he could have asked, but on the other hand he also said that he did not wish to know more than his adoptive parents had told him. B. told his wife-to-be about his adopted status. She had already known of this but had said nothing. She felt that had she been adopted she personally would have been curious about her biological parents. B.'s attitudes however were as follows: why should he be curious; he was happy with the parents he had; bearing a child did not make a mother; it was the parents who brought one up whom one felt were one's real parents. Evidence of this identification with his adoptive parents emerged when he recounted how, when asked for a family health record at hospital, he gave details about his adoptive parents, and it only occurred to him later that it was relevant to mention that he had been adopted.

He considered that only if someone were unhappy in their adoptive home would they want to know about their biological parents. He also commented however that if he had been offered information he would have accepted it, although he would not have looked for it. He felt that there was no reason to feel ashamed that his biological mother had not cared for him herself. It emerged that his adoptive mother had never been critical of unmarried mothers.

In appearance he was not dissimilar to his adoptive parents, but the question of physical characteristics had never occurred to him as important.

He does not care if people know he is adopted but he would not tell them unless there were some special point in so doing, as for example, when asked for a health record at hospital. He felt that it was best to be told of adoption but he would not have wanted his adoption discussed much. He certainly would not have wanted to be introduced as an adopted son.

The other man in this sub-group, *E.L., No. 23* presented a similar picture in so far as good adjustment was concerned. He had a good relationship with others and he was interested in and competent in his work. He was brought up in the middle of a family of three biological children.

The history of *P.T., No. 28*, is given as the first illustration of of the sub-group of seven unmarried girls in their late teens and early twenties who showed no problems.

P.T., aged 20, was a semi-skilled worker in a local manufacturing mill who appeared to have the ability to do work of a more skilled type. Although finding interest in the whole manufacturing

Group A—Good Adjustment

process, which was the traditional industry for her adoptive family, she was yet often bored with the particular process on which she was engaged. On the other hand, this work offered her good remuneration and so the opportunity to pursue her many out-of-door leisure-time activities with her several female friends. She had stayed at Junior Secondary School until the age of 16, preferring domestic subjects to going to Senior Secondary School although she had passed the entrance examination. She had no health problems. She had been engaged for three years, but had recently broken this off because of incompatibilities.

P., illegitimately born, was adopted at three months by a couple aged 34 and 35 who had married in their early twenties. There was a son of the marriage, aged $9\frac{1}{2}$, and a daughter had died two months earlier at the age of eighteen months. Another girl was born to this couple four years later. The adoptive father was a machine operator with a steady work record. He was a stable reliable person who had ambition to get on and to do all that he could for his family. The adoptive mother, who had also worked in the local industry prior to marriage, was also a stable, mature person, fond of domestic activities and centred on her family. She had died one year prior to the interviews.

Finances were always adequate and the home was a comfortable one. They had always lived at the same address in a small industrial town.

The adoptive parents were happy as a married couple. They were companions to each other, always going out together and enjoying family holidays and outings. They both tended to worry about the children but there was no question of curtailing their activities. They were all encouraged to follow their own particular interests and inclinations and each to have his or her own circle of friends. P. was treated exactly as the others in the family and she was encouraged in her many sporting activities, ski-ing, horse-riding, etc., although her adoptive parents had had no chance to do such things themselves. P.'s comment about her middle place in the family was that it was 'good to have one above you to look after you and one below you to depend on you'. She had a good relationship with both of her siblings. Her brother had served an apprenticeship, as also had her sister.

The parents were both members of the Church of Scotland and the children were sent to Sunday School.

All relatives completely accepted P. as one of the family.

Some time before P. was twelve, she began to wonder if she were adopted. She noticed that her brother was very like her mother and her sister was very like her father, whilst she was like neither, either in colouring or in physique. She was several inches taller than either of her parents.

When she was twelve, in a quarrel at school, a girl '. . . let me have it all . . . that I was adopted and so on'. P. was hurt by this and told her mother who spoke firmly to the girl concerned. Her mother did not tell P. whether it was true or not that she was adopted. It did not occur to P. to ask her parents about this. She was happy and felt her parents would tell her some time if it were true. There were no further comments at school.

When P. was fifteen, her mother and father, in an unembarrassed way, asked her if she would meet a lawyer. They explained that she had been adopted and that she could choose whether to stay with them or not. P. accepted this information and found that she was not surprised. While waiting for about a week for the lawyer to come to see her however she wondered what the visit would entail. (This visit was in fact in connection with the legalisation of her adoption and it can be assumed that the lawyer was the curator *ad litem* appointed by the court. Consent to the adoption would have to be given by P. herself since as stated in the Adoption Act, 1950, due consideration will be given to the '. . . wishes of the infant, having regard to the age and understanding of the infant'.)[3]

By chance, during the visit of the lawyer, P. overheard her biological name and thus learned that a person, known to the family as Aunt A., and who had visited them for years, was her biological mother. After she knew this, she was able to see a physical similarity between herself and her biological mother and she was able to piece together the story of her early history. Her biological mother had lived in the same street as her adoptive parents and her biological aunt had been a friend of the adoptive mother. When P. was three months old her biological mother had been considering placing her for adoption or in a Home.

For many years, however, the biological family had lived in a town at a distance of several miles from the adoptive home and contact had been maintained by three-monthly visits. P. and her 'aunt' had always exchanged birthday cards but to P. this was because, by a co-incidence, their birthdays fell on the same day. Aunt A. had never appeared more interested in her than in the other children in the adoptive family.

The family had not seen Aunt A. since P. was fifteen, when her adoption was legalised and Aunt A. had not replied to a letter sent to her by P. at the time of the death of the biological grandmother.

Group A—Good Adjustment

P. had sometimes thought about going to see her, especially after the death of her adoptive mother when 'everything seemed to be tumbling about my ears', She did not however go . . . 'well—because, she does not bother about me'. She said that if she happened to be in the area where her biological mother lived in the future, she might go and see her . . . 'but just as a friend'. She would not mention adoption and she would not be looking for a mother. Her biological mother had remained unmarried and had worked as an assistant nurse. (Throughout this discussion P. always referred to her biological mother as 'Aunt A.' or 'the woman'.)

P. stated that, had she not overheard at fifteen who her biological mother was, she would have wanted to know about her. She thought she would probably have been able to ask her adoptive parents about this, but she also wondered if she might have lacked the courage to do so, for she would not have wanted to hurt them. She considered that children should be told of adoption and that, had she not been told of this until she was twenty-one or more, she would have wanted to know full details of how the adoption was arranged, and of her biological mother and also of her biological father.

Adoption was never talked of in her home apart from the incidents at twelve and fifteen. Until the research interviews she did not know if her sister knew. She asked her adoptive father about this and he told her that he had told her sister when her adoptive mother had died. P. was certain that neither of her siblings knew who her biological mother was and she considered that neither were ever likely to think of this. P. and her sister had never mentioned the fact of adoption to each other. Her adoptive brother had told his wife about P.'s adoption, since when P. had felt that her sister-in-law had been jealous of her. There certainly was a poor relationship between them, with the sister-in-law being critical of P. This had hurt P. and her adoptive father was helpful and understanding to her here.

P. was not ashamed of adoption but she did not talk of it to outsiders, confiding only in one special friend and her former fiancé. She considered adoption was 'something personal'. Although she was quite indifferent to the fact that quite a number of people in her home area would know of her adopted status, she would not have dreamt of talking of it and in turn she did not want it to be discussed. She was happy in her adoptive home and clearly identified with her adoptive family.

The second illustration of this sub-group is *C.S., No. 9*, who was an attractive and sophisticated girl of twenty with a large circle of teenage friends of both sexes, interested in the latest pop records and in having as gay a time as any other teenager in a large city.

C. had attended a well-established co-educational and fee-paying school, where she had been active at sport, in the drama club and in the Girl Guides. Although she reported that she was in the top stream and passed her qualifying examination, she left school at 16 without her Scottish Higher Leaving Certificate. Her teachers had hoped she might become a teacher and go to Training College if not to University, but C. had periods off school, first, at eleven for one year with rheumatic fever and again when at fifteen or sixteen she suffered from insomnia. Her friends were a class ahead of her and so she wanted to leave school when they did. She attended commercial college for four months and thereafter had three posts as a shorthand-typist and secretary. She had some regrets about not having taken her Higher Leaving Certificate.

At the time of the interviews she was convalescing from pulmonary tuberculosis which had been diagnosed ten months earlier and for which she had had sanatorium care for three months.

C., illegitimately born, was adopted when 6 weeks old by a married couple aged 30 and 27. There was no information about how the adoption was arranged. All that was known by C. was the name of the town in the North of England where she was born. There was also no information about the adoptive parents' duration of marriage or about their inability to have children. C. was brought up as an only child.

Her adoptive father had a small business, which employed several journeymen, and which was financially successful. He was skilled in his trade and took some interest also in oil-painting and in ballroom dancing. He was a rather anxious self-uncertain man. Her adoptive mother, who had attended the same co-educational school as C., had been a milliner before marriage. She was a warm, welcoming, placid and tolerant person, again with an interest in ballroom dancing.

Finances were always very adequate with extra money available for expensive outings. The family had always stayed in the same urban area.

There was a good relationship between the adoptive parents, although temperamentally they were different. C. had a good relationship with her mother but a rather strained one with her father. She was at the age of resenting the fact that her parents 'fussed' her. As an only child and rather a spoilt one, she was able in most cases to obtain what she wanted from her adoptive father

Group A—Good Adjustment

by constantly asking for it. She and her adoptive father had frequent quarrels, but not more frequently than she found occurred between many of her girl friends and their fathers. These quarrels were never over major issues. C. found her interests were not those of her adoptive parents and she found her adoptive father rather old-fashioned. Her mother, however, encouraged her to have friends and interests appropriate to her age group.

The family were nominally members of the Church of Scotland.

The relatives all accepted C. and she was a particular favourite with her maternal grandfather.

C. said she had always known she was adopted and could recall no incident when she was told. Adoption was not talked of in the family nor with outsiders. C. knew only the place of birth and her age at placement. She was occasionally curious, wondering who her parents were and who she was, but she said she was not really concerned to know. She would never ask about her adoption or about her biological parents as, 'it might hurt Mum'. Also on the whole, she thought it was probably as well not to know about this, especially if the circumstances of the biological parents were very different from those of the adoptive parents.

Her adoption made no difficulties for her at school or with her friends. C. in fact never thought of it and so felt there was no need ever to mention it to people. The only exceptions to this were that she had mentioned it to a school girl-friend whom she had known since she was five and who was illegitimate, and also to a special boy-friend. The only occasions on which she had been embarrassed about her adoption were when she had to show her birth certificate for work. This certificate was an 'Extract from the Adopted Children Register'.

She considered that she was 'lucky in landing in the home I have', compared with what might have happened. She also considered that it was important for children to know that they were adopted. She wished that she had had a sister. It was clear that she assumed that she had been illegitimately born.

C. did not feel that she was like either of her adoptive parents. Outsiders saw her and her adoptive father as alike in appearance, whilst others saw her as having her adoptive mother's mannerisms. C. could not see any of these likenesses. She was amused by these comments.

From a brief conversation with the adoptive father, it emerged that the adoptive parents, and himself in particular, were rather anxious about the adoption situation. He reported that when C. was 8, she came home from school one day very upset saying to

Description of Histories

her mother that the children had said 'You're not my Mammie'. This gave the parents a shock. They had explained that they were not her real mother and father and had also explained about her adoption 'as nicely as we could'. (Specific details were not given.) C.'s reply to this had been 'Well, I don't want any other father and mother'. The adoptive father was anxious to know from the research worker whether, now that C. was older and able to judge for herself, she still was of the same opinion. The adoptive father, though thus showing his anxiety, failed to meet the research worker although C. and himself had agreed to this. When it had been diagnosed that C. had pulmonary tuberculosis, the adoptive father had been anxious about the possibility of inherited disease, and had talked this over with the doctors concerned.

It was clear that there was a certain lack of communication in this family and also a lack of homogeneity, which was not apparent in the other history quoted in this sub-section. This, however, seemed to be less a problem for C. than it was for the adoptive father, who, as a tense and anxious man, was worried about adoption and about his adopted daughter. It seemed unlikely that he would ever break through his own reserve to have a frank talk with her. It seemed likely therefore that he could continue to be unsure of his relationship with her, and so would tend to give her a great deal in a material way to compensate for his lack of confidence.

It is difficult however to separate out exactly how much of the parents' anxiety here was due to adoption as such, to C's illness, or to the fact that at 20 she was going through the normal developmental stage of wanting independence and of resenting the control of parents. There was evidence, however, to conclude that at least part of the father's anxiety related to his apprehension that, because C. was an adopted child, she might not be satisfied with her adoptive parents as parents.

C., though inarticulate about her adoptive parents, clearly viewed them as her parents. She had a close and easy relationship with her adoptive mother and there was no indication but that she felt secure in her adoptive home.

The other five histories in this sub-section present a similar picture of good adjustment to those just quoted. There were two, E.A. No. 2, and G.F. No. 19, who were particularly close to the first history quoted, whilst the remaining three, C.G. No.

Group A—Good Adjustment

44, P.C. No. 14 and V.O. No. 29 were nearer to the second quoted, in that there was evidence of some tensions in the adoptive family relationships. V.O. was an example of a child brought up in a family of two adopted children.

The third sub-group, that of five married women with children, is illustrated by the history of:

G.H., No. 21, a happily married, quiet and attractive woman of 29 with a daughter of eighteen months. She was a very competent housewife with a tendency to be anxious about her first child. Before marriage she had worked as an assistant to a dispensing chemist, having been to Junior Secondary School until the age of fourteen. She was very conscientious at work. She had many friends at school, and her own 'crowd' as an adolescent, and in this way she had met her husband. She had married at twenty-two and had continued to work until five years later when they obtained their own house. Her husband was in a minor executive post in a factory. She had had no health problems.

Illegitimately born, she had been adopted at five weeks through a mother and baby home, by a married couple of 46 and 39, who had been married for two years and who had no other children. As far as was known there had been no medical consultation or treatment about their inability to have children of their own.

The adoptive father was a semi-skilled factory worker with a steady work record. He developed a heart condition when aged 58 and thereafter was frequently off work for several weeks each winter. He died when G. was 24. The adoptive mother, a factory worker before marriage, was still alive at the time of interview. Both parents had been kind, gentle people, who were happy with each other and who were accepted in the community. The adoptive mother was prone to worry and to be easily moved to tears. The adoptive father was understanding of a child's point of view.

The family finances were often strained because of the father's ill-health. The family had had two addresses but had always lived within the same area of a small country town.

G. was encouraged to have as good an education as possible but the final choice about sitting for examinations was left to her. As she grew up she was given freedom together with guidance to have her own interests and friends. Her adoptive mother had herself suffered from a too strict father and she determined that this should not happen to G. G. was lonely as an only child and in her teens she noticed that her mother was too old to join in

Description of Histories

her activities. Her adoptive parents, aware of this age gap, would like to have adopted another girl, so that G. could have had 'someone of her own'. The father's ill-health, however, with the consequent financial difficulties, prevented them from doing this.

The adoptive parents were members of the Church of Scotland and G. later became a Sunday School teacher. All the relatives accepted G. as one of the family and she felt that she was. One uncle and his wife adopted a girl eight weeks after G. from the same mother and baby home.

G. was not dissimilar in appearance from her adoptive parents.

This placement, which occurred before the first Adoption Act of 1930, was made as formally as possible at the time of placement. It was subsequently legalised after the introduction of the Adoption of Children (Scotland) Act, 1930.

G. had no idea that she was adopted until she was eleven when in a conversation with a girl at school, she had referred to her mother. The girl said 'She's not your mother—you're adopted'. G. was upset by this and, on arrival home, told her parents, who also became upset. Her mother had said, 'Well, it may be so. But you're ours and we're your mother and father still . . . We have brought you up as if you were our own'. Her mother had also explained that she was unable to have children herself. Her adoptive father told her that if anyone ever said this again to her she should say that her parents chose her; that others have to take what they get.

When G. was 12, another girl did comment on adoption and G. gave the reply suggested by her father. The girl had departed 'stunned' and G. was quietly pleased at this effect.

About thus finding out that she was adopted, G. had been hurt by the cruel comments of children, and she felt that it would have been better if her parents had told her. It made no difference, however, to her attitude to her adoptive parents . . . 'still my parents, the only ones I have known'. Her adoptive parents had meant to tell her of her adoption but not until she was older. After the incident at eleven, her adoptive mother was reported as saying that G. had asked 'many awkward questions' about where they had got her and about her early history.

When G. was about fifteen she was given details by her adoptive mother about her biological mother. She was told that she was a school teacher whose parents did not wish the baby to interfere with her career (and so G. assumed she was young). She was also told that her adoptive parents had gone to a mother and baby home in another town to fetch her. The adoptive mother reported that she had always been afraid that the biological mother might

Group A—Good Adjustment

claim her back, and that neighbours, at the time of the adoption, had said she 'did not know what she was bringing up'.

G. knew that she had three different certificates and documents relating to her birth and adoption but she had never been required to show any of these for any official purpose.

Adoption was mentioned by the adoptive mother within the family when the subject occurred naturally in general conversation, but it was never discussed with relatives and friends. G.'s female cousin, who was also adopted, had always been a close friend, being G.'s bridesmaid at her wedding. Adoption, however, had never been mentioned between them, although G. considered her cousin would probably know of her own adoption and also of G.'s adoption. G. had told her fiancé that she was adopted and he had mentioned it to his parents, to discover they already knew. They had felt however, that it was for G. to tell him or not as she thought fit.

G.'s attitude to her biological mother was that she was glad to have information about her. She would really, however, have liked to know also what she looked like, what she was like as a person and what were her present whereabouts. Sometimes she fantasied about her. She would like to see her once, but without the mother knowing who she was, to satisfy her curiosity. She was certain her biological mother must wonder about her on her birthday. But 'the parents who bring you up are your parents'.

In the four other histories in this sub-group, a similar picture of good adjustment emerged although each had its own particular and individual variations. They were all competent women, happy in their marriages and in the rearing of their children. These were N.J. No. 22, J.H. No. 5, M.T. No. 34 and S.L. No. 11.

The history of the sixth married woman in this group is given since it illustrates how a person whose own adoption proved a happy one, was having difficulties as an adoptive parent herself.

C.H., No. 38, was a happily married woman of 46, who before marriage at 29, had been a dressmaker. She had an adopted daughter aged 9. She had always had severe dysmenorrhoea, but no other health problems, and no medical reason had been found for the inability of her husband and herself to have the children they wanted. Her husband, a semi-skilled transport worker, was like herself an easy-going person. They were devoted to each other and to their adopted daughter. Neither, however, had faced telling their daughter of adoption and they had no intention of doing so unless they had to. C. made it clear that she 'dreaded this'.

C.II., presumably illegitimately born, was adopted at 10 days straight from hospital by a married couple both aged 30 who had been married approximately one year. It was reported that the adoptive mother had said they adopted as she feared she was not going to have a family. Ten months after adopting C. a girl was born to the adoptive parents.

The adoptive father was a railwayman, who, after several years of ill-health, died of an intestinal obstruction at the age of 48. The adoptive mother became a domestic worker on the father's death. Both parents were people of integrity who had been very fond of both their children. They had been very devoted to each other having known each other since childhood. They had a pleasant social life with many friends, each being members of masonic organisations, enjoying dancing and the like. They were both members of the Church of Scotland.

Finances had been adequate though not abundant, until the adoptive father's ill-health made for some financial difficulties. The adoptive parents moved to a new area soon after they adopted C. and remained at this address until C. was 17.

C. and her adoptive sister were brought up as if they were sisters and, although different in temperament and achievement (the girl born to the adoptive parents had become an established civil servant), each was accepted for herself, and no comparisons were apparent. For example, they were each given music and dancing lessons. The child born to the parents was more successful in the musical field and the adopted child had success as a dancer. She ultimately became a teacher of dancing in her spare time. C. and her sister found that they chose different friends. This was accepted by the adoptive parents and each group was made welcome at home. Both parents took a share in the childrens' upbringing, and there were many family outings, holidays and so on.

Relatives always accepted C. as one of the family and treated both girls alike.

The child born to the adoptive parents had not married and she continued to stay with the adoptive mother. She was a reserved, rather self-contained individual, whilst C. was emotionally labile and an overtly friendly, easy-going person with a sunny disposition. In physique and in colouring they were dissimilar. C., however, in these could be seen as like her adoptive mother, whereas in both these respects, the sister was like the adoptive father.

Group A—Good Adjustment

C. reported that she had no idea that she was adopted until she was about to be married at 29, and her birth certificate was then required. This was given to her fiancé who was asked by the adoptive mother to tell C. of her adoption. This he did and the adoptive mother later asked C. how she felt about it. C.'s reply was that her adoptive mother was the only mother she had known and it made no difference to her. Her adoptive mother at this point had described how sad C.'s biological mother had looked when she took the baby from her. There had never been a further discussion of adoption since then. Adoption had not been mentioned to outsiders.

C. in thinking back, reported that perhaps it was a shock at the time when she was told of her adopted status, but she denied that it had worried her. Once she had been told of her adoption she could recall that, when she first went to work at 15, her birth certificate had been put in a sealed envelope, and, although at the time she had thought this rather odd, it never occurred to her to open the envelope. Even if she had thought of so doing, she would not in fact have done this since in her upbringing, amongst other things, the privacy of other people's letters had always been stressed. As a growing child, and as an adolescent, she had also noticed the differences between her sister and herself, but she had never thought of them as significant. After she knew she was adopted she saw them as due to the fact that they were not biological sisters.

C. was unsure if her adoptive sister knew of her adoption. She assumed she must know. She thought she could recall on one occasion that her sister had said to her 'You're adopted anyway'; but she was so unsure about this that it seemed that she probably wanted to deny that any such comment could have been made.

There had been no comments from outsiders about adoption. Neighbours of the family did not know of this since the family had moved to a new area when C. was a few months old.

C.'s stated attitude to her adoption was that she was not interested in how it had been arranged; there was no disgrace in it and no point in enquiry. 'To this day I don't know who my mother is'. When, several years after marriage, she was first given her birth certificate, C. had thought that perhaps she 'ought to look her up'. (Since this placement was made before legal adoption, the original birth certificate would give the name, address and occupation of the biological mother.) She had decided, however, not to do this, and she had never even looked at the address given for her biological mother. At the time of the interview, she could not recall what was on the certificate. C. reported

Description of Histories

that even if she had been curious, she would not have asked her adoptive mother. She would have left it to her adoptive mother to tell her.

A completely accurate assessment of this adult's real attitude to her adoption was complicated however by the fact that at 46 she looked at adoption also through the eyes of an adoptive parent. After eight years of marriage, C. and her husband adopted a baby girl through an adoption society after a wait of two years. C. wanted a very tiny baby girl, in order to know that she had done everything for her, and thus feel that the child was her own. C. also wanted everything to be as like her own adoption as possible. She had therefore not told her daughter that she was adopted and she only would do so if her daughter asked directly. The subject of adoption had already appeared several times on television, but her daughter did not seem to have noticed this, and C. had avoided using the word. C. felt that she could never introduce the subject herself as she was so easily upset, and she saw no real reason why her daughter's adoption should not parallel hers. Although neighbours knew of the adoption of her daughter, C. felt she had warded against any comments being passed, by her request to them not to talk of it.

She realised intellectually to a certain extent that she was avoiding seeing the situation here but she also knew she would use her own adoption situation as her guide. Here in fact she became illogical. As an adopted child she had felt that any details about her own adoption and about her biological mother had to come from her adoptive mother. In her daughter's case, she again felt that any questions about adoption had to come from the other person in the situation, this time her adopted daughter. She did not see that the rôles were now reversed. She paralleled too her lack of curiosity about her own mother with the lack of curiosity she had about her adopted daughter's biological mother. She had seen the biological mother's name and address on the original birth certificate but had made no effort to memorise these. In fact, she wanted neither to know these details nor to remember them.

In all this, C. emerged as someone who was very accepting of situations and who suppressed what she did not wish to think of. In this respect she could be viewed as not well adjusted, although in fact it was her way of successfully adjusting to her own particular adoption situation. It seemed likely however that in the future it would lead to difficulties for her, as an

Group D—Poor Adjustment

adoptive parent, if things did not go exactly as she had planned with her adopted daughter. That she herself reached the age of 29 without needing to be told of adoption seemed to have been the result of a series of chance occurrences. These might not recur similarly in the case of her daughter. C., however, would not acknowledge that there need be any difference.

GROUP D—POOR ADJUSTMENT

The second group of histories to be described is at the extreme other end of the scale of adjustment. Ten have been viewed to be in this group. Two were men and 8 were women and the age range was 60 to 31. Three were legitimately born and 6 were definitely known to be illegitimate, whilst in the tenth case there was good reason to assume illegitimacy. All the 5 who were married showed evidence of maladjustment in their marriage relationship or in their attitude to their children, or in some other way. Of the 5 who were unmarried, 2 had never been given any chance or freedom to develop their potentialities, and of the 3 remaining cases, one had a very abnormal personality and 2 were tense, nervous people unable to mix easily with others. Both of these last mentioned had had problems in their relationships with those of the opposite sex.

With regard to occupation, only 2 were happy and successful in the occupation of their choice, and there was evidence in all cases that their achievement or their choice of occupation had been affected by their unhappy adoption situation or their poor relationships with their adoptive parents. The two men had both served apprenticeships and one had gained promotion to become a colliery electrical engineer, while the other, after a period in the merchant navy, had also been promoted and was a foreman coach builder. Of the women, one was a factory worker, one a dressmaker and then a clerk, one a shop assistant and also a music teacher, one a qualified librarian, and one was a state registered nurse and a health visitor. Of the remaining 3, one had never been able to do full-time regular work but had done part-time work during war-time as a shop assistant, later working spasmodically as a seamstress. Another had been a nurse in training for a year and a half and then did voluntary Red Cross work during the Second World War, soon after

Description of Histories

which she married. The third had a domestic science qualification but worked only for a year and a half. After this she stayed at home to look after her parents' home for 21 years, when she became the proprietrix and then ultimately the manageress of a small draper's shop.

Only one of the 10 had had no health problems. One, though healthy in all other respects, had agoraphobia. Another had had severe tuberculosis of the knee, together with a phobia about birds. One man had had a reported nervous breakdown when aged 12, described as due to over-training for running for parental monetary reward. At 18 he sustained a severe hand injury which left a residual disability and so prevented him from enlisting in the armed forces. One woman had been a stammerer as an adolescent, and always had had severe dysmenorrhoea. Two had asthma and two had developed thyrotoxicosis in their thirties. In one case of the latter it was viewed as cystic in origin, but the other was recognised to have a larger psychological element in the aetiology. One woman was a very disturbed person, who had had night terrors as a child, a reported nervous breakdown in her teens, and showed marked hypochondriacal and hysterical behaviour.

To illustrate the first sub-group, that of the two men whose histories and adjustment presented many similarities, the history of T.D. is given.

T.D., No. 41, aged 56, was a foreman, intelligent and well read but slight in build, nervous in manner and lacking in self-confidence. He had left school at 14, not having achieved much at school. At 16 he had started an apprenticeship but went to sea a year later. He had intended making the Merchant Navy his career, and at 24 he had planned to go to nautical college. He became ill, however, with rheumatic fever at this time and he had also recently married. He decided to obtain a shore job and to finish his apprenticeship. He gained promotion at work and at 49 was promoted to the position of foreman. In this position, however, he had difficulties because of his poor relationships with others. At 55 he developed very severe bronchial asthma which was considered by the consultant chest physician to be largely psychological and to relate to his inability to cope with the responsibilities of supervising the men under him at work. He had difficulties also in his relationships in other fields. His first marriage ended in divorce and his second one was lacking in

Group D—Poor Adjustment

mutual understanding and sympathy. When at sea he had started to read widely and he now found satisfaction in reading and in having discussions with others on religion, atheism and the like. He was in the habit of using whisky to give himself confidence and to stimulate him for such discussions. He would not reveal however exactly to what extent he had drinking bouts. After the break-up of his first marriage he had had considerable recourse to alcohol.

T. was adopted when 1 year old by a married couple each aged 40. There was one daughter of the marriage, then aged 8. Prior to this and from the age of a few weeks, T. had been cared for inadequately by his biological mother's brother and wife, who were neighbours of the adoptive couple. His biological mother, a domestic servant, was unmarried. The adoptive parents, seeing he was not well looked after, offered to care for him permanently if they could adopt him and bring him up as a Roman Catholic, the biological family being Protestant. There was contact with the biological mother and aunt for about one year, after which the biological family moved from the area and contact was lost. T. used his adoptive parents' name and was brought up as if he were their son.

The adoptive father was a roadman in steady employment, a devout Roman Catholic of Irish extraction, who carried out his religious ideals in his everyday life. He had had little education but was intelligent and well read, being very interested in politics. He was well respected in the community. The adoptive mother's family was also of Irish extraction and she too was a devout Catholic. She was not intelligent as was her husband, being in fact almost illiterate. She was a competent housewife but had no other activities or interests apart from her attendance at Church. She had few friends and saw little of her neighbours. The adoptive father died when T. was 19, and the adoptive mother when he was 22 or 23.

Finances were always adequate and the family lived throughout at the same address in a small closely-knit country-like community near the city.

The atmosphere in the adoptive home was respectable and very religious and although the parents had quarrels they were not of a very serious or constant nature. They had occasional visits from relatives, all of whom accepted T., but otherwise few people visited the house and as a result the family was socially isolated.

His parents were kind to T. and he considered that they were fond of him in their own way, but he was very unhappy with them. He found he was temperamentally different from them and he felt this particularly in relation to their attitude to religion. He stated that he suffered from 'claustrophobia' whenever he went to Church, which he had to do regularly, and that he found that his parents instilled fears into him in connection with their faith. He was also sensitive that, being a Catholic, he was different from all the other children in the area and thus went to a different school. His reaction was to hate school.

His mother was very strict with him, using frequent physical punishment, and he found that he was 'checked and thwarted at every turn'. He was not allowed to play with the other children of his own age. The general tenor of his relationship with his parents was that he was 'to be a credit to them'. They were not interested in what he did at school so long as he behaved well, nor in what occupation he followed so long as he was earning. He had no real relationship with his adoptive sister, who was so much older that he had no interest in her. She was also very religious and a devout Roman Catholic.

After T. was 16 he was given a little more freedom and he began to have friends of his own age, all of whom were Protestants. He was ashamed of being a Catholic. At 17, he decided to go to sea in order to escape from home. Once he was away from home, he broke with the Roman Catholic Church and read widely on atheism, agnosticism and such authors as H. G. Wells and Bernard Shaw. He knew his parents would disapprove of such literature. This break with the Catholic Church worried him a great deal, and at the time of the interviews he still could not rid himself of the fears engendered in him by his parents. From 17 until his mother's death when he was 23, he sent money regularly to his parents. He was seldom, however, at home, and from the time he went to sea he did not feel responsible for them. Emotionally too, he made a break with his home, and from age 17 he felt that now he was on his own.

T. did not know he was adopted until he required his birth certificate for his application to the Merchant Navy. He noticed that his parents hesitated over this. They were both upset and his mother wept. He was given details about his early history and placement and he learned that his biological family were not Roman Catholics. T. was sure his parents had not meant to tell him of his adoption, as being illegitimate was viewed by that generation to be a disgrace as much for the child as for the unmarried mother. He stated also that they would not think there was any need to tell him, for endorsement of the birth certificate by the priest would make the adoption legal in their eyes.

Being told of adoption upset T. and gave him a shock. 'What

Group D—Poor Adjustment

I had been led to believe all along was true, was not true.' He wondered to what other things he had been told by his parents this could apply. He stressed such doubts as the main problem for him in his adoption situation.

Once he knew that he was adopted he could recall having heard whisperings from adults and children. 'Then what I feared might be true, was true.'

He reported that he had worried about all this for a time, but that once he got away from home, having new interests and activities, he soon forgot. He insisted that, in other ways, knowing of adoption made no difference to his attitude to his adoptive parents. This knowledge, however, together with the realisation that his biological mother was a Protestant, was one of the factors in his decision to break completely with the Roman Catholic Church. In fact it was this break which he considered worried him far more than being adopted, since he felt in making such a break he had done something very wrong. He was however very ashamed whenever he had to show his birth certificate (which would state that he was illegitimate), although he admitted that no one had ever treated him differently because he was illegitimate.

In his teens he was not curious about his biological mother and did not want to find out any more details about her—at least not sufficiently to take any action about it. He stated that if a person were unhappy in his adoptive home, he would want to get away from it, and not want to go and find another mother. He also considered, however, that his biological mother must have been totally indifferent towards him, since she had been unconcerned that he would be brought up as a Roman Catholic.

T. married at 24 and two years later, unknown to him, his wife traced his biological mother. T. stressed that he himself would never have done this. As well as lacking in curiosity about her, he did not think such an action was fair to her. His wife, however, was inquisitive. T. wondered if women were not more curious about such matters than men, and he considered that his wife might have wanted to know because of their children.

T. visited his biological mother several times and he met his half-siblings. His biological mother was more 'easy-going' than his adoptive mother, and she seemed to him to be a nice person though unhappily married. He did not maintain the contact.

T. had thought a great deal about how he felt towards her when he met her. To him she was 'just a woman, not a mother' ... 'The D.'s were my father and mother, even although I'd been told they weren't.' He was sure that it could be no other

Description of Histories

way for adopted children. It was the people who brought you up whom you looked on as your parents. He had, however, no feeling for his adoptive sister as a sister.

T's first marriage ended in a divorce when he was in his early thirties. This was a serious personal blow to him and he said, "I lost my head for a while'. The children of the marriage were looked after by his wife, but he had access to them from time to time. When he remarried (date not available) he did so on a very different footing. It was on the understanding that there was 'nothing romantic' about their relationship. There were no children of this marriage, and although it had lasted longer than the first marriage, there was evidence of constant tension.

T.'s attitude to adoption was that he wanted to be told of it and something of why he had been adopted. He felt very strongly however against any child being placed with any couple who would want to indoctrinate the child into any particular firmly-held religious belief. He thought he himself might have been able to accept the Roman Catholic approach to life had he been born of similar Irish parentage.

It is of course not possible in this history to assess exactly what weight to give to all the factors in the total situation. Although T. saw his difficulties as due to differences of temperament with his adoptive parents and also to their religious ideas, it could equally well be that his strong negative feelings about their religion were really an expression of his feelings against them as parents and that he projected these feelings as antagonism to Roman Catholicism. There is also the possibility that T. was already an emotionally deprived and insecure one-year-old when he joined the adoptive family, and, as already mentioned on the basis of Bowlby's thesis,[4] inadequate mothering in the early months may have permanently damaging effects on personality and on a person's capacity for good adjustment.

These considerations apart, however, it is clear from this history that the adoptive parents were far from adequate parents since they did not offer T. the basic requirements for a child—security, warmth and affection, and freedom with guidance to allow the child to develop its own personality. T. had always to be a 'credit to them', and they had adopted him 'out of pity' for his plight and not from a genuine and spontaneous love for children. They also conveyed to T. the feeling that illegitimacy was something of which to be ashamed and

Group D—Poor Adjustment

that they would want to hide this. The adoption situation itself created for T. the problem that if his parents had implied an untruth about his parentage, in what else in his upbringing by them had there been untruths. This too, could also have contributed to his revolt against Roman Catholicism.

Similar in many respects from the point of view of adjustment was the other man in this sub-group, C.McD., No. 45.

The second sub-group, that of 2 unmarried women who had never had any opportunity to develop their capacities for full and normal living is illustrated by:

T.W., No. 50, aged 60. Socially apparently confident, she now lived alone in a small comfortably furnished suburban house. She owned a small shop, and took an intelligent interest in the events in the community. She found, however, that because of her particularly restricted upbringing, she had never been able to use her abilities or her intelligence to the full. She had little schooling since from the age of 11 she was viewed as an invalid because of tuberculosis of the knee. Her parents did not arrange any alternative education for her, taking the attitude, as did their medical adviser, that as a girl she would 'just marry anyway'. T. greatly regretted her poor education. She was handicapped in many ways by her health record. From 14 to 16 she was confined to bed at home and subsequently used a caliper for a year. She then developed a chronic tuberculous condition, which was cured only when she was 30 and went to stay in a sanatorium in Switzerland. She had had good physical health since then, but continued to have a phobia about birds, with specific fears of feathers, this dating from her childhood before the age of 4.

T., presumably illegitimately born, was adopted when she was about 4 by a married couple in their twenties, who had married when they were 20 and 18, and who had no children. She knew that, immediately before this, she was cared for by an elderly woman of whom she was very fond and she assumed that she would be a foster-mother. She was brought up as an only child until she was 15 when her adoptive parents adopted a boy 18 months old.

Her adoptive father had a retail business, this being the family tradition. He was meticulous about all aspects of his business being unable to delegate work to others and his officious manner made him unpopular. His interests were in his business and in gardening and he was not sociable. He had, however, a sense of humour and from T.'s point of view proved to be more tolerant than her adoptive mother. He had suffered from asthma throughout his life.

T.'s adoptive mother had not had much schooling as a child and had spent 2 or 3 years prior to marriage training to be a dressmaker. She had met the adoptive father when buying materials in his shop. She had been given a great deal of attention as a child and was used to getting her own way, and this continued into her marriage. She was obsessional about the care of her house, about her clothes and those of T., and she was also obsessional about adhering rigidly to a particular routine in the house. Fond of social life and anxious to climb the social ladder, she had a circle of similar friends of her own, in which the adoptive father played no part. She was according to the family doctor a 'spinsterish kind of person of the type who are frequently afraid of pregnancies'. She had no warmth of personality and she was not motherly. She was reported as always 'delicate', but she was in fact hypochondriacal seeking frequent attention from her family doctor.

The finances in the adoptive home were very adequate and we can assume that the adoptive father was successful in his business since between the time T. joined the family and her reaching the age of 29, the family moved 8 times, usually to a larger house or one with a larger garden. The last two moves, when T. was 27 and 29, were to suburban villas built by the adoptive father. One of the early moves to a completely new area was timed to coincide with the adoption of the second child so that those living roundabout need not know that either was adopted.

Both parents were members of the Church of Scotland, with the adoptive mother being very religious and more active in Church affairs than the adoptive father.

The adoptive father and mother had frequent quarrels. The adoptive father was devoted to the adoptive mother and was dominated by her, but she resented the fact that he did not give her the social life she wanted. He also was lavish in giving money away and of this she only approved if it brought social prestige, as in giving to the Church. T. hated to hear her parents shouting at each other. She wondered if her mother regretted marrying her father. Their quarrels were less frequent as they grew older.

T. received a great deal materially in her adoptive home, such as clothes, toys and medical care, but her mother had no understanding of her emotional needs as a child. She could recall that at age 12 she said to her mother that she wished she gave her fewer dresses and more love. This poor relationship existed from

Group D—Poor Adjustment

the age of 4 or 5. T. was afraid of her parents and started to tell lies because she was afraid to tell the truth. She was punished physically for this, which made her even more afraid to tell the truth. Her mother became so distrustful and asked so many doubting questions that T. continued to tell lies to stop these questions. Her adoptive mother was afraid she would inherit a tendency to untruthfulness, and was, as a result, so very much on the outlook for lies that it seemed to T. that she was almost wanting her to be untruthful. A further confusion here for T. was that she noticed that her mother told lies about T.'s early history to avoid telling people that she was adopted.

T. was a sensitive child who disliked being talked of. Her mother frequently did this to her friends and if anyone commented that T. was well dressed or well mannered her adoptive mother would say that this was thanks to her.

Her adoptive mother was very strict with T. but not consistent in her discipline. After punishing her she would go out and buy her a lavish present as if from remorse. She also expected T. to conform always to her wishes in how she behaved, what she did, and what she thought. This in later years was taken to include even religion and T. was made to join the Church at a time dictated by her mother and not at the time when T. felt she was honestly able to do this. When T. was in her early teens and began to have ideas of her own, she and her mother came frequently into conflict. Her mother then stopped kissing her good-night saying there was no point in so doing if T. would not do what she wanted.

Her parents were not interested in her schooling or education and her mother did not encourage the interest T. found she had in politics and the affairs of the world in general. Later her parents could not understand why she wanted a domestic science training for a year. Her mother, however, gave her meticulous care when she was ill as a child. She was encouraged to have friends of her own age but her mother tried to dominate her as to who these should be, and her parents were always very distrustful if she came home a minute later than instructed. Because of her health record and absence from school, T. never had an opportunity to experience the usual group activities of a child growing up.

There were frequent quarrels in the adoptive home when T. was in her teens and early twenties. Her mother's distrustful attitude made T. very unhappy, sullen and sulky for days. She frequently threatened to run away, but this was to gain attention and sympathy since she found herself unadventuresome. In any case she had nowhere to go, and with her tuberculous knee, no training and little education, she knew she could not support herself. She often wondered how she would be able to live through this period of unhappiness. In these quarrels, her mother frequently said that she ought to be grateful to them for what they had done for her, and her mother related this also to their having adopted her.

In these conflicts her adoptive father was more tolerant than her adoptive mother, saying that after a certain age, a child has to make its own decisions, but in any actual quarrel he always took the adoptive mother's side. T., however, was fond of her adoptive father.

When T. was 19 she insisted on one year's domestic science training and thereafter worked in a Children's Home for 2 years. Then her adoptive mother said she was needed at home as she was unwell. T. felt obliged to return. She was tempted one year later to take a good post away from home which she was offered, but she felt that, although her mother was not genuinely ill and did not really need her, she was expected to stay at home. Thereafter she was used by her adoptive parents as the person responsible for all the house-keeping, but she was given no definite money allowance from her father. T. resented this and she was very unhappy at home. Her parents interpreted her desire to go to Switzerland for treatment for her tuberculosis as a desire to get away from home, and they agreed to this only very reluctantly and after many quarrels.

T. knew one or two boys when in her teens and early twenties and she had gone to social activities at the church. She always, however, had to meet any boys secretly since her mother disapproved of any such friendships. T. said that in any case she had put marriage out of her mind because of her tuberculosis and so she never encouraged a close relationship with anyone of the opposite sex. There was also some evidence, however, that she was influenced by her mother's extreme disapproval and her fear that if she had 'disgraced' her parents in any way they would never have forgiven her. Her adoptive mother used to say dogmatically that T. was certainly not going to marry at 18 as she had done.

The relationship between T. and her adoptive parents improved in later years once they saw that as an adopted child she was not going to do all the things they feared, and also when she herself, 'feeling so battered' gave in to their wishes. She nursed them devotedly in their terminal illnesses, her father dying when T. was 55 and her mother when she was 58.

T.'s adoptive parents were less strict with her adopted brother

Group D—Poor Adjustment

13½ years her junior. He however was also more self-assertive than T. and she felt he would have insisted on going his own way. He was clever at school, going to fee-paying schools on scholarships and reaching university entrance standard. He chose to train as an actuary, although his parents would have financed him through a university course. T. felt her parents obtained 'more pleasure and satisfaction' from him and from his achievement. He 'was more of a credit to them' than she was.

T. and her brother were completely accepted by all relatives on both sides of the family (being particular favourites with the paternal grandmother because the adoptive father had been her favourite child).

Though this adoption was arranged many years before it could be legalised in any way, the arrangement was a permanent one and T. always used her adoptive parents' name. Although she was brought up as if she were their daughter and although her adoptive mother took precautions to prevent it being known that she was adopted, T. never felt that she belonged in her adoptive home. She knew vaguely that she had another home although she could recall no details of it. She could recall someone elderly and of whom she was very fond, bringing her to her adoptive mother. When this person left her, she tried to run after her and wept bitterly.

When T. was 14, her adoptive mother told her that they were not her real parents and that she was adopted. Her mother also led T. to understand that she was telling her this in case someone else did. T. had said there was no need to tell her; she had always known; she had never felt they were her parents.

Adoption was thereafter mentioned frequently in quarrels between her adoptive mother and T., as . . . 'After all I've done for you' . . . 'You don't know where you'd have been if we'd not taken you' . . . 'If this is how you treat me, I should just have left you where you were'. To this T. used to say that she would have been much happier if she had. Her mother then said that she would not have been so well off, nor have had such a nice home. T's. reply was that she would rather be happy.

The attitude that T. ought to be grateful made T. very angry, and she was also very hurt by it. She considered it a dreadful thing to say to a child. She came to feel that her adoptive mother was not her mother and when she was asked by her to do anything, she felt "Why should I"?

She considered that her adoptive mother had adopted both children 'on the whim of the moment' and not from any love of children.

Description of Histories

The adoptive mother hid adoption from outsiders. She viewed the fact that she had not borne children as something to be ashamed of and she was always afraid T. would tell her friends. Trying to hide adoption led to embarrassing situations, such as, for example, when other women were talking of their pregnancies and confinements and the adoptive mother would not admit that she had not had T. in the usual way.

There was some physical similarity between T. and her adoptive father, and outsiders saw her speech and mannerisms to be like those of her adoptive mother. In physical appearance she was very different from her adoptive mother. T. did not consider that this question of similarity mattered one way or the other.

T. knew nothing of how her adoption had been arranged, nor about her life before she came to her adoptive home, except that she realised that she had then been in a much poorer home. She did not wonder about this period, nor did she ask. She considered that she was the kind to accept things, but she also admitted that there would have been no point in asking since her parents never answered her questions anyway.

During the years of conflict with her adoptive mother, T. felt she was not her mother. She dreamt of other parents and longed for a mother and father and brothers and sisters of her own.

Her adoptive mother gave her no details about her biological parents, but her attitude was that they had 'weak wills' (as unmarried parents) and so she must keep a close check on T. to see that she did not 'go the same way'. T. in fact saw all her problems in the adoption situation as stemming from this distrustful attitude.

Her adoptive mother and her particular generation appear to have viewed illegitimacy as a shocking social disgrace.

T. herself would not have dreamt of telling anyone of her adoption, since she viewed it as a very 'personal affair', but she was very opposed to the secrecy with which her mother enshrouded it. She would have liked it to have been accepted openly that she had been adopted, and then there would have been no need to talk about it. She certainly would have been cross if any of her friends had introduced the subject. Although she was against the fact of adoption being made secret she was opposed to the idea of frequent reference to it. For example, she would have hated to be introduced as 'an adopted daughter'. If this had happened she felt she would have been 'like a flower always being pulled up'; she would have had no chance to grow roots.

Group D—Poor Adjustment

T. knew nothing about how her brother's adoption had been arranged. Although she was 15 at the time she was given no details. She had never been curious about his parents. She knew her brother knew of his adopted status, but she does not know how or when he was told.

Her attitude to adoption in general was that it should not be made a secret but should be made known by the parents, as, for example, by a notice put in the press. Then everyone knew, and it need not be referred to in general conversation. She felt it important that both parents should be equally enthusiastic about adoption and that no one should be allowed to adopt in order to have someone to look after them. She also considered it was much better to be adopted as a baby and then one could not remember even shadowily an earlier home.

It is clear from this history that T. was not given affection and emotional security in her adoptive home, nor was she allowed to develop along her own individual lines. It could be considered that as she was not placed until she was 4, and had already built up a warm relationship with one mother-figure, such a change when placed in the adoptive home was damaging to her. Although her education was restricted, part of the difficulty here was her medical condition, which appears to have been acquired from a contact when aged about 9 or 10. It must also be borne in mind that many women of her generation who were brought up in middle-class homes were not offered educational opportunities, and it was automatically assumed that, if they did not marry, they would stay at home and care for their parents. It was also common not to give daughters a regular money allowance but to expect them to ask for what they wanted from their parents. It is clear that T. was not accepting of the dependent rôle which her parents expected her to fill. One might argue that if she had a different temperament, or one similar to her adoptive brother, she would have revolted and possibly left home. It could however equally well be contended that her circumstances prevented this possibility; first there was the problem of her chronic ill-health, and secondly, she felt an obligation to her adoptive parents, it being the social norm at that time for single daughters to stay at home.

The description of this history and of the relationships in the adoptive home might then find many parallels among single

Description of Histories

women now aged about 60, of good intelligence, who had unimaginative, rigid, possessive, dominating and unhappily married parents. Such women, however, born to these parents would not have faced several additional tensions which arose out of the adoption situation itself. First, there was the ever-recurring theme throughout this history of the adoptive mother's fear of what this child, illegitimately born, might inherit from its 'weak-willed' parents. This fear was a further factor in the adoptive mother's disapproval of T. having male friends and in her concern that she should always know where T. was going and what she had been doing. Secondly, there were the comments of the adoptive mother that T. ought to be grateful for what she had done for her. This might also be said in anger by a mother who had borne a child, but only in the adoption situation could the cruel comment be added that the mother ought to have left the child where she was. There was also the added insecurity that the adoptive mother might send the child back. Thirdly, there was an abrupt change of permanent parent-figures for T. when she was 4, as may arise in any late adoption placement. Fourthly, when T. was resentful of parental control in adolescence, a normal experience, she had the added feeling of resentment in having to do what her adoptive mother told her, yet knowing and feeling that she was not her mother.

The second history in this sub-group, B.Y. No. 33, showed again an unmarried woman, who had spent her life devotedly helping in her adoptive parents' home and who had had no opportunity to live a life apart from them.

The third sub-group here, that of the three unmarried women who showed more outward signs of their maladjustment is illustrated by the history of:

> M.M., No. 46, aged 36, a competent conscientious nurse, welll liked by her patients, but tense and ill at ease in general socia-situations. She had always denied her femininity and though potentially attractive had dressed in severely tailored tweeds and she had always avoided close relationships with others either of her own sex or the opposite sex. Her interests were athletic and out-of-door activities, and she had a deep emotional feeling for music. She had always been interested in nursing, 'particularly the macabre aspects of it', but had spent the first 6 years after

Group D—Poor Adjustment

leaving school at 14 in a commercial firm, where she had studied at evening classes. She did not, however, have suitable ability to be really successful here and at 20 she started her full nursing training. Having qualified as a State Registered Nurse, she then took further specialised nursing training. Her ambition was to join one of the international health organisations but she considered that her first duty lay with her ageing adoptive parents. She was tense and unhappy in relation to her adoptive parents, yet she felt very responsible for them and was very conscientious about caring for them. She smoked moderately heavily to assist herself to feel more relaxed. Having had a previously clear health record, she developed at age 33 thyrotoxicosis. At the time of interview this was considered by the family doctor to have arisen from a cystic condition of the thyroid gland.

M., who had been legitimately born, was adopted when 3 or 4 weeks old by a married couple, aged 41 and 35, who had been married for 4 years but had no children. There was no known medical reason for this. When visiting one of Mr M.'s sisters in a city a considerable distance away from their home, they heard that one of the guests in her boarding-house, a married woman, whose husband had died a few months earlier, had had a baby and had placed it with a foster-mother for adoption. Mr M.'s sister suggested to Mr and Mrs M. that here was a baby needing a home and they had no children. Mrs M. responded to this at once and felt that 'it was God's plan'. They stayed for 4 months with Mr M.'s sister and then returned to their home area with a five months old baby girl. It was not therefore known in their home community that the child was adopted. She was brought up as their only child.

The adoptive father, a semi-skilled worker in industry, became during the 1930's Depression years an investigating officer for the Unemployment Assistance Board. He thereafter was employed on various clerical jobs. Interested in politics, he became elected to various positions in local government. He had, however, rather a passive type of personality and he was dominated at home by the adoptive mother. Brought up in an evangelical missitonary family, his father having been a missionary in an English ciny, he adhered to this religious teaching though less strictly tha the adoptive mother. He retired when he was 73 and at the time of interview was in poor health. The adoptive mother had been the eldest in a family of five where her parents had been very religious in the puritanical sense. Her siblings all showed instability, three of them with tendencies to morally irresponsible behaviour. Emotionally she was very much tied to her mother, and was always expected to help out in family crises. Her parents had also controlled whom she should marry. She met Mr M. through their common interest in evangelical work. She was intelligent but had no opportunity to train for an occupation suited to this. During the Depression she supplemented the family income by running a small business and taking in boarders. She was attractive and always interested in dress, jewellery and her appearance, and she was anxious to be successful socially. She was also, however, very opinionated, and critical of those who did not follow the moral principles she advocated. She retained all the strictly religious and puritanical teachings of her parents. The family were members of the Congregational Church. She was in poor health at the time of the interviews, having previously had a clear health record.

Because of Mrs M.'s concern for social position the family always lived above their income and there were considerable financial difficulties during the Depression years. For the first few years of their marriage the parents had lived with relatives, but for most of M.'s childhood they stayed in a house purchased by them in the suburbs of the city.

The marriage was not a happy one. Both parents, because of their strict upbringing, were inhibited and undemonstrative. The mother was the dominant partner but she did not find the marriage satisfying emotionally and the father spent a great deal of time and energy outside the home. Though the parents got on well together on the surface, there were frequent quarrels during their financial difficulties in the 1930's.

M.'s upbringing was left almost entirely to the adoptive mother who, although she desperately wanted a child, was not really a child lover. She lavished a great deal of affection on M. and was possessive of her, becoming jealous if M. saw much of anyone else. She therefore discouraged M. from having friends of her own age. She also dominated her and had high aspirations for her, picturing her at University and considering her to be very clever. M. passed the examination for Senior Secondary School but because of financial difficulties, the parents could not afford the extra expense of this.

Her mother was very strict about her regular attendance at Church and about her strictly following her religious principles. She did not, however, worry if M. stayed out late in the evenings. She said she trusted her.

When M. was 16 or 17 she began to resent her mother's domination and she wanted to be free. She dressed like a boy and would not wear the pretty clothes her mother bought for her

Group D—Poor Adjustment

and she never used make-up or jewellery. She also did not want to grow up, preferring to remain a 'tom-boy'. She revolted against her mother's way of life and her religion and, unknown to her mother, she went out to 'have a beer with the boys' from her place of work, and she smoked. When her adoptive mother found out about this she was very hurt saying 'What have you done to me'. Her mother did not encourage her to have boy-friends, but M. found she was not interested in boys and, in fact, she did not want to have a close relationship with anyone.

When M. was in her late teens she was very anxious to train as a nurse. This was partly because of her interest in this profession, but also as a means of getting away from home. Her mother was opposed to the idea until she saw that she could talk about her daughter being in a profession. She wanted M., however, to train in her home area. M. was determined not to do this and as it was war-time she was able to use this as an excuse to go to the first training Hospital that offered her a vacancy. This happened to be a Scottish one.

In this struggle to gain freedom she found that, whereas her father had always supported her mother in any decision when she was a child, he gave her a measure of support in her desire to train as a nurse. She could not, however, rely on him since he would only express an opinion after he knew what attitude his wife was going to take.

After M. became a nurse she spent only holidays at home, although she always sent money regularly.

The adoptive family were regular Church-goers and as a child M. had attended Church three times on Sundays. She had been 'saved' in the evangelical sense at the age of 8. When she was in her teens she lost all sympathy with Church-going but continued to attend. On leaving home she gave up all Church connections, a decision which was a continual source of tension between M. and her mother. Her mother also brought religion into the adoption situation which added to the difficulties there. The adoptive father was less strict than the mother about some of the implied religious principles of their forebears, and he, unknown to his wife, would for example take alcohol on social occasions. This further influenced M. to feel he was not to be relied on to have a point of view or the courage to stick to it.

M. was accepted by all the relatives on both sides of the family but she never felt she belonged. She noticed her adoptive mother was emotionally very demonstrative to her relatives and she contrasted this with her own detached attitude.

Although this adoption was arranged before there was an

Description of Histories

Adoption Act in England, it was a permanent placement, with M. always using her adoptive parents' name. The adoption was legalised when M. was 8, which was two years after the Adoption of Children Act (1926) was passed. M., however, did not know that she was adopted.

When she was 10 or 11, she found a paper which referred to her by another surname (her biological one). She pushed this paper away from her at the time, saying that her parents would tell her some time. She told no one of her discovery.

When she was $15\frac{1}{2}$, her mother told her about reproduction and made it clear that M. had been born as a result of union between her adoptive parents. M.'s attitude to this was that if her mother said it was true, then it must be so.

When she was 16, M. without any introduction, asked a friend of her mother, with whom she had a warm relationship, if she knew whether she was adopted. The friend, who was taken by surprise, said it was something for her mother to tell her. On returning home M. tried to ask her mother about this but found she could not. Later her mother, having heard from the friend, introduced the subject by asking why she had asked. Her mother admitted that she was adopted and gave her details about how they had adopted her, saying that she had been unable to have children and that God had given her this one. M. asked who her parents were. Her mother said she did not know much about them, and had not wanted to know. It was God's plan and will that M. come to them; the rest did not matter. Her mother had said it several times very insistently that she had not been illegitimate. (This was important to her adoptive mother as she 'had a horror of illegitimacy'.)

M.'s immediate reaction was that she did not mind so much about being adopted, but she was very cross that her parents had not meant to tell her and she said so to her mother, and also about what if she had wanted to marry. She was unable, however, to get her mother to see things from her point of view, and she was unable also to argue with her about it as her mother used religious arguments and M. knew that there was no use arguing with her about religion. Talking about adoption was very upsetting to Mrs M. who asked that there should be no further discussion of it. M. said at the time she would view it as a 'closed book' but she later saw this as a mistake as she was never able to re-open the subject and did not feel that this one inconclusive discussion had really cleared things for her. M.'s later reactions were twofold. First, to find out that she was in fact adopted was 'shattering'. She had believed her mother completely when at $15\frac{1}{2}$ she

Group D—Poor Adjustment

had implied that M. was born to her. Until then she had always thought her mother 'was right and wonderful', but now she knew that she had deceived her and had not meant to tell her the truth. From then on she doubted her and did not feel sure of anything she said, since she felt she would dramatise and exaggerate. Secondly, she felt 'rootless' . . . 'not an individual if one was adopted' . . . 'in a vacuum if I do not know my forebears'.

From 16 to 17 M. was very aggressive, she wanted to dress like a boy, to get away from home and to be free. Mrs M. was reported as saying that M. had changed after the age of 16, that she became less docile and that the change in her continued after she left home. Mrs M. blamed Scotland and the others whom M. met when nursing for her break with the Church.

Mrs M. was always very anxious that M. should not tell any of her friends that she was adopted and she became angry at any hint that this had happened. Her attitude was the 'Victorian' one that it was something to be ashamed of that she had not had a child, and also she very much wanted to believe the child was hers. She could not see that for M. in discussions with nurse friends, for example, about breast feeding and baby care, M. could be placed in the position of telling lies if she did not say she was adopted. M., who felt that there was nothing to be ashamed of in adoption, talked of it to her nurse friends. When in her late twenties and doing private nursing one of M.'s employers to whom she mentioned that she was adopted, became very curious about her biological family, suggesting she might be from 'a sprig of the nobility' and urged her to consult Somerset House. With encouragement in this way, M. went to Somerset House and learned about her place of birth, that her mother had registered the birth and that her father was an engineer. A complete search could have been made, which would have given details from the marriage certificate, whether her parents were still alive, and so on, but M. 'let things go at the time'. She had discovered she was not connected to any nobility and she was 'scared' in case by accident any correspondence should go to her adoptive mother.

Over the years M. learned a little about her biological parents from her mother's comments. She learned thus that her biological mother was a nurse. On one occasion when M. wanted a sherry, she was told that her biological father had been killed in a motor-cycle accident a few months before she was born and that he had been drunk at the time. Her adoptive mother, who referred to 'the curse of drink' had been afraid that M. too would be affected by a desire to drink.

Description of Histories

M. had never discussed adoption again with her mother. She could never introduce the subject. If her mother introduced it, then she listened to what she had to say but would not ask anything.

As a nurse living in a group, M. gradually built up for herself a life of her own with her own friends. She had had one or two male friends, but she never allowed any such friendships to develop. In connection with this, she said 'Whatever would I tell anyone about adoption?'—and about not knowing her own parents. She also said, however, that she never wanted to marry or to have a special boy-friend.

M.'s relationship with her parents remained a tense and unhappy one. On her father's retiral she took on considerable financial responsibility for them, and they moved to near her place of work. She maintained, however, her own life as a nurse apart from them. Her mother still centred everything on her, was critical and disapproving of her way of life with its lack of Church attendance and of observation of the Sabbath, its cigarettes and occasional drink. M. resented that her mother was thus critical of her, her comments hurt her, and she worried about her own lack of religious belief. M. found that, because of her mother's domination, she had had difficulty in being sure she was right to have her own opinions, and yet intellectually she knew she was. This led to tenseness and unhappiness for her and there were frequent family quarrels. Her mother too remained possessive and very jealous of any friends M. had made.

One year after her parents moved to be near her, and at a time when they were guests in her house and there had been many tense and unhappy scenes, she became aware that her thyroid was not functioning normally. A year later this was diagnosed as thyrotoxicosis of a cystic nature, and after removal of a cyst the condition was controlled by drugs.

M.'s comment about adoption in general was that she felt an adopted child either gave more than a biological child to its parents, or else it walked out. If she had had one other person of her own age she would have left home for good, or else she would have stood up for herself more. In providing for her parents financially, and in her general care of them, she feels that this is 'what I owe them'.

She felt all parents should tell their child of adoption at an early age but she was against the idea of saying the child was chosen . . . 'for then you feel more obliged than ever that they gave you a home'. Also she could not see how a parent could explain to a child that they were chosen from amongst a large number of other children. In any quarrel between herself and

Group D—Poor Adjustment

her parents she, as an adopted child, felt in a more dependent and difficult position since such a child can never say 'I didn't ask to be born'. She found her parents' strong religious beliefs and her mother's use of these in the adoption situation added to her problems. She felt so strongly about this that she felt people like her parents should not be allowed to adopt, yet she realised that people of similar religious convictions were particularly likely to adopt children.

Although M. gained a certain freedom and independence through leaving home and leading her own life as a nurse where she built a up circle of her own friends away from her mother's jealousy, this history shows that she was still emotionally very much tied to her parents and to her adoption situation. It also shows that had she had no valid excuse, such as the need for nurses in war-time, she might not have been able to gain even this measure of freedom through training far from her home area. She felt she owed her parents a great deal and she was very conscientious about caring for them, but she clearly resented their intrusion into her own life. She was still unsure of herself and of her right to have her own opinions apart from them. She found herself temperamentally very different from her adoptive mother who wanted to shower affection on her and for her to respond, whereas she found that her way of coping was to remain detached.

In her revolt against her parents at 16, it is not possible to differentiate exactly how much was due to the poor relationship with her mother which resulted from hearing of her adoption, and how much was a natural reaction against her mother's possessiveness. As however, a factor in this possessiveness was related to the mother's need to believe this child was born to her, it seems appropriate to give considerable weight to the adoption situation. M'.s feelings of resentment against her mother appear to have been made more acute by the fact that she suspected when she was aged 10 or 11 that she was adopted, and then was more or less convinced by her mother when she was $15\frac{1}{2}$ that this was not so. She must still have wondered, however, but probably was hoping for confirmation that it was not so.

Her adoptive parents were clearly not ideal parents and her mother emerges particularly as rigid, possessive, egocentric and

Description of Histories

with no insight. She always saw situations from her point of view and had no understanding of the need to allow M. or any child to leave their own individuality and opinions.

This revolt against her mother at 16 coincided with the time in early adolescence when it can be regarded that many boys and girls normally pass through a phase of homosexual psycho-sexual attitudes. In later adolescence they gradually develop with maturity normal heterosexual inclinations. This last phase for M. would have meant wearing pretty clothes, jewellery, and so forth. Since this was just what her mother wanted her to do, M.'s motivation at this age to do exactly the opposite of identifying with femininity was strongly reinforced by her strong negative feelings towards her mother. Her wanting to remain at what she referred to as the 'tom-boy' level also reflected her insecurity with regard to more mature emotional attitudes.

Furthermore her mother had not been able to talk easily about the sexual aspects of marriage, her attitudes here being influenced by her puritanical religious approach to life.

All such factors in M.'s total life situation, together with her fear deriving more specifically from the adoption situation of any kind of close relationship, can be seen to have influenced M's. level of adjustment, where she denied her femininity and that she should marry and have children of her own.

Of the two other histories in this sub-group, one, K.McI, No. 10, presented a very similar picture of reactions and adjustment. She was an attractive intelligent professional woman, who had been completely dominated by her adoptive mother. She too made efforts to trace her biological mother. The other history, A.P., No. 7, gave a picture of severe maladjustment and social inadequacy.

Finally there is the group of 3 married women whose adjustment is illustrated by giving in detail the history of J.M.

J.M., No. 4, aged 38, had been married for 5 years and had a son aged 4, who was suffering from asthma and attending a Child Guidance Clinic. At the time of interview, J. was desperately trying to adopt a baby girl and apparently hoping thereby to repeat the pattern of her own adoption. She was, at the same time being rejecting in her attitude towards her son. Because the adoption of a baby girl was not proving possible, J. felt very

Group D—Poor Adjustment

acutely that she was being punished. She was a competent housewife, doing much home-baking and the like. She was however very adolescent in her attitudes and manner towards others, and she had no real friends. In mood she appeared somewhat cyclothymic.

Before marriage J. had done clerical work and had been a dressmaker, having served an apprenticeship for this after leaving school at 14. During the Second World War she was in one of the women's services.

After her discharge from the service, J. reported that her 'nerves' were affected. She became a chronic bronchitic, and suffered from asthma, and was frequently off work. Her health had improved since her marriage.

J. had been taken to her adoptive home from hospital when 10 days old. The original arrangement had apparently been a fostering one, the adoptive family having been asked to help the biological mother. This had been done willingly by the adoptive mother because she loved babies. When the biological grandmother wanted J. admitted to a Children's Home, since she disapproved of her daughter keeping this illegitimate child, the adoptive family at once said they would keep the child permanently. If the biological mother made any payment for the fostering, it was a small one and only for a short time. There was no written agreement between the two families. There was, however, a formal arrangement that the biological mother would not contact the child, and that the elder daughters of the adopting parents would undertake to care for the child if the adopting parents should die.

The adoptive father, aged 50, was at the time of J.'s placement in the armed forces during the First World War. Being very fond of children, however, he was in favour of the adoption. He was a hard-working master decorator and painter, but at that time such employment was seasonal. He died when J. was 19.

The adoptive mother was also aged 50. She had been married at 21 to a serving soldier in the regular army, and there were 5 children of this marriage. After the death of her first husband, she worked for some time to maintain her family and then remarried at 36. There were 4 children of this second marriage. She took in boarders to supplement her husband's seasonal income. She, like the adoptive father, was hard-working, and she was gentle in manner and fond of children. She was reported as 'old-fashioned' in her attitudes to child-rearing in that she always tried to shield J. from any unpleasant situation. She died after 2 years of ill-health when J. was 21.

Description of Histories

J.'s siblings, by the first marriage were aged 28 to 19, and by the second 14 to 8. Six were girls and three were boys. All were still living at home, except first, the eldest daughter who was married and had a daughter of about the same age as J., and secondly the one adult son who was in the army. The second eldest daughter, also married and with a son 3 years older than J., was living at home at the time of J.'s placement, since her husband was in the armed forces at that time. She had taken an active part in the original decision to take J. for fostering.'

The home was described by J. as 'a house full of women., and with the men in the forces 'a baby was a great attraction' This second eldest sister continued to take an active part in the up-bringing of J., who, from the age of 3 spent the summer months with her, her husband, who had by then returned from the Forces, and with her son, who was 3 years older than J.

There was never much money in the adoptive home, although finances were always adequate. There was, however, more money available when J. was a growing child than there had been when some of her adoptive siblings were children. This may have contributed to some of the future jealousies which sprang up in the family.

The family lived at the same address until J. was 14, when they moved to a new area in the city.

The adoptive parents were members of the Church of Scotland and J. went to Sunday School and later became a member of the Church of Scotland.

In spite of there being a step-father, who at first was resented by the children of the first marriage, the home was a happy one. The adoptive parents were happily married. J. was given every encouragement to lead an active and full life with others of her own age, and to join in their activities. Later she had many energetic activities; skating, tennis, swimming and cycling, and she was always given the necessary equipment to pursue these interests. She was encouraged in the occupation of her choice.

J. and her adoptive mother were very close to each other. The whole family in fact gave J. a great deal of attention and 'babied' her. She never felt she was treated differently because she was adopted. As an adolescent she was not interested in boys, being 'always with the family'. Her adoptive mother was never able to discuss sexual matters with her. The family had approved that 'there was no trouble with boys'. Although there was this acceptance of J. by her adoptive siblings while her parents were alive, it was found on her adoptive mother's death that the adoptive sister nearest to her in age, that is, 8 years older, had

Group D—Poor Adjustment

removed J.'s name from her adoptive mother's will. The other members of the family rectified this. This sister, however, remained jealous of J. and later quarrelled with the adoptive family because of this.

All older relatives accepted J. as one of the family. As a child, J. did not know that she was adopted. When J. was 9 or 10, the daughter of the eldest adoptive sister told the other children at school that J. was adopted. J. asked her mother about this and she denied that it was true. J. accepted this and there were no further comments at school. When J. started work at 14, her birth certificate was given to her in a sealed envelope. She did not see this as significant at the time.

When J. was 15 and visiting her eldest adoptive sister, who had moved to another town, her daughter (that is, J.'s adoptive niece), again said that J. was adopted. The relatives did not deny that this was so and J. at once came home. This time her adoptive mother did not deny it either. J. was very upset when she knew it was true. She commented that it was 'a dreadful blow' . . . and that she had 'felt besmirched and inferior ever since'. Her niece had told her of her adoption in a spiteful and cruel way. J. realised that her niece had done this out of jealousy because J. had taken the place with the adoptive mother which this niece would otherwise have had as the eldest granddaughter.

For a time after this incident, although J. still felt she was one of the family, she wanted to die. She threw the clothes off her in bed at night hoping to catch pneumonia and die. She became aggressive and resentful saying many things to her adoptive mother which she afterwards regretted.

At the time of the interviews, J. could still not give the details about this incident at 15 without being very emotionally upset. She could recall it as clearly as if it had just happened.

J.'s adoptive mother, although admitting that J. was adopted, did not tell her much of how the adoption was arranged, nor did she give her any details about her biological mother. J. related this to the fact that her adoptive mother always tried to shield her, including shielding her from the fact of her adoption. J. was certain that, even if her adoptive mother had been told that she ought to tell her of adoption, she would not have done so.

J. could not have asked her adoptive mother for details, nor even have mentioned the subject of adoption again. She was able, however, to ask her adoptive sister to whom she was very close, and she continued to ask her about her biological mother over the next two to three years. J. again asked for details when she was about to be married. J. thus learned about her early history, and that her biological mother had been a tailoress who had also worked as a clerkess. She had been engaged to a sailor who was lost at sea. J.'s adoptive sister was sympathetic towards the biological mother and had described her as a 'nice, respectable girl'.

Adoption was not discussed in the family, nor was it mentioned to outsiders.

J., who was ashamed of being adopted, never told people about it, with the exception of her family doctor and her minister when she was trying to adopt a child herself. She was very sensitive about the whole question and found it hurtful even to overhear anyone talking in a general way about adoption and about illegitimacy. J. felt children should be told of their adoption by their parents and not by anyone else.

When J. returned home from the forces, both adoptive parents were dead and she lived with her eldest adoptive brother and her youngest unmarried sister. This sister was very jealous of J. and there were frequent quarrels. As a result of these the sister ultimately left home. It was during this time that J. complained of suffering from her 'nerves' and that she developed bronchial asthma.

At 33, J. married her eldest brother's friend, aged 33, who was building up a small business of his own. He and J. lived in the brother's house. This brother, aged 50 at the time of interview, had been engaged for 20 years.

J. and her husband had one child, a boy, and when he was 18 months old he developed asthma. All three adults in the house shared in the care of this child. The adoptive brother, however, played a much larger rôle as father than did the husband, who, because of working longer hours spent less time at home. Both brother and husband, however, were at home at week-ends and this time coincided with the child's asthmatic attacks. The family doctor reported that it was considered that the child was reacting to this triangular situation. J., however, had no insight into the fact that her marriage situation was abnormal or unusual. It seemed likely that the adoptive brother, though engaged, would not marry and that he was viewing J.'s son as if he were his own.

Following the birth of her son, J. had a severe prolapse. When operative treatment did not effect a complete cure, J. appears to have wanted a sterilisation operation. This was performed, and J. had said at the time that she could always adopt a child. At the time of the interviews, however, J. was finding that it was not as easy to adopt a child as she had anticipated. Because adoption societies had not accepted her application, J. felt that

Group D—Poor Adjustment

she was being punished. Because of her immaturity, J. in turn wanted to be punishing. Her overt way of doing this was to stop attending Church and to discontinue helping children's charities. She interpreted her rejection by adoption societies in terms of being herself an adopted and illegitimate child.

J. wanted the child she adopted to be a girl, so that . . . 'I can repay the good time they (the adoptive family) gave me'. She also said that she would not allow such a child to be hurt by outsiders as she had been.

Later in the contact with J., it emerged that she had had a further gynaecological operation to restore normal function. She was optimistic that she would now have a further child and, although she acknowledged intellectually that one could not be certain about such matters she was sure in her own mind that when she had this further child it would be a girl.

In her relationships with her adoptive family, J. kept in touch with nearly all her siblings and she did a great deal for them. She reported that she helped them 'because I feel I ought to, as they did so much for me'. She even wanted to keep in touch with the youngest sister who had been jealous of her. J. said here that she 'bore her no grudge'.

From this history, J. emerged as someone very immature and childish in her attitudes. Because of this she was concerned primarily with her own needs and so was an over-protecting, frustrating and rejecting mother to her own son. She was very accepting of the behaviour of any of her adoptive family and showed no aggression or resentment towards any of them. In her relationships much of J.'s motivation appeared to derive from wanting to repay and to gain approval. This too could be seen as her motivation in wanting to adopt a baby girl. If she were to have further children she would clearly identify with girls and reject boys.

This adjustment could be seen to be related to J.'s experience in her adoptive home, where the pattern established for her had been that of the baby and the youngest of a large family. As she entered the family at a time of great stress for the female adults because of war-time conditions, it would be inevitable that they would give the baby a great deal of attention in part at least as a means of distracting themselves from their own worries. J.'s unusual adjustment in adolescence where she did not, as is normal in adolescence, seek to establish her independence from

Description of Histories

her adoptive family, showed that her main identification was with the female members of her adoptive family. She was still emotionally very tied to her adoptive siblings particularly her eldest sister.

Her adoptive mother had viewed adoption as something from which to shield J. This attitude must have re-enforced J.'s feeling of inferiority and of being 'besmirched', which resulted from being told spitefully about her adoption by her jealous adoptive niece. Once J.'s adoptive parents were dead, she began to be absorbed in illness. After her marriage, she replaced this with a preoccupation with her home. Although her adoptive parents had been warm and very accepting towards her, it could be seen that it was the total family situation, together with the attitudes, not just of the adoptive parents but of the whole family, which ultimately influenced her adjustment.

The other two histories in this sub-group, P.H. No. 25 and J.G. No. 48, are of married women whose own problems so dominated their situation that they too were unable to have good relationships with others. Their marriages were insecure and they were facing problems in their relationships with their children.

GROUP C—INTERMEDIATE ADJUSTMENT

The third group of histories is the largest in number and is a rather heterogeneous group. When adjustment is viewed as on a sliding scale, the group is not so obviously maladjusted as the last group but none are or have been without problems.

The twenty-one histories have been broken down into three sub-groups. First there are those, 2 in number, who had problems in their adoption situation and adoptive home, but who could now be regarded as being more or less free of these. Secondly, there is the group of 8 who at the time of interview were in a stage of transition and whose adjustment was improving. Thirdly, there was a group of 11 still involved in and affected by their adoption situation, but functioning adequately in many areas of their lives Of the total twenty-one cases, 4 were men and 17 women, and the age range was 42 to 19. Five were legitimately born and 16 were illegitimate. Sixteen

Group C—Intermediate Adjustment

were married. In occupation, of the 4 men, one was a doctor, one a first mate on a large trawler, one a butcher and one was in semi-skilled employment. Of the women, there was a non-graduate teacher, a state registered nurse in training, an assistant nurse, 8 who were or had been shorthand-typists or secretaries, one who had been a skilled factory worker, and one an unskilled factory worker, while 3 had done domestic work and one was a sewing-maid.

Health records over the years showed that only 7 had had no health problems, but of these 7, two were potential unmarried parents themselves and one ran away from home. Two showed symptoms of hypochondriasis, with in one case, an attempt at suicide. One had hysterical paralysis and another had a functional aphonia. Several complained of sleep disturbance, 2 had tension headaches, one suffered from migraine, and 2 had had enuresis. One had had asthma, together with infantile eczema, and one had a recurrent puerperal psychosis. It will be noticed that in all of the above complaints the condition could be regarded either wholly or in part as attributable to psychological factors.

To illustrate the first sub-group, the history of B.C. is given.

B.C., No. 51, aged 24, was a large pleasant, easy-going country woman, happily married for 4 years to a farm worker and tractor driver, with two children aged $2\frac{1}{2}$ and $1\frac{1}{2}$. She moved frequently from farm to farm as is still the custom with many of the less skilled farm workers. She had good relationships now with her neighbours and was a reasonably competent housewife and a devoted mother. Apart from obesity which she had suffered from since the age of 10, she had no health problems, although at 11 she had had rheumatic fever which kept her in bed for 9 months and off school for one and a half years. Before marriage at 19, she had worked in a series of unskilled jobs, on the railways, in hospitals and in laundries, and had left school several months before the statutory leaving age of 14 because of her adoptive mother's death.

B., illegitimately born, was adopted when aged 18 months or 2 years, by her biological mother's uncle and his wife. She had previously been boarded out by the local authority with a foster-mother who proved unsatisfactory and had spent two periods in a Home run by the Scottish Society for the Prevention of Cruelty to Children.

Description of Histories

The adoptive father, a 'kindly' man, aged 64, was a carter. He was employed until his death at 80 when B. was 17. Her adoptive mother, aged 60, had no health problems, and was described as 'a good manager'. They had been married since their early 20's and had three children; a daughter, aged 48, widowed with no children, and living away from home, an unmarried son, aged 45, who lived in a common lodging house, and an unmarried daughter of 36 who did farm work, living at home and taking over the housekeeping when the adoptive mother died. Irritable, unstable and very unreliable about money, this adoptive sister was later admitted to a Mental Hospital. There was also an adopted boy of 15, legitimately born, whose biological mother had died at his birth. When his siblings were adopted into other families, he had been cared for since a few days old by the C.'s and legally adopted. He achieved more than the rest of the family becoming a clerk in a Roman Catholic newspaper office and later in a law office. He left home to go into the Army when B. was 7.

The family lived in a quarry worker's cottage for 30 years and although the adoptive father never had a large wage, finances were adequate because the mother was a good manager.

The family were nominally Roman Catholic by denomination and the children attended Catholic schools, but the adopted brother was the only practising Catholic.

B. was not articulate about her parents, but it was clear that her adoptive father had accepted her and been kind to her. Her adoptive mother and the younger of her two adoptive sisters were however constantly critical of her and were always asserting that she would be like her biological mother. Thus she was given toys, but not allowed to take them outside the house in case she broke them; she was not allowed out of her parents' sight for long, or to go out and play with the other children from school. It was said that she would just want to go away from the house and that she would be like her biological mother. She received frequent physical punishment. She always felt she was treated differently from her adoptive brother, 13 years older, on whom her adoptive sister (referred to as 'aunt') lavished gifts and who in B.'s eyes was given greater freedom. She resented this, particularly because she knew his name had had to be changed to that of the adoptive parents. Her name, on the other hand, because of the relatedness, was already the same as theirs, although she was told she too had been legally adopted. Her brother tried to be friendly with her, but she only became angry and quarrelled with him. Later they were able to discuss this together and he realised how she had felt.

Group C—Intermediate Adjustment

Her parents took no interest in her activities and frequently when she had been scolded at home she truanted from school.

B. knew she was adopted from the age of 7. By chance, when shopping in a large multiple store with the elder of her two adoptive sisters, they had met a woman in her 40's who had given B. a present. She was told later that this woman was her biological mother. This elder sister was in no way critical of her biological mother, but the unmarried sister and the adoptive mother were very critical. Now that B. knew she was adopted they told her that she was the youngest of four illegitimate children whom her mother had borne all to different men. They also told her that she had been neglected and poorly cared for during the first 18 months to 2 years of her life, and that she had had at least three moves.

B.'s reaction was that it was at first a shock to be told this; not so much that she was adopted, for she had had her suspicions about this because of her adoptive parents' age, but that she had been moved so frequently and neglected. Gradually, however, she became used to such ideas for whenever she was 'given a row', her mother and her sister would 'cast up' that her biological mother was unmarried and had had four illegitimate children and that B. would turn out just like her. When B., remembering the gift from her biological mother, said there must be some good points about her mother, her unmarried sister became particularly angry.

B. considered that but for this chance meeting, her parents might not have told her of adoption—certainly not when she was so young.

At school, B. found the taunts of the other children about the age of her adoptive parents embarrassing. They used to ask if her sister were not her mother. Her way of coping was at first to run away. When the children further taunted her that she ran away because they were not her real parents, she used to reply, 'I know they're not, but they're the only ones I've got; and there is no need for you to talk about it too'. She became angry and fought the other children, until gradually they stopped commenting.

These incidents started when B. was aged 8 or 9 and went on until she was about 11 when, with a change to secondary school, fewer children knew her circumstances. B. also made it clear that she would fight anyone who passed any comments, and her adoption was seldom mentioned.

B. revolted against the critical attitude at home, feeling it was unfair that she should be blamed for what her mother had done.

Description of Histories

The fact that her own mother had been unmarried made B. resolve . . . 'No one was going to make a fool of me'. She told her adoptive family this, but they paid no attention. When she became unusually fat at 10 or 11, they feared she was pregnant. If she behaved well, no one commented. She felt therefore, that she might just as well be bad; she was at times 'so angry' that she 'wanted to go around smashing things'. 'I'll go and get into trouble . . . be put away and so get away from them.' She realised now that this would only have been hurtful to herself, but at the time her feelings were so strong that she saw it as the only means of escape. In her revolt against her adoptive mother and sister, she used to say that she need not do as they said, for although they said they had legally adopted her, she could never find any papers to confirm this.

She said that she used to keep going by saying that she would be free of them at 16. She never felt that she would have cared if anything had happened to her adoptive family, for then she would be free.

When her adoptive mother died when she was 14, and her adoptive sister took charge of the house, life was unbearable for B. In quarrels her sister threatened her with a bread knife.

B. obtained exemption from school after her adoptive mother's death, and with her first week's wages she ran away from home going to her younger adoptive brother, who was married by then and living in England. She was traced by the police and a Welfare Officer interviewed her to see whether she should be sent home. She was allowed to stay and she continued to live there for a further 2 years. She returned home at 16, partly because she felt her brother and his wife were exploiting her to care for their children, and partly because she was home-sick for her home area, though not for her home, and was anxious to see her adoptive father again. The situation for her on her return home was in no way different.

The family were evicted from their home about this time because of non-payment of rent by the adoptive sister, and they had to live in a farm shack. When the adoptive father died when B. was 17, B. did not want to live with her sister, but she was 'not ungrateful' and felt 'I should give her a home as her father had done for me'. By working together on a farm they were allocated a farm cottage.

B. remained very unhappy living with her sister who, now that B. was at the age of having boy-friends, did all she could to disrupt any friendships. She intercepted letters and told the boys about B.'s biological mother and her four illegitimate children.

Group C—Intermediate Adjustment

B. was so unhappy that she 'would have taken the first opportunity to get away'. Until then B. had not told people about being adopted, but she now realised that she should tell any boy-friend herself, rather than allow her sister to do so.

When B. became engaged, her sister again tried to intervene, this time by telling B.'s fiancé that she was out with other men. Her sister became more disturbed as B. planned to marry. She became violent, threatened suicide, and was ultimately certified. After she had been 18 months in a Mental Hospital, B. and her husband 'took pity on her', applied for her release and acted as surety for her during her parole period. The sister obtained a resident domestic post, and spent all her off-duty with B. Though now less disturbed however, she still had not changed in her attitude, but B. was now able to say outright what she thought of her. Although irritated by her, B. was able to tolerate the situation, and she wanted to help her adoptive sister because of what the family had done for her.

It was clear that B. was happy in her marriage and that her husband trusted her, otherwise the sister's persistent comments might have made for difficulties. B. was very proud of the fact that her first child was born 10 months after her marriage, whereas her adoptive brother's child was born 7 months after marriage.

B. had wanted to meet her biological mother again since the age of 7, but she could never ask her adoptive family about her or about her whereabouts. When she was very unhappy in her adoptive home, she never thought of trying to trace her biological mother, since, she said, her adoptive family would never have agreed to this. In her teens she met her biological half-brother, who had written to her adoptive father. They met unknown to the adoptive family and tried to trace their mother through the local authority department which had originally boarded out B., but they were given no information. She also met her biological sister twice. Her brother would possibly have kept in touch, but again her adoptive sister intervened, telling him when he called that B. had gone to work elsewhere.

When B. married, she put an advertisement in a local paper giving her biological mother's name and asking her to contact her. A person of the same name, but not her mother, replied.

B. would still like to meet her mother, but she thought one meeting would satisfy her except that she would like her children to have a grandmother. She realised that her mother might not want to meet her and that it might be embarrassing if she were now married. B. frequently talked to her husband about this desire to trace her mother. She would not consider advertising

Description of Histories

again as she did not want her neighbours to know of her adoption.

B. did not want her adoption talked of when she was a child, nor did she tell people now about it, for she felt she would then have to tell them the whole story. When asked about her parents, she said they were dead.

B.'s attitude to adoption was that adoptive parents should not know too much about the biological mother. In her own case, this had meant that her adoptive parents could recall all her biological mother's faults. She felt she would have been better brought up in a Children's Home or adopted by people who did not know her biological mother. She also felt that at 60 and 64 her parents were too old to adopt. She was sure that had they died when she was younger and she had thus been left even more to the care of her sister, she would have 'gone wrong' and ended in an Approved School.

Though similar in having had problems and now being free of most of them, the adjustment of the other married women in this sub-group, A.K., No. 17, was not as good or as normal as that of B.C.

The second sub-group consists of 8 whose histories showed an adjustment which was improving, and will be illustrated by giving 3 histories; one of the two men in this sub-group, one from the 4 married women and one from the 2 unmarried women.

H.G., No. 20, aged 33, is an example of a man whose adjustment was improving and where this improvement came about with the passage of time rather than through a radical change in his environment. Legitimately born, he was adopted at 4 months old, because his biological parents had separated. His biological mother had felt that she could care only for one child, his sister 2 years older, at the same time as going out to work. He was adopted by his biological maternal uncle and his wife, aged 33 and 34, who had been married for 3 years, and had no children. They lived in the city, some distance away from the village where H. was born. He was brought up as if he were their only son, used their name, and it was not intended that he should know either that he was adopted or related. The whole family acted together in this.

The adoptive father, a shopkeeper, died of a malignant disease when H. was 8. He was rigid and critical of H. The adoptive mother, country bred, a head table-maid before marriage, was also rigid, and possibly frigid, having a universally Calvinistic

Group C—Intermediate Adjustment

attitude to life. When the adoptive father died, she took in University students as boarders. At 49 she developed angina and died at 55.

A third adult in the house was an unmarried friend of the mother, also a waitress but more intelligent. She had known the mother before her marriage and continued to live with her after marriage. The relationship appeared latently homosexual.

The household then was an rather unusual one and all three adults centred very much on the one child and competed for his affection. Both parents were inadequate personalities and were not well adjusted to each other. They were unable to give warmth or affection to H. They had, however, social and educational aspirations for him and made considerable financial sacrifices in order the he should go to a fee-paying school. This continued after his adoptive father's death when finances were strained, for H. was intelligent and won yearly bursaries until he attained the Scottish Higher Leaving Certificate level. He was expected to do well at school but he resented very much that his adoptive mother could take no interest in his developing intellectual interests. Neither could his 'aunt', although she, with more money than his mother, bought him 'improving books'. He was socially isolated, not being allowed to play with the children round about who were viewed as too rough, and since he did not want to bring his better-off school-friends to his shabby home. He became increasingly self-orientated, and the situation at home accentuated this, since he found that he could play his mother and aunt off against each other to achieve the greater material gain for himself.

When H. was disobedient, his mother punished him physically until he was stronger than she was, and also used the threat 'Wait until I tell you something that will make you sit up . . . then you'll be grateful for what I've done for you'.

He had persistent nocturnal enuresis as a child which recurred at 12 on admission to hospital for a few weeks.

At 12, H., when looking through drawers which he was forbidden to enter, found his birth certificate. He learned thus that the person he had viewed as his aunt, but never met, was his biological mother. He was surprised at this, and then accepted it. He gave no indication to his adoptive mother that he knew. When he was 16 or 17, and details of birth were required for a formal application for a school bursary, his mother with difficulty told him of his adoption, and of how he was related. H. accepted this information, again without comment. From the age of 12 he had been very curious about his natural parents, but he could

Description of Histories

not ask his adoptive mother, and although after 16 or 17 he asked his 'aunt', she gave little information.

Over the years, however, he gradually pieced together the story and learned about both his natural mother and father. She had since re-married and none of the relatives really approved of her, describing her as 'flighty'. She had been more intelligent and had a better education than the rest of her siblings.

Although intelligent, H. never used his capacities to the full. At school, where he wanted acceptance from his peers, he found no one admired the 'swot'. Later at University, where he studied medicine, he put a great deal of energy into doing well at sport, rugby, boxing, and the like, not so much because he enjoyed the sports for their own sake, but in order to compensate for previous inadequacies, and to win. Again he had few friends, finding conflict in the fact that he was a fellow student with his mother's boarders. With his adoptive mother he had no real communication. When he qualified, his biological sister came to see him, and out of curiosity he went once with her to see his biological mother towards whom he felt very resentful since she had placed him for adoption. He had no desire to see her again. He was, however, very curious about his biological father and learned all that he could about him.

His relationship with his biological sister was a very close one, and in fact it developed abnormally since they found they were physically attractive to each other. They were both already engaged by this time. Each subsequently married but kept in touch with the other. They found it very difficult however to adjust their relationship to one between siblings since they saw so little of each other.

H. married at 22 and he continued to be self-orientated both in his social attitudes and in his marriage. He admitted that when he volunteered as a para-trooper during his peacetime National Service he was again over-compensating. Later his ambition was to be a neuro-surgeon, but he achieved little towards this.

By his late twenties his attitude became more mature, and more realistic. He took an administrative post which did not use his medical skill to the full, but gave him and his wife the chance of an adequate income and a home of their own. He had now also time to pursue his artistic and intellectual interests.

Having feared responsibility and that he would be an inadequate parent, he had previously avoided parenthood. He and his wife now sought to have a child and having achieved this he found himself maturing and dwelling less on the past.

Group C—Intermediate Adjustment

This man in his childhood had little warm feeling for anyone. He felt that he had never had parent-figures and being interested in psychiatry and psycho-analysis, his diagnosis of his own situation was that he was one of the affectionless personalities as described by Bowlby.[5]

The emotional isolation which he experienced as a child was possibly no different in kind from that felt by many children who are much more intelligent and better educated than their parents. In fact one can see him as the 'classless person' described by Hoggart.[6]

The factors, however, peculiar to the adoption situation were two-fold. First, he was brought up by a mother, who had had no child of her own, and who was considerably less intelligent than his biological mother. Secondly, there was her insistence that he should be grateful to her for what she had done for him.

Although this man's adjustment was apparently improving at the time of interview, he had not resolved many of his problems of relationships with others. Although he had good relationships with patients, these were very poor with equals and those in authority over him.

The other history of a man whose adjustment was improving, W.L., No. 52, is similar to H.G. The improvement in his adjustment, however, could be seen to date from the death of a rejecting adoptive father, who appeared to have agreed to adopt only to please the adoptive mother and who always preferred the later-born biological son.

Of the four married women in this sub-group, the history of M.N. is given.

M.N., No. 37, aged 21, was an attractive girl dressed in brilliant colours and heavily made-up. She had married at 18, had a daughter of two and she was again pregnant. She and her husband, an apprenticed tradesman who was doing National Service at the time of interview, had made an attractive home out of a single attic room in a tenement.

M. had gone to Junior Secondary School until the age of $15\frac{1}{4}$, having stayed for an extra term at her father's insistence to obtain some commercial training. She did clerical work and then residential domestic work.

She had had no health problems of a physical nature, but she reported that since 14, her 'nerves' had been affected by her

Description of Histories

unhappiness at home. She had been referred to a psychiatrist because of stealing, and at 17 she had attempted suicide.

Although M. was excitable and irritable, and behaved in an attention seeking way whenever her husband had to leave her to return to his unit, her adjustment had greatly improved since her adolescent years.

M., illegitimately born, was adopted when 9 months old, through the appropriate department of the local authority, by a married couple, aged 30 and 33, who had been married for 5 years. She was brought up as an only child, her adoptive mother having had 2 or 3 miscarriages before adopting her.

The adoptive father had steady employment as a machine operator in a factory. He had no health problems. He was unassertive and very quiet. He read a great deal, and although he had no real leisure interests, he was more sociable than the adoptive mother. His weekly outing was to visit his step-mother. A strict adherent of the Roman Catholic faith he became more religious as he grew older.

The adoptive mother was a competent housewife but 'always delicate and nervous', and she frequently attended the family doctor. At 50 she was admitted to a Mental Hospital with a rare kind of anaemia which produced psychotic symptoms. After treatment for the anaemia, the psychotic symptoms cleared. She was, however, basically unstable with a cyclothymic personality. She had no friends and no interests outside her home, although she enjoyed the cinema and theatre.

She had been emotionally very close to her own mother, but she had also been tied to her and dominated by her. She wanted to repeat this pattern with M. Originally she had been brought up as a Roman Catholic but she did not attend Church regularly.

The family finances were always adequate and the family lived at the same address, in a centrally situated working-class area of the city.

There were constant quarrels between the parents. During these the mother behaved in an hysterical way, and, following them there were frequently silences between the parents lasting for up to 2 weeks. These quarrels dated from before M.'s adoption but later she was always involved in them. For example, if M. spoke to her father during such a quarrel, Mrs N. accused her of taking his side. If the father commented on how Mrs N. was bringing M. up, then he was accused of being on M.'s side.

The mother was reported as saying that the happiest years of her marriage were the 3 years when her husband was in the army. She had letters from him, but M. and she were then on

Group C—Intermediate Adjustment

their own. The mother was very possessive towards M., discouraging her from having friends of her own age. There was a very close relationship between them until M. was 12. The adoptive father took no part in M.'s upbringing during these years.

After 12, M. began to want to have friends and activities apart from her mother, and by the time she was 14 she and her mother were constantly quarrelling about this. Her mother, who had an exaggerated idea of how M. would grow up 'into a lady', was critical of any friends M. made. She constantly watched M. and was very distrustful in case she should become friendly with any boys. If M. ever came home later than expected, her mother did not believe her explanations.

As M. felt that her mother never believed her when she told the truth, she decided that she might just as well tell lies. She kept a diary, however, of her daily activities and when she was 14 her mother found this and read out the contents to her. Here M. had recorded various innocent meetings with boys and how she had not told her mother of these. M. reported, 'My mother never really believed me after that'.

M. felt, however, that her adoptive mother's whole attitude towards her was wrong. She was sure she should have a life of her own, and choose her own friends, who always came from homes like her own. She was determined not to be dominated in this by her mother. In these constant adolescent quarrels, adoption had been frequently mentioned by the adoptive mother.

M. had had no idea that she was adopted until she was 12 when children from school taunted her that they knew something about her—that she was adopted. M. could not believe this and was at first afraid to ask her mother. Her mother, however, urged her to have no secrets from her, and then denied that it was true that she was adopted saying 'Don't be silly'. M. would have dismissed the whole subject from her mind if her father had not told her that evening that it was true. He had said 'But you'll always be our little girl'. M. burst into tears at this and continued to weep all evening. Her adoptive mother then also became upset saying that she had had no idea M. would react in that way. M.'s father remained calm, and her mother, who had not wanted M. to be told of adoption, was very angry with him. M. herself was upset, not so much because she was adopted, but because she had been moved to tears by the nice way in which her father had told her. M. never felt that knowing of adoption made any difference to how she felt towards her parents. She thought about her adoption for some time after this, but then it slipped into the background. Her adoptive mother, however, maintained that M. hated her parents because of it from the day that she knew, and the adoptive mother frequently quarrelled with the adoptive father for ever having told M.

At 12, M. was given no details about her early history. When she was 16 or 17 she was very curious about this, but she would not ask in case it hurt her mother. She decided to wait until the information came out gradually. On several occasions when her mother was in an amiable mood, M. heard about how she had gone to a 'big house' to fetch her and how there were no clothes for the baby as there should have been. M. worked out her own interpretation of this which favoured the biological mother. M. learned too that her adoptive mother had been the prime mover in wanting to adopt. When her mother was angry with her for not doing exactly as she said, M. was told 'You ought to eat humble pie . . . we gave you a home . . . you ought to be grateful'. M. commented that she realised that she should be grateful but she found she could not show her feelings. Her mother had also commented, 'My mother said you would bring me nothing but trouble'.

Later when there was a family quarrel about M.'s break with the Roman Catholic Church, M. was told she was born a Catholic and that her parents had answered an advertisement that a good Catholic home was wanted for a baby girl.

Her adoptive mother however, never gave M. any details about her biological mother. Her only comment about her was when M. stole. The adoptive mother had then said . . . 'what can you expect—bad blood'. M.'s reaction to this comment was to be very hurt and angry, but she indicated none of these feelings to her adoptive mother.

The family had no real contact with relatives. The maternal grandmother, who died when M. was 5, had been opposed to adoption.

In the years after leaving school at 15, M. was very unhappy and rebellious at home. There was constant conflict between her desire to have a life of her own like all the others of her age, and her mother's desire to be possessive of her. M. also found the adult world which she entered on starting work to be rather frightening, and, because of her restricted upbringing with its few social contacts, she found she knew little about life in general.

M. showed signs of maladjustment. She defied her parents and went to dances, and to other teenage activities. At her first dance, after she had alcohol for the first time, she had sexual relations and it was later feared that she might be pregnant. Her mother

Group C—Intermediate Adjustment

had given her no information or help about relationships with those of the opposite sex.

When employed in two positions in a cash desk, M. stole sums of money ranging from £3 to £14. She reported that she did not want or need the money, but that she stole because her mother did not trust her. She knew that she was doing wrong and she appreciated why her parents became very upset. She thought however, that they had been too strict with her. On the second occasion she was seen by a psychiatrist who advised that she should leave home. M. had frequently threatened to leave home and, after a particular quarrel when her father in anger had said she had better go, she used this at once as an opportunity to get away. This was viewed by her parents as running away.

Later, however, her father saw that M. would be better away from home, and she was put in touch with a social work agency to arrange this. Thereafter M. took residential domestic work, not from choice, but in order to have somewhere to stay. She reported that if she had been charged with stealing and sent to an Approved School, she felt sure that she would never have improved. About this time, however, she became friendly with and fond of her husband who was one of her so-called adolescent 'crowd'. It mattered to her that he should have a good opinion of her.

M. was in a series of residential posts, staying only a few weeks in each one, being dismissed because of day-dreaming. She was unhappy away from home, worrying about her mother if she did not see her, and longing to have a good relationship with her parents. When she went home however there was constant tension. M. was an attractive, sophisticated teen-ager by this time, and her adoptive mother never trusted her alone with the adoptive father. If he indicated that he was fond of M., the mother would say that he was fonder of M. than of her, and that their relationship was not a father-daughter one. M. denied that this was so.

During this time, M. had nowhere to sleep on one occasion between two jobs. Her adoptive mother would not allow her to stay alone in the house, as she and the father were going on holiday. M. spent the night in a large railway station, accompanied by her boy-friend. She never forgave her mother for this apparent lack of feeling for her. Soon after this, following influenza, she took an overdose of barbiturates. Her adoptive mother showed concern and M. was allowed to stay at home for a short time.

At 18 M. married a stable, kind and competent young man,

Description of Histories

no older than herself, who was a Protestant. He had been very understanding of her problems, and gradually she was maturing and her adjustment was improving. After marriage she had still hoped for good relationships with her adoptive parents, but these fluctuated as before, and gradually M. was learning to lead her own life and become independent of her adoptive mother. On leaving home, M. had given up any contact with the Roman Catholic Church and this caused tension with her adoptive father, particularly over the baptism of his grandchildren.

There were problems in M.'s marriage, since the husband was away and they had bought more expensive furniture than they could afford on a National Serviceman's pay. When the husband returned, however, to a job which was assured to him, this would alter. It seemed likely also that M.'s adjustment would continue to improve when she had a reliable husband constantly with her on whom she would depend.

In her attitude to her own adoption, M. said she would like to have known about her biological parents. She wondered if her mother was living and why she had placed her for adoption. She assumed that her biological mother had been unmarried. M. accepted, however, that she would never learn anything of this from her adoptive mother, whom she thought probably knew nothing about her biological mother. In spite of her poor relationship with her adoptive home, M. viewed her adoptive parents as her mother and father, and she was sure that, had there been less talk of her adoption in her home she would have forgotten about it.

This history again shows the pattern, already mentioned in this series, of a possessive mother who dominated her daughter. In this case the daughter did not acquiesce, but became rebellious. This led to a period of quite severe maladjustment for her. In fact, if she had not met her husband and grown very fond of him when she did, she might well have become a confirmed delinquent. She herself realised this. She found that now she was 'honest to excess', and she commented about her stealing 'I shall never live it down to myself'.

Although the situation of an adolescent rebelling and becoming a near-delinquent could happen in a similar kind of home where there were biological as opposed to adopted children, there were clearly specific tensions in this home due to the adoption situation itself. For example, there was the adoptive mother's fear of 'bad blood', and her comments about adoption

Group C—Intermediate Adjustment

and gratitude. There was also the question of her interpreting the relationship between the adoptive father and M., who was not his biological daughter, in an incestuous way.

Similar in present adjustment, and in some respects in the problems of adolescence, are the other three histories in this particular sub-group. In all three their adjustment was improving through gaining emotional freedom from their adoptive home with the help of a warm relationship with an understanding husband or fiancé. In one case, B.W., No. 18, uncertainty about adoption details had resulted in dramatic hysterical paralysis before marriage. In another case, M.F., No. 13, uncertainty and then conflicting stories about her biological background led her into fantasy and contributed to her having ill-health of a hypochondriacal nature and feelings of unreality. She saw making enquiries about her biological mother as a way of ending her uncertainties. She was helped to do this during the period of this study. L.H., No. 12, had been acutely unhappy in her adolescence, feeling that no one belonged to her, these feelings of insecurity being partly related to uncertainty and veiled comments about her adopted status.

The two unmarried women in this sub-group were also in a state of transition in adjustment at the time of interview, and the history of one of them is given in detail.

P.P., No. 30, aged 20, was slight in build, pretty in a quiet way, and quietly spoken though poised and outwardly composed. She worked as a sewing-maid in a hospital, having been unable to pursue any of the occupations of her choice because of severe bilateral flat foot resulting from untreated fractures of the toes. She had been educated at a fee-paying convent school, where it had been anticipated that she would sit her Scottish Higher Leaving Certificate. Circumstances in her adoptive home, however, were such that her schooling was irregular from the age of 13. It was also doubtful whether she had the basic intellectual ability for such an educational standard. At the time of interview, she found that she became extremely tense before going to any social function and she was only happy in situations where she knew everyone. She had a male friend, however, who was now helping her to lead a more normal social life than had ever been possible for her before her adoptive mother's death a year before the interviews.

P., legitimately born, was adopted when 2 months old, probably through a fee-paying nursery in the Edinburgh area, by a well-educated unmarried woman of 32. The adoption was legalised. The adoptive mother, who had been brought up in a comfortable middle class home, had, from the age of 19, nursed her invalid father until his death when she was 31. She was a director in her father's business, her one brother having left the city to become an engineer. A year after her father's death she adopted P. and devoted all the emotional energy that had previously gone into caring for her father to the care and upbringing of P.

The adoptive mother was fit until the age of 45 when she developed disseminated sclerosis. Her gait and speech were affected and she became bed-ridden, dying at the age of 51. She would not accept her illness, was very difficult in behaviour, and was constantly changing her doctor. She had a dominating personality and strong opinions. She was an enthusiastic member of a political party and of the Episcopal Church in Scotland. She was limited in her understanding of situations, being able to see things only from her own point of view. Her friends were either widows or unmarried professional women.

The finances were always very adequate and the adoptive mother owned a pleasant house and garden in a semi-residential area of the city.

The adoptive mother centred her whole existence around P. They were always together, and P. led a very sheltered life, her mother choosing whom she should have as friends and planning even her leisure time activities.

The adoptive mother put considerable educational pressure on P., always doing home lessons and music practice with her, and not allowing her to accept invitations out during term time. P. was taken to Church from the age of 18 months, and when she could write she was expected to write down parts of the sermon for discussion with her mother afterwards. She was not sent to Sunday-school, her mother instead teaching her at home. P. was allowed to join her school friends at sports, and Girl Guides, but in all her activities a high standard was expected by her mother who compared P.'s achievement with her own when at the same age. P. managed to obtain good marks at school until she reached the age of 12. Then she found that the additional subjects, such as two languages, were confusing for her. She was not very interested in school-work and only worked hard because her mother was so concerned that she should do well. The relationship between P. and her adoptive mother was poor. P. reacted to the excessive pressure on her by not confiding in her mother,

Group C—Intermediate Adjustment

by hiding things, and by with-holding from her items of information which in themselves were of a trivial nature.

The social life of the family was restricted to friends of the adoptive mother. There was no real contact with relatives and only occasional visits from the adoptive mother's brother. P. 'hated' when he came to stay, feeling that . . . 'it was all wrong to have a man about the house'. She did not consciously miss a father, but, looking back on her home life, she realised she accepted many things because she knew of nothing different.

When the adoptive mother became ill, she expected P. to look after her, to do the housework, and to continue with school. As a result P. only attended school irregularly from the age of 13 to 15 and was soon behind with her school-work. P. was also very lonely during this time.

Her mother required hospital care when P. was 15, and after a short period at a day-school, P. returned to her convent school as a boarder until she was aged $16\frac{1}{2}$. She was then admitted to an orthopaedic hospital for operative corrective treatment for her severe bilateral talipes planus. This prevented her from continuing her studies with a tutor at home, and also from sitting any of the usual examinations. Her mother was extremely upset about this. Her fractures had occurred when P. was $15\frac{1}{2}$, but she had not admitted this to her mother. Her reasoning here was that she was determined to continue with ballet lessons which she greatly enjoyed. Her mother was not observant enough to notice the injury although friends commented on the way P. was walking.

The hospital treatment lasted for 2 years and although P. was an in-patient only for a few weeks, she was subsequently sent to 'a hostel for cripple girls' in another city as there was no one to care for her at home. She learned there to sew.

Although this kind of training was not that envisaged by her adoptive mother, P. enjoyed the experience and it gave her her first chance of independence. She learned, for example, to wear adult clothes. Her mother strongly disapproved of this, since she tried to keep P. a child.

When 18, P. went for a year's course to a domestic science school. It was planned by her mother and one of her friends, a Church deaconess, that P. should thereafter care for her mother at home. This was viewed as P.'s duty after all that her mother had done for her. Other friends and the family doctor opposed this plan and P. ultimately took a post as a resident domestic.

The adoptive mother, however, was very unhappy in hospital, and took her own discharge, ignoring the fact that she was seriously ill. P. nursed her at home for the last 9 months of her life as well as working as a daily sewing-maid in a hospital.

With regard to the adoption situation in this case P. was not told by her mother that she was adopted. Those living in the home area would know of adoption since the adoptive mother was always referred to as 'Miss P.' but no comments were ever passed to P. P. was also aware that her mother was Miss P. but it did not consciously occur to her that this was significant. When P. was 9 she took a letter to school in a used envelope addressed to Miss P. The girls seeing this said that Miss P. could not be her real mother. P. was very upset and she asked her mother on her return home. She noticed her mother was unsure at first whether to agree or not, but eventually she admitted that P. was adopted. P. and her mother were both very upset, her mother shutting herself away in her room and P. running out of the house. P.'s reaction was to feel annoyed. 'I felt I had been cheated', but she said nothing of this to her mother.

P. was curious about her biological parents and she asked her mother about them from time to time, although often afraid to do so. Her mother always became annoyed and usually replied emphatically . . . 'Well, you're not illegitimate anyway'. Sometimes her adoptive mother would give no further information. At other times she said crossly, 'It doesn't make any difference to you now . . . It does not concern you. I'm in charge now'. Her anger here apparently related to her fear that P. was more anxious to talk about her biological parents than about her.

P. wanted especially to know who her biological father was, and why her parents had placed her for adoption. She obtained information from her adoptive mother from time to time about the former, but her mother gave her differing stories, for example, that her biological father was 'a medical doctor' but also that he was dead. P. wanted information about him in order to cope with the comments of the girls at school. She knew these details given by her mother were not true and so in order to avoid telling lies, she avoided her friends when they talked about their fathers. P. gave up asking her mother the second question when she saw it always hurt her. P., however, remained curious about this.

One of her mother's friends, a widow, had also an adopted daughter of about the same age as P. This girl did not know that she was adopted. When she talked about her supposed father, that is, her adoptive mother's late husband, P. felt very angry and resentful. 'Why should she not need to know when I've been told.' P. was frequently tempted to tell her.

Group C—Intermediate Adjustment

P. found that when her mother was ill, she could obtain more information from her, for, being confined to bed, she could not walk away when P. questioned her. P. thus learned that her adoptive mother had taken her for adoption from a large house where there were other babies, and that she had met her biological parents. When P. questioned her as to where her parents now were, she simply replied, 'Far away'.

Her adoptive mother gave P. the impression that adoption was something to hide and to be ashamed of. She tried to hide it at P.'s school by wearing a reversed signet ring and by being referred to as 'Mrs P.'

P. and her adoptive mother were not dissimilar in colouring and build.

P.'s attitude to her adoption was that it would have been much better if her adoptive mother had told her all that she wanted to know. She found she could only forget about adoption for a while and then it came into her mind again. She was annoyed that she did not know. She considered her mother's reluctance to tell her would be in case she was not satisfied with her as a parent.

When her mother died, P. wrote at once to Register House and obtained the extract of the original entry about her birth entry. She learned thus her original name, and that her father was a medical student. She also learned the name of her mother and the place of marriage. P. was very pleased to have this information. Although she admitted it did not give her much detail, she found she was satisfied. She had wanted particularly to know her original name. She now had no desire to meet her biological parents.

P.'s attitude to talking of adoption had changed over the years. Where previously she had been ashamed of it, she found that with the passage of time, it embarrassed her less. She stated however that she would 'not go out of my way to mention it'.

P.'s health record reflected something of the stress that she had experienced when a child. From the age of 8 she walked in her sleep and on one occasion dressed and went out of the house. On another night, before a school concert, she tore up her music. Such symptoms cleared, to appear again when her adoptive mother was ill. At $15\frac{1}{2}$ P. fractured both great toes, and as already mentioned required hospital care for 2 years. She was left with a considerable residual disability which made it impossible for her to take work which involved long periods of standing. Six months prior to the interview, she had been losing weight and her appetite and sleep were disturbed. This was

Description of Histories

viewed as reactive to the stress of the last few months of her mother's life.

P. was now leading a more normal life with friends and activities of her own choosing. She had never complained nor wanted to leave her home, and in all her unhappiness, she had remained loyal to her adoptive mother. It was only when she had experienced something different that she realised how restricted and abnormal her upbringing had been. Her adoptive mother had left her her house and all her money and P. was looking forward to the day when she could marry and live in her own home.

The other history, C.A., No. 1, showed a similar picture of an adjustment which was improving. In this case, however, this was a gradual process of maturing through experience rather than a change made possible by a radical change in environment. Again there was no father-figure in the adoptive home, and again uncertainty about adoption details.

The final sub-group in this second main grouping of histories are eleven in number. Of the two men, one history is given in detail, and of the 9 women, one illustrates the married women and one the single women.

M.B., No. 8, aged 29, was a weather-beaten first mate of a large trawler, slight but strong in build. He was intelligent with a good vocabulary, and a quiet manner and way of talking. He had attended Senior Secondary School but had left at 14, although his adoptive father had urged him to stay on for further education, and on leaving school to undertake a definite engineering apprenticeship. M. however, was anxious to go to sea and he did so in the fishing fleet. At 16 he was offered a merchant navy cadetship. Again he preferred however to stay with the fishing fleet where he had remained, except for a 3 years' break in the army doing war-time national service. He attended nautical college and had obtained his skipper's qualification. He anticipated being offered his own boat in the near future. He now had regrets however about his lack of education and apprenticeship, since with these extra qualifications, he could have worked on ships where he had better living conditions. His pay in the fishing fleet, however, was on a higher rate and this he felt compensated.

M. had been married since 25, and he had two sons, aged 3 and a few weeks old. He and his wife had bought their own house in slum property hoping one day to move to a better area. M. did not approve of his son playing with the other children in the neighbourhood, and he and his wife had unrealistic educational

Group C—Intermediate Adjustment

ambitions for their son. They hoped to send him to one of the more expensive fee-paying schools in the city.

M. had many friends among the sea-faring community. His wife was also of a sea-faring family. His relationship with his adoptive mother, however, was a very tense one, and it had led to considerable unhappiness and tension in his marriage.

He had no health problems as an adult, although at 7 or 8 he reported he was 'a bundle of nerves'. This he related to difficulties at school, but these symptoms could have had origin in particular tensions in his adoptive home at that time.

M., illegitimately born, was adopted from hospital at 10 days, by a married couple aged 40 and 23 who had been married for 6 years. There were no children of the marriage although the adoptive mother had borne an illegitimate child before marriage.

The adoption was arranged through the Public Assistance Department of the local authority and a welfare officer from this department had visited M. and his adoptive parents until he was 7 years old. The adoption, however, was a permanent one, though at that time *de facto*, since it occurred prior to the Adoption of Children (Scotland) Act. M. always used his adoptive parents' name, and he was brought up as their eldest son. Five years later Mr and Mrs B. adopted a girl through the same department and 18 years later a second girl.

The adoptive father was a marine engineer with a technical college qualification and at sea until the age of 31. When he married, he obtained a shore job and had regular employment in a responsible post as a foreman in an engineering firm. He was a competent and conscientious workman. His work was his main interest and he worked long hours. He talked very little about his own early life which had been unhappy. He was unobtrusive except when he lost his temper. He drank heavily.

The adoptive mother was a member of a very large family. Of poor intelligence, she was self-opinionated, quarrelsome, very talkative and very possessive towards all her children, and later towards her grandchildren.

The finances in the adoptive home were always adequate. There had been three changes of address but from the time M. was 5, the family lived in approximately the same sea-faring area. It was generally known in the area that the children were adopted.

In the adoptive home the mother was the dominant partner and there were frequent quarrels between the parents. Some of the difficulties related to the talkative relatives of the adoptive mother. They 'gossiped' about everyone's private affairs, but

Description of Histories

they could learn nothing from the adoptive father about his early history.

There was a very close bond between M. and his adoptive mother until M. was 12, when he came to resent her possessiveness. Their relationship had deteriorated since then. M. felt that his adoptive mother was too possessive to be a parent and that this related to the fact that she had not given birth to any of her family. He was also irritated by the gossiping of her relatives with whom she identified.

M. had a good relationship with his father and found that he had influenced him a great deal.

M. was fond of the older of his two sisters, although he did not feel very close to her. He was protective towards his younger sister who was then 11, a mental defective in the feeble-minded range. She had had hospital care for 4 years because of dislocation of hip, and she was pallid and of poor physique. This child had been adopted on the adoptive mother's insistence, the adoptive father feeling that he was too old to become responsible for a third child. The adoptive mother found it difficult to accept that nothing could be done to improve this child's mental condition.

Also a member of the family for 3 years was the adoptive mother's illegitimate child, J. The adoptive mother had found J. by chance, when he was aged 8, and being inadequately cared for in a foster-home. The relatives of the adoptive mother had, at the time of his birth, insisted on his adoption. J. came to stay with the adoptive family when he was 12 and M. was 6. The adoptive mother, however, always preferred M. to her biological son, and this was resented by him. After a family quarrel over this, when J. was 15, J. left the home and went to stay with one of the adoptive mother's sisters, who had originally insisted on his adoption placement. J. had started an engineering apprenticeship under the adoptive father and this continued, although thereafter the rest of the family saw little of him. It should be noted that M. reported that, between 7 and 8, this coinciding with the stay in the family of his step-brother, he was a 'bundle of nerves'. He was sent away from home for convalescence, but he ran away from the convalescent home.

Through the Public Assistance Department, the adoptive mother fostered babies temporarily for unmarried mothers until adequate arrangements could be made for the future of these babies. These infants were remembered clearly by M.

The adoptive parents were members of the Episcopal Church in Scotland but seldom attended Church. M. sang in the church choir.

Group C—Intermediate Adjustment

The family were in constant contact with the adoptive mother's relatives. A maternal aunt had made M. feel that he did not belong in the family. She never included himself or his siblings in any invitations extended to the rest of the family.

M. was not told that he was adopted although he always knew that his sisters were. When he was 12, he found his birth certificate and another document relating to his adoption in his mother's handbag. Before this, however, he had wondered about adoption. He had observed that he was not like his adoptive father, and that he was especially unlike, both physically and temperamentally, his adoptive mother and her relatives. There was a marked family resemblance between all the members of his adoptive mother's family. At 12, M. accepted that he was adopted. He made no comment, however, about his discovery.

After 12, M. came to resent the over-possessiveness of his adoptive mother. He did not feel he 'belonged' in the family, and, although fond of his siblings, he had no close emotional bond with them. He reported that he 'felt detached'. Because of this it was very important to him to have a home and family of his own, and when he was 16 he became engaged. At the same time, when thinking of marriage, he 'felt bitter' that he did not know more about his adoption. He wondered what he would tell his girl-friend and whether it would make any difference if she knew.

He was engaged for 5 years and during 3 years of this he was in the Army. His fiancée's family were opposed to marriage and M. considered that this could have been related to his being an adopted child. After his engagement was broken off, M. became engaged for a second time at 23 and he was married at 25.

At 20, when he had wanted to join the Palestine Police Force and his full birth certificate was required, his mother avoided mentioning adoption and gave him a shortened certificate. This would give no indication of parentage. When M. was 28, at a New Year celebration a cousin asked him if he and his sister knew about their adoptions. This cousin wanted to tell M.s' sister about this, but M., fearing that she did not know and not wishing such information to come to her from an outsider, himself told her husband. This led to difficulties with the husband. He said that he would not have married this girl had he known that she had been adopted.

M. was very angry about this incident, not with his cousin personally who, he knew, bore him no animosity, but with the fact that his adoption had been mentioned casually in front of strangers. What also angered him was the realisation that all the

Description of Histories

details about his adoption were apparently known to his 'gossiping relatives'. He had an angry quarrel with them about this.

As a result of this, M.'s adoptive mother went to see his wife and told her about his adoption. She also told the wife something about his biological parents. Until then M. had only known his place of birth. He thus learned that his biological mother had been a domestic servant. He also learned her married name and that she had gone to Australia. His biological father was reported as being a doctor. M., however, was unsure whether to believe this or not since he had found his adoptive mother untruthful over other things.

This visit from his adoptive mother confirmed for M. that everyone in the family knew about his adoption, and also that it was generally known in his home area. M. now felt that 'people were laughing' at him, although intellectually he knew that they were not. He felt that for years he 'had been made a fool of', and this made him self-conscious and resentful.

After his adoptive mother's visit, M. and his wife talked of adoption for the first time, although before their marriage, she had had hints from others in the community that he was adopted. She was very curious about M.'s biological parents. She could not understand why M. did not want to try to trace his biological mother whose married name was that of a well-known fishing firm in Australia. M.'s attitude was that he was 'not interested', and that he preferred 'to let sleeping dogs lie'. He further said, . . . 'I might find out something I would prefer not to know'.

He considered that, had he always known about his adoption, and if he had been told when he was very young, a very few factual details would have satisfied him. He personally felt it was more important to know about his biological mother than about his biological father. Even now he was not curious as his wife was. He would have preferred not to have had it suggested to him that his biological father was a doctor. He considered that this kind of information would make a child feel he would have had more opportunities and a better social position with his biological parents than with his adoptive parents. He considered that a lie was justified in such circumstances.

The adoptive mother always looked for physical resemblances between her family and M.'s children and those of his adoptive sister. M. found it difficult to remain silent when he listened to 'such nonsense'.

M. had never at any time had a conversation with either of his parents about his adoption, since he was unable to introduce the subject. He felt . . . 'it was up to my mother to start' such a

Group C—Intermediate Adjustment

conversation. Although there was no barrier between himself and his adoptive father as there was between him and his adoptive mother, M. still could not bring himself to discuss his adoption with him.

M.'s relationship with his adoptive mother had been tense since his adolescence. She had interfered in his first engagement. She had opposed the second engagement and interfered so much in his marriage that he and his wife had moved to a completely new fishing town for a while. The relationship deteriorated even further after the incident when he was 28. He felt that, as his adoptive mother had been secretive with him for all these years, he would now in turn not tell her anything. He found he told her lies without any embarrassment even when she asked about simple everyday activities. A further motive in lying was that he and his wife thus gained some freedom from her possessiveness and inquisitiveness.

Although there was this very bad relationship with his mother, whom he now actively disliked, M. continued to visit his home occasionally because he had a positive feeling for his adoptive father. He also continued to think of his adoptive parents as his mother and father, and in any discussion about his antecedents, he found it confusing to try to think of another mother and father.

M.'s attitude to his adoption was that adoption in itself had not worried him, but the secrecy about it had. What had hurt him particularly in his childhood was the fact that one of his aunts had never accepted him as one of the family. As a result of this, he considered that the attitude of relatives should be enquired into before any child was placed for adoption in any particular home.

This history shows excessive possessiveness on the part of the adoptive mother and an obvious denial by her that these three children were not born to her. Further evidence of her immaturity was her emotional rejection of her own illegitimate child while at the same time she cared for other people's illegitimate children.

M.'s own problems centred round his feelings of detachment from his adoptive family. He was unlikely to make a mature and relaxed parent, since he was not allowing his own child freedom to have friends and activities of his own. He was also quite unaware that he would create problems for his son by sending him to an expensive fee-paying school while he lived socially isolated in a slum community. It seemed possible that these social and educational aspirations related to M.'s feelings that he might have had such an education from his biological father. M. himself, however, would not have acknowledged any such association, since he was trying to deny to himself that this piece of information about the occupational status of his biological father was in fact correct.

The other man in this sub-group (J.A., No. 16) showed similar problems of adjustment for a man who had had a very possessive adoptive mother, although in this case the adoptive mother was also rejecting.

Of the seven married women, the history is given of *E.S.*, *No. 6*, aged 42. E. was a competent, energetic housewife, who had been happily married to a hard-working skilled mechanic for 19 years. She had an adopted son, aged 7, and a daughter born to her, aged 19 months younger. The husband had steady employment, finances were adequate, and the couple had their own flat.

Before marriage at 22, E. had been a clerkess, having left Junior Secondary School at 14. During the years of the Second World War, when her husband was in the Forces, she had done the detailed and exacting work of a wages clerk in a large garage. She enjoyed this kind of mental activity and she found routine house-work boring and rather dull. She now satisfied her interest in intellectual pursuits by studying Gaelic at evening classes and being a member of a Drama Group. Her husband did not have similar interests, but was happy that she should pursue these. It emerged that she had passed the appropriate examination at 12 for entrance to Senior Secondary School, but her adoptive father was unwilling to pay the small fees necessary at that time for such schooling.

E. had had no serious illnesses. As a child and adolescent, she had many friends and had enjoyed the usual social activities, many of them attached to her Church, typical of a young girl growing up in a city. She and her husband continued to have a pleasant social life with many friends.

E. was devoted to her children, but if anything appeared to be more fond of her adopted son. She was very protective towards him and anxious to shield him from being hurt as she had been. Her relationship with her adoptive father continued to be a tense and unhappy one. Her attitudes in both of these relationships found their origins in her adoption situation.

E. talked easily and in a relaxed and pleasant way about her childhood experiences and her present life, except when these

Group C—Intermediate Adjustment

related directly to the adoption situation. Then her whole manner changed, her face narrowed, she became tense and resentful, and expressed considerable negative feeling about various aspects of this situation.

E., illegitimately born, was taken for adoption when 5 weeks old by a couple aged 34 and 39, after she had been fostered unsatisfactorily for the few weeks after leaving hospital. The adoptive mother, hearing of this through an ex-employer, was anxious to care for the baby. She had seen the biological mother briefly but, realising the latter had no love for the baby, she had undertaken to care permanently for the child. E. always used her adoptive parents' name and was brought up as their only child. The family had moved to a new area of the city when E. was 4, and so no one in the home area knew of her adoption.

The adoptive parents did not talk about their respective early histories and so it was not known when they had married nor was there accurate information about pregnancies of the marriage, although it was likely that there had been miscarriages. The parents had wanted children and the adoptive mother had had some medical treatment for this.

The adoptive father, a journeyman joiner, was a good craftsman, but obsessional about his work, and intolerant of mistakes both in himself and in others. He had, as a result, poor relationships with others at work, who tended to be afraid of him. Although he was employed mainly by the one firm, he left it from time to time because of disagreements with his fellow-workers. At home he was a strict disciplinarian and liable to violent outbursts of temper. He was reserved, unsociable and undemonstrative. He had quarrelled irrevocably with his own family, and particularly with his parents. He had no contact with them, not even attending their funeral.

The adoptive mother, from a country area in the North of Scotland, had planned to train as a teacher. The relative who would have provided for this financially died however, and the adoptive mother became instead a companion in a well-to-do home in the city.

Having had no previous health problems, she developed in her forties severe arthritis, and at 51 she had an arthrodesis of one knee. Thereafter she wore a raised boot and, being very sensitive about this, she seldom went out of the house. As the arthritis became more crippling, E. did more of the housework and she also helped her mother to dress. In her sixties, the mother developed angina. From 64 she was a chronic invalid, dying 15 years later, after 2 years of being completely bed-ridden.

Description of Histories

She was a warm, affectionate and kindly person who had been very attractive in her youth. She read a great deal, and, although confined to the house for many years, remained actively interested in current events. She became difficult in behaviour, however, when her health deteriorated after she was 64.

Finances in the home were always adequate, in spite of the father's brief periods of unemployment.

The adoptive parents were fond of each other, with the father the dominant partner. They had few friends, however, and little social life because of the father's critical and opinionated manner.

E. found her father provided for her in a material way, but gave her no love or affection. She wanted these and not material things from him. He was strict and 'Victorian' in his attitude to children. E. was very afraid of him and she was unable to discuss anything with him. She was given no choice where her education was concerned. She resented this as she wanted to go to Senior Secondary School and her father could have afforded the small fees. She assumed, however, that he would view education as relatively unimportant for a daughter. E.'s fear of her father continued until a traumatic incident when she was 36.

By contrast, E. had a very close and intimate relationship with her adoptive mother. She was able to confide in her and discuss with her all aspects of her life, except her questions about sex and reproduction and later E.'s own inability to have children. E. felt she owed everything to her adoptive mother.

Both adoptive parents had been brought up in close touch with the Church of Scotland, but neither were regular Church attenders. E. however was sent to Sunday School and later became an active member of Church youth groups.

E. was allowed normal activities for a girl in her social group, and at 22 she became engaged. She had contact only with her adoptive mother's relatives, and, as a child, she was accepted by them, although when she herself adopted a child she found her cousins were prejudiced against adoption.

E. did not know she was adopted until she was 21, when one day her adoptive mother, without any kind of introduction, told her of this. Her mother also gave her some details about her early history and biological parents. Her biological mother had been a young shorthand-typist and her biological father was a law student. Marriage between them had not been considered possible because of the differences in social class. Her biological mother had been put out of her home by her own family, and the baby had been fostered unsatisfactorily until taken by the adop-

Group C—Intermediate Adjustment

tive parents. The biological mother had visited the adoptive mother twice to make a small payment, but when asked to hold the baby 'she had shuddered'. The adoptive mother returned her payments and wanted no further contact with her.

There was in fact no further contact, although the adoptive mother said she had always feared the biological mother might come and claim E., especially when the adoptive mother learned through her ex-employer that she had married a captain in the army and had had no children. From the details given, however, it was in fact clear that the biological mother was very unlikely to do this since she completely rejected the baby. E. considered that it was this fear at the back of her mother's mind which 'made her blurt out' that E. was adopted.

E.'s reaction to this information was to feel 'very resentful about the whole situation'. She was very upset, and wept a great deal. She felt she was 'something different' . . . 'an odd man out'. She did not want to meet any relatives of the family since they must have always known of her adoption. She told her fiancé at once, saying that there was no need for him to continue being engaged to her. His response was to reassure her that it made no difference to him. She also told his relatives and then became anxious about how they would react. Because she was so upset she found that she even told her fellows at work.

Once she recovered from the initial shock, she reported that having been told of adoption made no difference to her relationship with her adoptive mother. She also commented, however, that if in the shock of being told thus suddenly she had left home, she would never have returned. She felt that this might have been her reaction if she had not had a particularly strong bond with her adoptive mother.

E.'s attitude towards her biological mother was to feel very angry . . . 'I felt she had let me down'. These feelings of resentment related both to her having been unmarried and to her having rejected E., as evidenced by the adoptive mother's description of her 'shuddering'. E. had not wanted to hear more about her biological mother or meet her, and she reported that she would have taken no steps to try to find out details about her. She had no picture of her as a mother. Her adoptive mother was the only mother she had ever known.

E. commented that, knowing the details of her biological mother's visits to her as a child and about her lack of real concern for her, 'did not help me'. E. did not express anger at her adoptive mother for having told her this, but it was clear that she would have preferred not to have known this information. In fact her

Description of Histories

attitude was to have wished desperately that she need never have known of her adoption at all.

It is interesting to note that when E. thus gave details about her early history, she never used the first person but always referred to 'the baby' and 'the mother of the baby'.

Although E. had never suspected that she was adopted, once she knew of it, she saw certain things in the past as significant. First, she recalled that her maternal relatives had asked her if her parents were good to her. Secondly, she felt her father's whole attitude to her was such as to suggest he had not really wanted to adopt her, but had been persuaded to do so by her adoptive mother. She realised later, however, that at 21, she may have seen attitudes as due to her adoption when in fact they were not.

Her adoptive mother, having once told her, was quite eager to talk of her adoption and of her biological mother. Whenever she introduced the subject, however, E. became irritated and said that she did not want to hear. She thus learned, however, further details about her biological parents, for example, that her mother had been an accomplished singer and that her biological father's parents had sent him to Paris at the time 'to be out of the way'.

In physical appearance, E. was not dissimilar from her adoptive parents and so outsiders would not think of her as unrelated. In fact the family doctor attended the family for 15 to 20 years before the fact of adoption emerged. No one in the neighbourhood knew that E. was adopted, since as well as the change of address, the adoptive mother concealed it from friends and neighbours.

When E. became engaged her adoptive father had said that she could not marry. He had just been told that the adoptive mother's medical condition would not improve, and he said E. must stay at home and look after her. E., however, insisted that she was going to marry, and her fiancé agreed to stay at first with the adoptive parents. This they did for 2 years after their marriage. The arrangement, however, led to tension, since the young couple could only look for a home of their own unknown to the adoptive parents. After 2 years, during which time E. became irritable and suffered from a series of minor complaints, her husband insisted that she go and live elsewhere. Thereafter, the parents had to agree that they look for a home of their own, and this they found in the same block of flats. E. thus kept in very close touch with her adoptive parents and continued to do housework and to care generally for her invalid mother.

E. and her husband hoped to have children following marriage,

Group C—Intermediate Adjustment

but during the first five years the adoptive mother was ill and E. did not give much thought to their lack of family. She assumed that there would be children in time. For five years following this her husband was in the Forces. On his return they consulted their family doctor who advised them that no organic reason had been found as to why they should not have children. When E. was 35, however, they applied to an adoption society, and a three-months-old baby boy was placed with them. This adoption was finalised by legalisation four months later and four months after this E. became pregnant for the first time after twelve years of marriage. E. and her husband were delighted about this, feeling that they could not have had their daughter but for their adopted son.

E. continued to take a very responsible attitude towards her adoptive parents. When E. was 36, an incident arose when she had been told by the family doctor that her mother, who was particularly unwell, was not to be disturbed. She had mentioned this to her father who was anxious to take her mother a cup of tea. The father suddenly showed his resentment and jealousy of her, saying, 'Who the hell said she was your mother'?

This one comment made by him after 36 years was very hurtful, but also in time helpful for E. She was deeply hurt, but she also found that she was no longer afraid of her father. Following this incident, E. viewed her first duty as to her husband and her children, whereas before she had always given her parents first place. She now felt she had no obligation to provide a home for her father if he became ill, and she also knew her mother would not now ask her to promise to care for him.

On her adoptive mother's death, when E. was 40, her father continued to live in his own flat although originally he had said he could not do so. E. was attentive in her attitude towards him and she felt responsible for him, but she was not happy with him. She never felt she 'could get through to him', and this lack of communication between them occupied a large part of her thoughts. She also felt that she, with her husband and children, should have a life of their own apart from him. She had however a continual emotional struggle to obtain this. Because of being ill at ease with her father, and because she felt that if he could, he would still try to dominate her, she found she frequently adopted a hard and uncompromising attitude towards him.

E. and her husband were very happy with their two children and no further children were either wanted or advised. E. wanted her children to do well at school but there was no sign of excessive pressure there. She mentioned, but without further

Description of Histories

comment, that her daughter was proving to be a good singer. She was, however, very protective towards her adopted son, fearing that as he was a sensitive child, he too might be hurt as she had been. Her adoptive father was very fond of him and so she felt that her adopted son would not be hurt from this source. She had told her son, when aged 7, that he was adopted, that his biological mother had died and his father, being a soldier, could not take him with him to the army. These details were not factually accurate, the mother being still alive and the father, though a soldier, having disappeared. E. thought that one day she might be able to tell her son the truth about his mother. E. became upset however, whenever she thought of her son's biological mother. This she did especially on her son's birthday, when she felt that his mother must think of him. E. had guarded against her son talking of adoption to outsiders by telling him that this was a secret to be discussed only within the home and not to be shared even with his younger sister. She was constantly afraid, however, that outsiders would say something to him about his adoption.

Her attitude to her own adoption had changed over the years. At first she had been unable to accept that her biological mother had not herself cared for her. She became able, however, particularly after becoming an adoptive mother herself, to accept that not all unmarried mothers are immoral people, and that in fact in the particular circumstances her biological mother had no alternative but to place her for adoption.

She still felt resentful, however, that her adoption had never been legalised, or at least that her name had not been changed officially. This could have been done either by legalisation under the 1930 Adoption of Children (Scotland) Act, or by a process equivalent to Deed Poll. Her adoptive father, however, would not allow a change of name. On her marriage certificate therefore E.'s maiden name was given as . . . 'known as E.W.', her adoptive name, and E. was resentful that the evidence of her adopted status was thus apparent. She did not wish her children to know of her adopted status, and yet she considered that it was inevitable that they would when they married and had to show their parents' marriage certificate for any official purposes.

This history showed, first, that this adopted adult was still ashamed of having been adopted, and secondly that she was still very emotionally involved in the adoption situation, especially that aspect which dealt with how and when she was told of adoption.

Group C—Intermediate Adjustment

Regarding the first, she would admit to outsiders that she was adopted only under very provoking circumstances, when there was a discussion about whether or not she should tell her son of adoption. She hoped desperately to hide the fact of her own adoption from her children.

Her emotional involvement was clear in her completely changed expression and tone of voice when she talked of the incident at 21. She became very angry and resentful, whereas when talking about all other aspects of her life situation, she was relaxed and happy.

The impersonal method she used when referring to the details of her placement by talking of 'the baby' and 'the mother of the baby' was found in other histories. In those histories, as in this one, the adopted persons did not want to identify themselves with the details of their rejection by their biological parents. In the same way she wanted to protect her adopted son from feeling he might have been rejected. She therefore chose to tell him details about his biological parents which implied that they would have cared for him themselves if they could.

Of the other six in this sub-group, C.T. No. 15, J.S. No. 38, S.R. No. 47, H.B. No. 35, and B.M. No. 24, were all resentful about adoption and ambivalent towards their adoptive parents, although very conscientious towards them. F.S. No. 32, had no problems in connection with her adoption until both her parents died when she was aged 15. Thereafter she joined the family of an adoptive aunt who had not approved of her adoption and who treated her very differently from her biological son.

Of the two unmarried women in this sub-group, the history of E.M. is given.

> *E.M., No. 3*, aged 19, was an inexpressive, rather affectless girl with no apparent individuality of personality and with little drive. She was pallid and not robust, but had had no health problems. She was, at the time of interview, training as an assistant nurse, having failed to reach the necessary academic standard for a full nurse's training. She had been educated at a series of fee-paying schools until the age of 16, but left without sitting any of the usual school-leaving examinations. Her upbringing in her adoptive home was such that Scottish Higher

Description of Histories

Leaving Certificate standard had been expected of her. It seemed likely, however, that she had never had the necessary intellectual ability for this and that in training as an assistant nurse she was operating at a level appropriate to her intelligence. She had always wanted to be a nurse, but her parents, who had social ambitions for her, had opposed this, and she had worked for two years in an office. She was training as an assistant nurse away from home in a small country town and this was her first essay into adult life. She was enjoying this, and she talked thoughtfully about her work. She had made her own circle of friends, who were of artisan level of achievement rather than professional. At the time of interview she was adjusting well to this new life and was asserting herself against interference by her adoptive mother's second husband. She was, however, potentially very vulnerable, first, because she still had many problems in relation to her adoptive home, and secondly, because she was seeking warmth and affection from someone who would accept her as she was, without wanting her to conform to a particular pattern of behaviour and achievement.

Later information about E. through the family doctor revealed that she had not been able to make her own adjustment away from her adoptive home. Had she been interviewed even only a year later, her adjustment would probably have been assessed as coming within the range of the next main group, that is, of those with a poor adjustment.

E., presumably illegitimately born, was adopted when 10 days old through a hospital in one of the large English cities by a married couple who had been married for 4 years and whose residence was in Scotland. The adoptive father, in his middle thirties was in a well-paid executive post in industry, but he was very maladjusted in his relationships with others and particularly in his sexual relationships, having required psychiatric treatment from time to time. His first marriage had ended in a divorce and he had the custody of his son who was aged 11 at the time of E.'s adoption.

The adoptive mother had been an attractive and vivacious girl, brought up in a wealthy middle-class home, where she had been able to pursue a gay social life. She was intelligent and had been educated to the standard appropriate to such a home. Four years after her marriage she had a baby who died. E. had been born in the same Hospital at approximately the same time, and the adoptive mother returned home with her. The adoption was subsequently legalised. This marriage, although unhappy, lasted a further six years. A divorce was then arranged. Both parents

Group C—Intermediate Adjustment

then remarried and E., after a year in a Boarding School from the age 6 to 7, stayed with her adoptive mother and step-father. Until the age of 16, she went occasionally to see her adoptive father and step-siblings, since he had two children by his third marriage. There were no children by the adoptive mother's second marriage. E. always used the name of her adoptive step-father and this change was made official by the equivalent of Deed Poll when E. was 16.

This second adoptive home was not a happy one. The step-father, younger than the adoptive mother, was also well-educated to University degree standard. He had an executive position in commerce. He appeared to be extroverted but ego-orientated and was fond of a full social life as was the adoptive mother. His salary, however, though in the professional range, was probably not such as to allow them to live in the way that the adoptive mother had done in her own home or in her first marriage.

The adoptive mother had warmth of personality but she was impulsive, unstable and restless. She was constantly moving to a new house. In her forties she suffered from an illness similar to anorexia nervosa, and was in a mental hospital for several months following a serious suicidal attempt. She made a good recovery, but it was not known at the time of interviews whether this was of a permanent nature. She frequently threatened to leave her husband.

E. and her adoptive mother had a very close relationship with each other, the mother looking for emotional satisfaction and companionship from her daughter. She resisted, therefore, E.'s desire to go away from home. She remained possessive of E., commenting frequently on what she had done for her.

E.'s relationship with her step-father was a very strained one, and there were constant quarrels between them, the adoptive father being particularly ashamed of E.'s occupational status.

Because of family disapproval of the mother's two unsuccessful marriages, there was almost no contact with relatives. E. felt that, because of this and because of the constant quarrels at home and the frequent changes of house, she had had 'no family life'. She had been very docile up to the age of 16, and she had not consciously been aware of the family quarrels. Thereafter she began to assert herself and this brought her into conflict with her adoptive step-father. She began to notice too that in the quarrels between her parents, her step-father always brought her into them.

E. had always been able to make friends easily, but she had never known any for any length of time because of the frequent

Description of Histories

family moves. After leaving school, however, and while still living at home, she had not been able to make friends. Away from home she found that she could make friends. She was also then much happier and commented, 'I know now where I stand'. She had a boy-friend, a stable young man who was an apprentice craftsman, and they both wanted to become engaged before he started his National Service. E.'s parents, however, were very opposed to this.

The adoptive parents had no religious affiliations or church connections.

E. did not know that she was adopted until she was 18. Her step-father had apparently threatened frequently to tell E. of this in his quarrels with her mother. It was in fact the fear that he would do so which ultimately made the adoptive mother tell E. herself. Otherwise E. considered her mother would never have told her.

The adoptive mother had told her that her biological mother was on the stage and had died at E.'s birth. E. had been born prematurely, and her biological father, fearing that E. was going to die, threw himself under a bus. E. considered her biological mother had been someone important in the theatre world, although she had never pressed her adoptive mother for details, since talking about adoption obviously upset her. E. was content to know no more at the time but she stated that she would in the future want to know more details, probably when she married.

It emerged, however, that the adoptive mother in fact knew little about E.'s biological parents. This apparently worried the adoptive mother from time to time since she wondered what kind of temperament E. might have inherited. When E. wanted to marry someone from a different social class, her adoptive mother wondered if her biological parents had also been from that social class.

E. reported that being told of adoption did not upset her and her relationships with her adoptive parents were unchanged. She considered that all her relatives must already have known of her adoption but this did not worry her. She felt that, as an adopted child, she had been given more materially and in affection than a biological child could have had.

People outside the family would not know that E. was adopted, because of the frequent family moves. Also the adoptive mother would not tell anyone, adoption being not entirely socially acceptable in her particular social group at the time.

In appearance E. was neither so similar nor dissimilar to her adoptive family that people would comment on it.

Group B—'Fairly Good' Adjustment

This history, as also the history of *P.P., No. 30*, showed an adopted child unable to achieve the educational and occupational standard expected of her by her adoptive parents. It was not possible to assess accurately how much of this girl's lack of achievement was due to lack of innate ability and how much to the blunting of her affect by the very disturbed upbringing which she had had. An assessment by a psychologist would have thrown light on this but this would not have been acceptable either to E. or to her adoptive family.

E.'s lack of affect and her apparent composure were her ways of adjusting to the many tensions in her adoptive home. She had witnessed many quarrels and her mother's threatened suicide. She defended herself against anxiety by denying that these incidents affected her in any way. For this reason it seemed that her assertion that she was not affected in any way by hearing of her adopted status at 18 should not necessarily be viewed as accurate.

The other history in this sub-group was of R.H., No. 39. Aged 20, and unmarried, she was also having difficulties in her relationships with her adoptive parents and she too was seeking to establish her right to a life of her own.

GROUP B—'FAIRLY GOOD' ADJUSTMENT

The fourth group of histories are those, 6 in number, who on the whole had maintained a good adjustment throughout their childhood and into adulthood in spite of difficulties in their adoptive home. Three were men and three were women. The age range was 34 to 18 and three were married. One was legitimately born and the remaining five were illegitimate. In occupation, of the men, one was an apprentice engineer, one a tractor driver and one a lorry driver, and of the women, two were skilled secretaries and one had worked as an assistant nurse.

Of the six, two had health problems of a fairly serious nature, one having epilepsy and the other diabetes.

The first sub-group here, that of the three men, is illustrated by giving the history of G.Y.

G.Y., No. 49, aged 30, was somewhat self-uncertain, though apparently happily married, with a daughter aged 3. He had steady employment as a lorry driver with a large firm for which he had worked, apart from War Service, since leaving Junior Secondary School at 14. During 9 years R.A.F. Service, he had been a staff car driver. He had no special ambitions about his work. His only health problem had been when he was admitted to hospital for about one year when 5 following mastoidectomy. He had good relationships with others of his own age and at work, and he enjoyed social activities at his R.A.F. Association club. He had, however, only gained real freedom to follow his own inclinations after the death of his adoptive mother.

G. was adopted when a few weeks old by a married couple of 29 and 26 who had been married for some time. He was brought up as an only child. There was no information available about the parents' ability or otherwise to have children of their own.

The adoptive father was an underground coal-miner until 37, when he became unfit for this work because of pneumoconiosis and bronchitis. He was unemployed for 6 years during the Depression, and then was employed on the railways. He was frequently off work, however, because of illness. He was easy-going and fond of social activities when younger, being an active member of the British Legion. In later years, however, he became taciturn and rather bad-tempered. He died when he was 55.

The adoptive mother, who had worked in a market garden before marriage, did domestic work to supplement the father's unemployment pay. She had rheumatic fever in her early 20's, which left a slight cardiac disability, and she was under medical care for many years. She died of angina at 48, when G. was 22. Liking to dominate, she was very labile and 'worried over trifles', especially if these related to G. She was very talkative, and loved company.

During the father's unemployment when G. was aged 8 to 14, there were considerable financial difficulties, and the family had received financial help from the British Legion. Later there continued to be financial difficulties because of the father's ill-health.

When the father had to leave the mining industry, the family had moved from their Corporation house in a pleasant country town to lodgings in a slum area of the city. They did not obtain a house of their own in this area until G. was 14. In spite of financial difficulties, however, G. was given what he asked for in a material way.

The relationships between the father and mother were fairly good, with the adoptive mother the dominant partner. The father took little part in G.'s upbringing, and in any disagreement

Group B—'Fairly Good' Adjustment

in the family, the mother always viewed G. to be in the right as opposed to his father.

Until he was 8, G. felt that he was given freedom to have friends and to join in all their activities. After the family's move to the city, however, the mother became possessive and protective and always questioned with whom he was friendly.

When G. was 16, he wanted more freedom and he resented his mother's control of him and her strictness about hours. His mother did not want him to have friendships with those of the opposite sex and so she did not allow him to go to dances. G. resented this, particularly as he knew both parents had been fond of dancing in their youth. He therefore occasionally went to dances and then told his mother lies about this. G. had frequent quarrels with her at this time, but as she always became upset and ill, he could never assert himself against her wishes.

At call-up at 18, G. was rejected on medical grounds for the army, because of the old mastoidectomy. A few months later, however, he volunteered for the R.A.F. and was accepted. His mother was furious about this, and wanted to tell the service authorities about his health record hoping that again he would be rejected.

On G.'s return from the forces, his mother was again possessive. She did not wish him to marry and he was of the opinion that if she had still been alive, he would not yet have been married.

The parents were nominally Protestant, and G. was sent to the Boys' Brigade, but religion did not enter into the home life.

All relatives accepted G. as one of the family.

G. was not told by his family that he was adopted until he was about to be married at 24. At 20, however, a boy from their first home area asked him if he were the 'adopted son of Mr and Mrs Y'? G. found this 'a shock' and felt embarrassed. His immediate reaction was to wonder how many other people knew. He realised that his cousins did not since they implied that he would inherit his adoptive parents' particular abilities. He could recall incidents which now took on a new significance. For example, when he was 16 an insurance agent had called and his mother had sent him out of the house. He noted that he had never seen his birth certificate. He recalled that on many occasions he had come into a room and found his mother and aunt talking in lowered voices. G. did not mention this episode to his adoptive mother. Although he was curious and tempted to ask, he never did, first since it might not be true, and secondly, because it might have hurt his mother. Also she was unwell by that time, and G. felt it would have been hurtful and upsetting to her, even to have asked indirect questions, which, if he were adopted, she would have had difficulty in answering. His attitude, however, was also that it was his parents' place to tell him. As his mother was dominant in the house, he assumed that she would tell him and not his father.

His suspicions about being adopted made no difference to his relationships with his parents.

The day before G.'s marriage, when his birth certificate would have to be shown, a paternal aunt called to see G. He anticipated what he assumed she was going to say by commenting that he already knew that he was adopted. The aunt found it very surprising that he had known for so long and had never mentioned it. He asked why his adoptive mother had not told him herself and learned that she had been afraid that if he knew he would want to go back to his original mother. When his adoptive mother was dying she asked his adoptive father to tell him but he too lacked the courage.

G. was resentful about this, feeling that his father should have told him himself and that he would have preferred to hear about adoption from one of his parents. He commented that this was something about which no child could ever ask. G. did not, however, express much aggression here. No details were given to him by his aunt, and he thought that, had he not spoken first, she probably would have told him something about his biological parents.

He learned, however, from his birth certificate, his biological mother's name and address, and that she had been a factory worker. He was curious about her and wondered about going to see her, but he would not have wished her to know who he was. He simply wanted to know what kind of person she was, and also why he had been adopted. He took no action, however, although while driving he frequently passed through the town where she had lived. He commented that he did not wish to cause any kind of upset for her. He was also, however, afraid that there might be something in his background about which he was better not to know. He was not looking for a mother in her; she would have been a stranger to him. His wife was also curious about his biological mother particularly with regard to any children they might have.

Although G. remained curious, and was particularly puzzled about how the original contact could have been made, since the two sets of parents had come from widely separated geographical areas, he never asked either his father or his aunt, and they, for their part, did not mention adoption to him.

G. had assumed that he had been placed for adoption when

Group B—'Fairly Good' Adjustment

eighteen months or two years old. This was not information he had been given, but which he had deduced from a particular snapshot of himself at that age where part of the snapshot had been cut off. He assumed that the person thus cut out had been his biological mother. During the interviews he learned from a conversation which his wife had with a neighbour that he had been only a few weeks old when placed, and so the snapshot had none of the significance which he had imagined.

G. was not ashamed of adoption, and he did not try to hide it, but he 'did not broadcast it'. He did not want his friends to know of it nor to talk of it.

His adoptive parents had not been critical of unmarried mothers nor of the illegitimate child, and both areas in which he had lived would also be accepting of adoption and illegitimacy. G. was also not physically markedly dissimilar from his adoptive parents.

The main problem for this adult in childhood had been the divided discipline in the home and the possessiveness of his adoptive mother. Such possessiveness of a mother for a son can be viewed as within the limits of 'normality' in that it can happen in any family, and in this history it was not possible to elicit any definite evidence to suggest that the mother's possessiveness as such related particularly to the adoption situation. The description of how she became more possessive and restrictive after G. was 8, could relate to her disapproval of the standards and behaviour of the slum neighbourhood children. On the other hand there was the suggestion in this history that because of her health record with cardiac involvement there would have been risks in her having pregnancies, and so once she had adopted a child, this one child mattered a great deal to her. This was borne out also by her fears about telling him of his adoption, and may again have been her motive rather than purely her possessiveness, in her preventing him from going to dances, meeting girl friends and so marrying. When he married his adoptive status would be revealed. G.'s comment about her attitude that 'She did not wish to lose me' could then have had a double meaning—to a wife or to a biological mother. Also the fear which must always have been present that someone else might mention adoption to him must have added to her own feeling of insecurity.

The other two histories in this sub-group, J.T., No. 42,

Description of Histories

aged 22, and T.N., No. 31, aged 18, showed similar adjustment in spite of possessive adoptive mothers. In the case of T.N., his adoptive home was clearly one from which he was escaping.

The sub-group of three women is illustrated by the detailed history of G.M.

G.M., No. 40, aged 34, was unmarried and was a quietly spoken, gentle, very competent and extremely conscientious person. She was well liked and respected in the small coal-mining community where she had always lived. She played a very active part in the life of the church (Church of Scotland), being a Sunday-school teacher and in charge of the large girls' organisation run in connection with the church.

G. had been educated until the age of 14 at a primary school where her achievement was always amongst the first three in the class. She won a bursary for a year's course at a commercial college. Thereafter she did office work in the city, book-keeping, shorthand and typing. After one change of employment she had gained promotion until she had considerable executive responsibility in her own right.

She became engaged when aged 20, but after a year and a half broke this off because of incompatibilities. She stated she had no regrets about this and that she accepted that she would not now marry.

Her health record was free of major illnesses. She had had diphtheria at 8, was viewed by her mother as 'chesty' when a schoolgirl, but this apparently was because G. simulated chest pains in order to avoid classes from a particular mistress at school. At 32 she had severe rheumatic fever which had left, however, no residual disability.

G., illegitimately born, was fostered for the first four months of her life. This arrangement proved unsatisfactory and the biological mother had asked a friend from a small mining town whether she knew someone who would care permanently for the baby. The friend approached the adoptive mother, who had married the adoptive father 2 years earlier, and she and the adoptive father decided to adopt the baby. The adoption was a permanent one, but being 8 years before adoption was legal in Scotland, it was never legalised. G. always used the adoptive parents' name and was brought up as their only child.

The adoptive father, aged 44 at the time of the adoption, had been a regular soldier. He then worked as a coal-face miner until at 57 he developed serious kidney and chest conditions. Quiet and good-natured he became tense, anxious and self-centred

Group B—'Fairly Good' Adjustment

after he became ill. He was probably depressed in the psychiatric sense and he frequently threatened suicide. At 68 he died by drowning, after having walked out of the house in an apparent fit of depression.

The adoptive mother, aged 47 at the time of the adoption, had been brought up in the north of England and at 22 had married a Scottish railway engineer. Ten years later the couple moved to the husband's home city, and as he had become a permanent invalid, they bought a small shop. The adoptive mother ran this and nursed her husband until his death twelve years later. There were no children of this first marriage. A year later, at 45, she remarried. There were no children of the second marriage. At 55, the adoptive mother developed diabetes, and when 66, following a fractured ankle she developed diabetic gangrene. By 68 she was confined to bed and a wheel-chair until her death at 73. Of good intelligence, with a certain ability with figures and at organising, Mrs M. had had little formal education. In personality, she was quick-tempered, obsessional, opinionated and dominating. She had poor relationships with others because of her aggressive manner. In the close-knit Scottish village community where she lived, she was also viewed rather as an outsider because of being English and an incomer.

Finances in the adoptive home were strained. The father received only a minimum miner's wage and the income was seriously reduced when he became unwell. The adoptive mother took in boarders to supplement the income. The family lived throughout in the same colliery company's house. The home area would be accepting of adoption on the whole, but there would also be some prejudices.

The adoptive mother dominated the father, who was emotionally dependent upon her. They had some social activity together and lived harmoniously until quarrels followed the father's ill-health and the consequent financial difficulties. Although the adoptive father was kind and fond of G. and participated fully in the decision to adopt, the adoptive mother played the major rôle in her upbringing. The mother used physical punishment, expected a good school achievement, but could not understand G.'s interest in reading. Very generous in a material way, she dominated G. as a child and continued to do so later, although encouraging her to have friends of her own age, particularly through Church activities. Both parents were Church members. The adoptive mother, however, was somewhat paranoid in relation to other people's attitude to G., fearing that they would treat her less favourably because she was adopted.

Description of Histories

G., who was a sensitive child with a vivid imagination, showed signs of insecurity in her adoptive home. She had a tendency to wander as a child. She felt acutely fearful when she heard her parents quarrel.

She was unable to confide in her mother over her fear of a teacher of physical education who had temper outbursts. Instead G. simulated illness or in collaboration with another girl of the same age, wrote letters as if from her mother saying that she was unfit for the lesson. G. knew she would have been severely punished if her mother had discovered this, since she 'could not stand deceit'. G. was extremely shy and had difficulty in mixing socially with others, especially if any were not already known to her.

The adoptive mother gave G. no help at the time of her menarche and in fact she was out of touch with a teenager's view of life. Her health was deteriorating by the time G. was 8, and G.'s life after 21 was spent in working and caring devotedly for her adoptive mother. She had no opportunity for any social activity apart from her weekly attendance at the Girls' Guildry. Co-incident with her mother's deterioration in health, G. broke off her engagement, but there was no acknowledged connection between these two circumstances. The adoptive mother was appreciative of what G. did for her and G., ashamed of her mother's critical attitudes, tried, in a quiet unaggressive way, to modify these.

The adoptive family had not had good relationships with the adoptive father's relatives who lived in the same village. The adoptive mother, however, had kept in close touch with her sisters, and holidays were spent at their home. G. felt very close to these aunts and cousins and, on her adoptive mother's death, they were anxious that she should make her home with them. G. however preferred to remain in her home area.

When G. was aged $5\frac{1}{2}$ and staying with relatives she overheard the word 'adopted'. On her return home six months later, she asked her adoptive mother about this and was told that her own mother had not been able to care for her and had asked the adoptive mother to do so. The adoptive mother stressed that she loved G., and that she had picked or chosen her. G. wept at this and the adoptive father was angry and upset that adoption had been mentioned to her at all.

It emerged that the biological mother had kept in touch with the adoptive parents until G. was aged 2. Also a welfare worker[7] had visited the home until G. was aged 7, but G. was not aware of these visits. After this incident at 6, G. did not ask about her

Group B—'Fairly Good' Adjustment

adoption, and she never thought about it, since she viewed her adoptive parents as her mother and father. The adoptive mother only mentioned adoption in connection with her fear that G. was not always given her proper place in the class at school because she was an adopted child. In this connection the mother later was sure that G., in not being made 'dux' of the school, had been discriminated against.

When G. was 8, and admitted to hospital, one of the nurses whom she had displeased, passed some remark about adoption which made G. 'feel different' and which she found hurtful.

When G. was in her teens, she heard her adoptive mother comment to friends that she should have adopted when she was younger. G. denied that she had felt that her mother was too old, but she felt bound to give people an explanation of how it was that her mother was so much older than most mothers.

From physical appearance, the fact of adoption would not be obvious since G. was not strikingly dissimilar from her adoptive parents.

When G. became engaged to be married at 20, she was curious about her biological mother 'as a person', and also in relation to 'what stock I came from'. G. had worried about telling her boyfriend of adoption when they were about to become engaged. It made no difference to him however.

After the death of the adoptive father, the adoptive mother wanted to talk about the biological mother from time to time. She told G. that she had letters from her. G. however did not want to hear such discussions, finding it 'confusing' to hear of another parent.

A chance meeting in hospital with a relative of the biological mother brought the subject into the open again. The adoptive mother by that time would have encouraged a continuation of the contact, but G. again found that this would have been confusing to her. She wanted, as she said, to keep 'the two sets of parents apart'. She learned, however, at this time that her biological mother had been a domestic servant at the time of her birth, and had later married a school-teacher. She was still alive. G. still did not know who her father was. She found it reassuring, however, to have this amount of information and to know that she 'came from a nice, respectable family'.

A year after the adoptive mother's death, G. was seriously ill with rheumatic fever and during this illness, which was the first time for years that she was inactive, she wondered a great deal about her biological mother. She wondered whether she would recognise her, should she by chance meet her. When G.

Description of Histories

had been admitted to hospital she had been asked if there had been any similar illnesses in the family. She commented ruefully, 'That's when you come up against it'. G. had in her possession letters written to her adoptive mother by her biological mother. She had only read one or two of them. She had kept them, however, not because she thought any money would come to her from her biological family, as her adoptive mother suggested might happen, but because it would be going against her adoptive mother's wishes if she disposed of them.

G.'s attitude to her adoption was to be embarrassed when she had to mention it. Gradually over the years, however, this embarrassment had decreased. G. had had to refer to it at the time of first being insured since her birth certificate was in her biological name. She had been reassured that she could use her adoptive name for official purposes.

G. had told no one but her boy-friend that she was adopted. She assumed, however, that all her friends knew, since the fact of her adoption was generally known in the area. She did not want anyone outside the family to mention adoption to her since she found it hurtful to have strangers talk of it.

G. felt she belonged in her adoptive family and she very much wanted to feel no different from anyone else. She achieved this, except when family backgrounds were being discussed.

This history shows a picture of an unmarried daughter devotedly caring for her ageing and invalid mother. Many such daughters do not take or have the opportunity to marry and in this G. was no differently situated from many daughters who were not adopted. There were, however, factors in her upbringing which were peculiar to the adoption situation. First she was daughter to a woman who was too old to bear children in the usual way. Secondly, this question of age made her feel that others would be more aware of her adopted status. Thirdly, the adoptive mother, by her fear that G. would be discriminated against because she was adopted, must have added to G.'s own feelings of insecurity, and of acute shyness in relation to others. Fourthly, G. found that reference to her biological parents was confusing to her, and from this it can be deduced that her identification with her adoptive family was not complete.

The two other histories in this group, M.K. No. 26, C.D. No. 27, were both married and had young children. M.K. had always felt detached from her adoptive family, whilst

Group E—Adjustment of Foster Children

C.D. had felt somewhat resentful about her adopted status there having been problems in her adoption situation and tensions in her adoptive home.

GROUP E—ADJUSTMENT OF FOSTER CHILDREN

This last group are the six children who, although they viewed themselves as adopted members of their respective families, yet had been in fact originally foster-children where financial gain had emerged as one of the motives for taking them into the adoptive home. In 4 cases amongst the series of 52 adopted adults, however, the payment of money had been in no way an influence in the decision of these particular parents to take these children into their homes and in their planning to become permanent parents to them.

Regarding adjustment, two of these six foster-children had made a reasonably good adjustment but the other four showed varying degrees of maladjustment. In age they ranged from 45 to 38. All had been illegitimately born and all six had married. In occupation none had had any apprenticeship or formal training, yet there was in at least two cases evidence of ability which could have taken them to the Scottish Higher Leaving Certificate level of education. Amongst the 3 men there was a factory worker, a window cleaner, and a fitter, whilst of the 3 women, two had married when they were very young doing unskilled work prior to this, and one had been a hospital maid. When the health records of this group are considered, one had bronchial asthma, one had dermatitis of nervous origin, and one had constant ill-health, which had been partially accounted for by hyperthyroidism, but which was now being viewed as due largely to psychological causes.

Great variety of circumstances arose amongst these foster-children. Only two histories, however, are given; one to illustrate the group of 3 men, and one the group of 3 women.

G.McG., *No. 58*, aged 45, was boarded-out from age 4 by a local authority in one of the larger towns in the Scottish Borders. He was brought up by a couple where the foster-father was the brother of another foster-father in this series. As a result these two fostered or adopted adults looked on each other as cousins.

Description of Histories

His foster-parents were aged 51 and 48 at the time of fostering. The father was a road and quarry worker, and was of limited intelligence. He was bad-tempered, brutal and moody, and this became more marked when his eyesight deteriorated. He tended to ruminate and from time to time had bouts of heavy drinking. The foster-mother, aged 48, was also hard, insensitive and mercenary. She was apparently parsimonious, but as she did a great deal of home-baking, her family were always adequately fed.

There were two girls in the family, both aged 10, when G. joined the household. He thought one was the foster-parents' own child, since she was always given preferential treatment by them, but he later learned that she had been legally adopted. The other girl, whom also he viewed as a sister, was a foster-child,

The material conditions in the foster-home were adequate. There was always plenty of food and the house was quite well kept. The home, however, was a socially isolated one.

The religious background of the foster-home was Roman Catholicism.

G. was acutely unhappy as a child. His foster-parents quarrelled frequently. They gave him no warmth nor affection, and they were totally indifferent to his interests or activities. His birthday was not remembered and he had no pocket money or social outings, whereas his adopted sister was given all these things. Moreover, in any dispute between G. and the latter, her word was always preferred to his, and she frequently 'told tales' against him.

Little physical punishment was used, although when drunk the foster-father became rather brutal. When G. was given a row, he was reminded that he was a foster-child and that he could just go if he did not behave. G. felt that a child born to his parents could have ignored such comments, but that for him this feeling of being unwanted had left a deep mark. His vivid memory of an incident when he was 8 added to his feelings of insecurity. The foster-father's own son, by a previous marriage, was convicted for theft, and the father totally rejected him, putting him out of the house. G. knew that this would happen to him too if he ever did anything viewed as wrong.

G. carried out a great deal of the housework, particularly after his foster-mother became crippled with arthritis when he was 12. He resented this but could make no protest.

G. pursued his own interests since he was only happy away from the home. He developed a very strong positive relationship with a nun who was his teacher at school. He transferred to her all the

Group E—Adjustment of Foster Children

feelings that he would normally have had for a mother. He was very good at school work and encouragement from her gave him confidence in examinations. Although he had very strong emotional feelings for this nun, as exemplified by his frequently kissing her cloak as it hung behind the door, he felt that she had 'let him down', since, because of her vows, she could not show warmth of feeling towards him.

During his teens, G. was so acutely unhappy that he wondered how he could go on. At 13 an incident occurred which made him feel that he must leave home. The cat had strayed, and G., because it had followed him, was blamed and physically punished. G. accepted punishment when it was deserved, but this, a trifling thing in itself, symbolised for him the injustice of his foster-parents' behaviour towards him. He walked out of the house and set off to march across the hills to the nearest large city. On that occasion he had been quite determined to leave and he reported that he would have gone on if his older sister had not found him about four miles from his home town.

During these adolescent years he turned for guidance to the religious instruction he had learned from the nun who taught him. He had learnt nothing of religion from his foster-parents. In his religion, he had been taught not to retaliate and so he followed this precept. He was determined 'to go straight', although he felt that his foster-parents' attitude could well have driven him in the opposite direction.

His school achievement had been such that his teachers wanted him to go on to Senior Secondary School. The local authority gave permission for this but his foster-parents would not agree. He thus left school at 14, when he worked as a labourer. He became unemployed during the Depression years. Then he gradually built up a small window cleaning business.

Although he had friends during these years, he withdrew from any close friendship, as he did not wish it to be known that he had little or no money. He gave his entire weekly wage to his foster-mother. He pursued interests which cost little and which he could enjoy on his own, for example, swimming, hill-walking and reading. Though short in stature, he became very muscular and physically very strong.

G. always knew he was a foster-child and he could remember vaguely something about his life in the Children's Home where he had lived until he was aged 4. He was curious, however, about how the arrangements had been made. He asked his foster-mother, who told him that it was none of his business. After such a remark he found he could never ask again, but he remained on

Description of Histories

the outlook for information. He found correspondence which gave him his biological name and the name of the local authority which had boarded him out. He wondered many times how his foster-parents had ever been allowed to care for anyone. He said, however, that he would never have mentioned his problems to the local authority visitor since he wanted to be loyal to his foster-parents. He also did not wish to admit to an outsider that as a boy he still wanted somebody to be a mother to him.

From the age of 12 he wondered about his biological parents. He felt that, with all the people there were in the world, he could not be alone. There must be someone coming to look for him. He felt that nothing could be worse than his present home and that his biological mother if he met her, would take an interest in him.

When he went to work his birth certificate was needed. He wrote for this to Register House, and learned that he was born in an English city, that his mother had been a laundry maid and that her home address was in a Scottish city. He also discovered that his birthday was in a different month from what had been assumed. He was shocked by this, interpreting it as showing a complete lack of feeling on the part of the local authority administrators.

He desperately wanted to trace his biological mother, fantasying that she would be a mother to him and that he would be able to help her. Through his nun friend, he was put in touch with a convent in the appropriate area. The house at the address which was on his birth certificate had been demolished and although nuns at the convent knew others who had lived in the same block of flats, none knew his biological family. They suggested that his mother must be dead and that he was best to take no further steps. G. accepted this reluctantly. He felt that perhaps he would be hurt again if he did find her, since she had only kept him for two months. He also felt however, that no one could really understand the 'turmoil' he was in, nor how important it had been to him to trace her.

G. had tried to picture what his biological mother would be like as a person, what she looked like and why she had left him. The uncertainty had always 'nagged' at him. The lack of knowledge, he reported, made him feel very alone . . . 'as if in a flood and searching for a straw to hang on to'.

Although G. had been very unhappy in his adoptive home, he was very conscientious about caring for his foster-parents and providing materially for them. He felt that he had a duty towards them, and he had always felt that he ought to be grateful to them. He did not marry until after his foster-father's death when he was 29.

G.'s marriage was a happy one and he and his wife had nine children. His wife died suddenly when G. was 40. Although the two youngest children, aged 10 months and 2 years, had then to be cared for in a Catholic Children's Home, G. was determined to look after the other seven himself and to have the youngest two home again as soon as possible. This he managed to do, and although he had to work extremely hard, he had remained cheerful and was determined to be a 'good parent' to them all. None so far had shown any signs of maladjustment.

G. still wondered about his biological mother. He still thought that one day she 'might turn up'. He found it hurtful when his own children asked about his parents. He told them that he had been adopted, and so did not know, but added that his biological mother was dead.

G.'s attitude to adoption was to feel that any child of any intelligence was bound to wonder about his or her biological parents, and that adults in general should give children credit for having greater understanding and intelligence.

Of the other two men in this group, H.McG., No. 56, aged 45, had made a good adjustment although he was somewhat lacking in drive in some areas. A.L., No. 57, aged 41, had made a poor adjustment being self-uncertain and somewhat affectionless. His aesthetic appreciation and cultural interests did not correspond with the social group into which he had been fostered.

Of the 3 married women in this group, one history is given:

D.W., No. 53, aged 40, married with three children, had been very unhappy in her foster-home particularly because her foster-parents treated her differently from the children born to them.

D.'s biological father had hoped to marry the biological mother but, on finding her unreliable about money, he decided against marriage. Although D. was unsure how the original arrangement had been made, she assumed that her adoptive parents knew her biological mother and had agreed to foster her from the age of 3 weeks, on the understanding that there would be regular payments for her, probably from both biological parents. In fact, as far as she knew, payments had not been made regularly.

The adoptive father was 35, a cabinet-maker, who was quiet, and good-natured but easily dominated. The adoptive mother,

Description of Histories

also 35, had had an operation for a facial tumour when aged 25. Since then she had complained continually of buzzing noises in her head. Talkative, dominating and irritable, she was very energetic and very concerned to achieve material success.

There were four children of the marriage. The eldest sibling, a boy aged 11, always resented D.'s presence in the house. He later trained as an engineer. The second sibling, a boy aged 10, also had apprenticeship ability. The third sibling, was a girl aged 9, who later married an unstable man. Finally there was a boy of 7, very small in stature with a congenital shortening of one leg, who was not as intelligent as his siblings and who apparently reacted to parental pressure by developing a stammer. As a child he identified with D.

The family finances were always adequate and when D. was 12 the family moved from an ordinary working-class area to a suburban bungalow area.

The foster-parents' marriage was not happy. D. insisted that they were 'good people' in the sense that they were never knowingly unkind and that they regularly attended church (Episcopal Church in Scotland). They were, however, very undemonstrative, both to herself and to her adoptive siblings They never, for example, exchanged birthday presents within the family.

Her foster-parents were openly critical of D. They complained to strangers that she had nocturnal enuresis, that she was left-handed although she had been told to use her right hand, and that she stole food from the kitchen. She was always introduced as their 'adopted' daughter.

D. felt that she never knew what was expected of her by her parents. She tried to gain their approval in many ways, for example, by doing housework but she was never praised. Being resented by her brothers, she also tried to win their favour by doing things for them. She tried to maintain a good relationship with her adoptive sister in the same way. Under these pressures she escaped from reality by reading a great deal. She also had many fantasies of all the wonderful things that she would achieve, of subsequently recounting these to her foster-parents and of their then accepting her and praising her.

D. always knew that she was a foster-child. She was known by her foster-parents' name but also by her biological name. She was constantly reminded of her position in the family by her foster-mother who told her that she was lucky, that she ought to realise this, and that her biological mother was 'no good'. D., however, felt that it must also be very obvious to outsiders that she was an adopted child, since her hair and eyes were dark in colouring,

Group E—Adjustment of Foster Children

and she was thick-set and short in stature whereas her adoptive siblings were fair, blue-eyed and tall.

Until the age of 12, D. called her foster-parents 'Mum' and 'Dad', but after the family moved to a socially better area, her foster-mother told her to refer to her as 'Aunt'. D. found this confusing, and out of defiance and because she could not understand this change, she continued to call her 'mother'. Several years later, when D. was working as a hospital maid, her adoptive sister, to whom she was devoted, asked her not to refer to her as her sister. D. was very hurt by this.

The only information which D. had about her biological parents was what her foster-mother had chosen to tell her, and so there were gaps in her knowledge. D. never asked about her biological parents since she anticipated being told, 'There you go asking for details about parents who just left you'.

D. learned that her biological mother had come to see her when she was 5, and that later she married, had a family and was still alive in England. D. also knew that her biological father, still unmarried and living in England, was a naturalised German, but she knew nothing of his occupation. From her birth certificate, D. learned that her biological mother had been a hospital domestic worker. From her adoptive mother she heard that when her biological mother had seen her at birth, she had commented on what an ugly baby she was. D. considered that it was cruel of her foster-mother to have passed on such a comment to her.

When D. was old enough to be able to write, her foster-parents insisted that she write letters to both her biological parents. D. never received a reply from her biological mother, although she may have written to D.'s foster-parents. Her biological father had replied. He also came to see her on three occasions, first, when she was 7 and secondly, when she was 15 and a premium was needed if she were to be able to train as a hairdresser, which was her ambition. D. had no private conversation with her father and she viewed him as a stranger. When she was 17, he asked her to go and stay with him. She agreed and then fear of the unknown kept her at home. Later that year he came for the third time to see her, since he had had no acknowledgment from her of money which he had been sending but which she had never received. He discovered then for the first time that her birth had not been registered in his name but in that of the biological mother.

The foster-mother, critical of the biological mother as a person, and as an unmarried mother, frequently told D. that she would be just like her mother. As a result, D. felt ill at ease

Description of Histories

with others of her own sex and particularly gauche with those of the opposite sex.

Her foster-parents made D. feel that 'to be left by one's parents and to be illegitimately born' was something of which she should be ashamed.

D., tired after having to rise every morning at 4 a.m. to deliver milk and do housework, had not done well at school, and she knew that this displeased her foster-parents. When she left school, her foster-mother arranged that she work in a dressmaking department, but D., reacting to her strict upbringing, was dismissed for misbehaviour. D. then had a series of unskilled jobs. At 17, she decided she would train as a nurse and whilst awaiting to start this at 18, she became a resident hospital maid. She reported that on her 18th birthday she developed dermatitis and that this prevented her from applying for training. Of interest here is that it seemed possible that D. did not have the necessary education for the full training of a nurse. Another factor in this situation was her exaggerated fear that, since she was illegitimately born and since this became known to employers when they saw her birth certificate, the only kind of work she would be able to obtain was domestic work.

When D. was about 20 she was persuaded by a girl-friend to go to London to work as a hospital maid.

D. was happy for the first time when she was thus completely away from home, since for the first time she was accepted for herself. D. was always very fond of music but she had been too insecure at home to sing in front of others. While in London she took singing lessons and she reported that she was advised that she could have been an operatic singer.

D. always spent her holidays at home although she knew she was not welcome. Again she tried to gain acceptance and approval by doing a great deal of housework.

At 24, D. married someone who also had had an unhappy childhood. With the outbreak of the Second World War, her husband persuaded her to return to her home area while he was in the armed forces. D. was happy in her marriage. After a period of financial strain she and her husband now had a comfortable home and a good income. Her husband was a whaler and she had come to accept his long absences. There were three children of the marriage, aged 12, 9 and 7.

When D. returned to her home area she found that, as her foster-mother had grown older she came to depend more on D., but anything given by her to D.'s children caused jealousy with the other siblings. The tensions were such that D. found it easier

Group E—Adjustment of Foster Children

to stop seeing her foster-mother and she had had no contact with her for a year at the time of interview. At first D. was very upset at the break but then she began to see her foster-family as they really were and to realise that they had simply found her useful.

Until about one year before the interviews, D. had had very negative feelings for her biological mother, blaming her for all her unhappiness in her adoptive home and being very resentful that she had not cared for her herself. Having had children of her own D. found it particularly difficult to accept that anyone could leave a baby. After giving up work, however, when finances were easier in her own home, she had time to think things through and she became more tolerant of her biological mother seeing that as an unmarried mother she was in a very difficult position.

Although D. did not view her biological parents as parents, she had always wanted to go and see her biological mother. She had, however, mixed feelings about this, since she wondered what she might learn and since she also felt that it might be unfair to her biological mother.

D. was very lacking in self-confidence and she felt that she herself was a 'bad parent', being too strict and telling her children too often that they ought to realise how lucky they were in their home compared with her own early home life. Of her three children, the two younger ones were reacting to her own insecurity and to the lack of a permanent father-figure in the home. The second child, aged 9, had diurnal enuresis and the youngest one, the only boy, aged 7, suffered from bronchial asthma and nocturnal enuresis. He clung to D. and was babyish in his ways.

D.'s health record showed something of her reaction to the tensions in her foster-home. Between 10 and 12 she had vague rheumatic pains which she did not mention to her parents. During this time too she developed a psychogenic torticollis following an incident when her adoptive brother tried to hit her and she jerked herself out of the way. She suffered from nocturnal enuresis until 15. At 18 she developed dermatitis which had recurred throughout her adult life. Afraid of the dark and with a generalised feeling of fear, she also had a slight stammer. When nervous she felt a tightening of her throat muscles similar to that experienced when, as a child, she had been unable to sing at her parents' request.

The dermatitis was viewed by the family doctor as largely psychogenic in origin, and the other complaints, apart from the rheumatic pains, would generally all be accepted as psychogenic. Since D. had made a complete break from her adoptive family the family doctor noted a marked improvement in her health.

Description of Histories

This history showed an adoptive home which produced maladjustment in the biological children as well as in the fostered one, since children in it were not accepted for themselves but for what they achieved. The theme throughout this history was D.'s longing to feel she belonged in her adoptive home and much of her behaviour as a child and as an adult appeared to have as its motivation a desire to gain acceptance by her adoptive family. On the adoptive family's side there was a total rejection of her as a child and later they were ashamed of her occupation status.

Giving this particular history appeared to be therapeutic for the adopted adult. She reported that it was the first time she had ever had an opportunity to verbalise all her feelings and attitudes about her adoptive home. As a result of this she felt that she was seeing her situation in perspective and her foster-home as it really was.

The other two women in this group, K.H., No. 54, aged 45, and G.D., No. 55, aged 38. both showed signs of maladjustment, which could be related to unhappy early experiences. G.D. suffered particularly as a result of uncertainty about her antecedents.

Chapter Four

ANALYSIS OF HISTORIES AND OF ADOPTION SITUATION

THESE detailed histories show that a wide range of adjustment is possible for the adult who was adopted as a child and they suggest that for an adoption to be a happy solution from the point of view of the child a large number of factors are involved. They also show that there can be many subtle attitudes involved in this adoption situation which are of a kind different from those found in the situation of parents bringing up children born to them. Looked at from the point of view of the adoptive parents, many of these adoptions classified in groups other than the well-adjusted group, would also be viewed as successful since the child was dutiful towards its parents and kept from them feelings of doubt or resentment about adoption. Also from the point of view of 'community value' in the sense used by Theis, in which an assessment was made on the basis of self-support, law observance and response to educational opportunity, by far the greatest majority would again have been viewed as successful, since there was only one who was not self-supporting (No. 7) and one other who because of particular social circumstances never had been self-supporting (No. 25), and there were only three (Nos. 37, 48, 51), who had deviated in such a way that they had or might have come into conflict with the law. On the question of response to educational opportunity the picture is much more complex, since the histories show that there can be many interacting factors here. This in some cases meant that opportunities were not offered by parents to their adopted children (for example No. 6), whilst in others there were problems in relationships or in the adoption situation affecting a child's ability to use its intellectual ability to the full (for example

Analysis of Histories and of Adoption Situation

Nos. 12 and 20). In some cases there was a definite lack of response on the part of the adopted child to opportunities offered, but again the picture here was complex and different factors were involved as influencing the situation in each case. In the case of M.B., No. 8, for example, there was evidence that M. did not accept his adoptive father's offer of further training, because of a desire to be financially independent. This related to his feeling of detachment from the family, and in the case of one of the fostered children, G.D., No. 55, non-acceptance of educational opportunity was because of the manner in which this was offered.

If community value, however, is also taken to include positive health, or lack of ill-health, then a different picture would emerge. Thus in the total 58, only 17 emerged as having had no health problems of any kind at any time, and a further 5 had had minor organic conditions, such as mastoiditis leading to mastoidectomy, congenital squint, and slight hypospadias. A further two had major organic conditions, diabetes and epilepsy, and two others had had tuberculosis. Nine of the 58 had suffered from rheumatic fever at some time. Another apparently frequent medical condition was thyrotoxicosis, which appeared as a diagnosis in 4 cases of women in their thirties. In one case this was definitely viewed as psychogenic, in another it was thought that there might have been psychological factors involved, whilst in the other two cases, an entirely organic basis was given to the illness. This disease is 'more common in females than in males', and '. . . is commonest in the second and third decades'. '. . . Mental stress, anxiety, shock and sexual neurosis are often precursors of the disease, but a constitutional vulnerability of the thyroid to such stimuli is probable.'[1] Of these 4 cases, 2 were classified as poorly adjusted, one was in Group C and one was among the group of foster-children.

Amongst the group of medical conditions generally accepted as psychosomatic there was a wide range of diagnoses and frequently overlaps with one person suffering from several different conditions of a psychosomatic nature. With the exception of one case of short-term dermatitis, all these occurred in those cases classified in the intermediate and poorly adjusted groups and in the foster-child group. Thus

Analysis of Histories

there were 4 who had suffered or still suffered from asthma. One had had urticaria of nervous origin, and another continued to have recurrent dermatitis, where no allergic factor had been found. Three were viewed as hypochondriacal and frequently required attention from their family doctor. One here also threatened to commit suicide and one in fact had attempted it. There were two instances of hysterical illnesses—an hysterical aphonia and an hysterical paralysis. There were two who were currently needing help with tension or migrainous headaches, two complained of phobic anxieties, and one was suffering from severe loss of weight and disturbed sleep.

In childhood, three had suffered from nocturnal enuresis, one had been a stammerer and two had had breakdowns of a neurotic kind, when they had been unable to attend school for periods of about 6 months. There was also one case of recurrent puerperal psychosis. Two others had had fractures which had left residual disabilities. In one of these cases the disability resulted from lack of early treatment and this situation arose out of tensions in the adoptive home.

These conditions, however, occurred over many years and so they could not readily be related in any quantitative way to the figures about stress illness in the population as a whole.

1. ANALYSIS OF HISTORIES

Before an analysis of the adoption situation as such, various factors will be taken which are stressed in adoption work and in many of the studies already quoted. These will be examined in turn with reference to the classification of the adopted adults' adjustment. Thereafter the patterns which emerged in the different groups will be discussed.

In this section the groupings will be those already described in Chapter Three, and in order to facilitate references, the same initial letter for each group will be used. Thus viewing adjustment as a continuum with variations from, at one extreme, a good adjustment to a poor adjustment at the other, and with a group who had had serious problems next to the poor adjustment group, and a further group called fairly well adjusted near the well adjustment group, then the initials used to show these gradations respectively are Group A (good

Analysis of Histories and of Adoption Situation

adjustment), Group B (fairly good adjustment), Group C (intermediate adjustment), and Group D (poor or abnormal adjustment). Group E includes those cases more accurately described as fostering placements.

Also where examples are given of histories which illustrate particular points, the number of the history is given and the reader may then refer back to such details as have been given of this individual history in Chapter Three.

Although comparisons will be made and percentages of these falling into particular groups given, it should be stressed that these can only be used as indications of possible trends. This is so for two reasons. First, the classification used is of necessity a qualitative concept and, as was clear from Chapter Three, the groups were in no way watertight compartments, there being in fact a good deal of variation even within each group. Also these histories described dynamic situations at one particular time in the person's life. There were several instances to show that had they been interviewed at a different time although the problems in the situation would have been the same, the person's adjustment would have been different and so the history would have been classsified into a different group. Secondly, since it is not known what are all the possible variations in the adoption situation, it cannot be claimed that this study of 58 adopted adults includes them all. This study in fact aimed at being purely exploratory.

With these reservations in mind, however, valid comparisons can be made in relation to particular factors, especially between the two extremes of adjustment, the group of 15 who were, and always had been, well-adjusted in all areas, and the group of 10 who had major problems and who were permanently affected in major areas of their total life situation.

Age of Adoptive Mother at Placement

Adoption societies and others concerned with adoption placements usually have a policy about the age limits within which adopters must fall before they will place a child with them. The law[2] stipulates a minimum age but no upper age limit. Thus if a couple, unrelated to a child, are legally adopting it, one of them must be at least 25 and the other over 21. For a

Analysis of Histories

biological mother or father to adopt their own child, there is no minimum age stipulated, but if the adopter is not related in this way, he or she must be at least 21 years older. Adoption society policy varies but many will not consider applicants much over 40 and few would consider those aged 45 or over.[3]

TABLE 2. AGE OF ADOPTIVE MOTHER AT PLACEMENT RELATED TO ADJUSTMENT CLASSIFICATION

Age of adoptive mother at placement	Group A	Group B	Group C	Group D	Group E
	%	%	%	%	%
Under 30	26·7	16·7	14·3	20·0	0·0
30–39	46·7	50·0	57·1	10·0	16·7
40–49	13·3	33·3	19·1	60·0	33·3
50 and over	13·3	—	9·5	10·0	50·0

When the age of the adoptive mother at the time of placement was examined (Table 2) in relation to the classified adjustment of the adopted adult it was found that in Groups A, B and C a progressively bigger percentage fell into the age group 30 to 39, while in the case of D, the poor adjustment group, the largest percentage fell into the age group 40 to 49. Also in the case of Group A, the well-adjusted group, there was a larger proportion of adoptive mothers aged under 30 than in any of the other groups. On the other hand there was a larger percentage also under 30 amongst the poorly adjusted group, than amongst the other two groups. Adoption societies as a whole would not place a child with adopters over 50 and yet here 13·3% of the well-adjusted had adoptive parents over 50. This, taken in conjunction with the histories, suggests that age of the adoptive mother as such does not account for the wide range of adjustment seen amongst this particular group of histories, although if the two extremes of adjustment are taken it is found that in Group A 73·4% of the adoptive mothers were under 40 and 26·6% over 40, whereas in Group D the percentages are almost exactly reversed, with 30% under 40 and 70% over 40. Also from the histories it emerged that the

Analysis of Histories and of Adoption Situation

children whose parents were very much older than the average parent did frequently meet comments in the community which emphasised to them their adoptive status.

In the cases of the fostered children, half were with foster mothers over 50.

Adoption by one Adoptive Parent (a Mother)

Although most adoptions occur where a married couple adopt a child, there is no legal bar to one person adopting a child and no definite universal policy in adoption societies about this. The adoption of children by single women, widows or divorced women, is in fact relatively common. In this series of 52, there were three brought up by only one adoptive parent, two of whom were widows and one was single. As far as adjustment classification is concerned, two fell into the intermediate group and one into the poorly adjusted group. An examination of the histories showed the difficulties for the child brought up by a widow without any father-figure in the house (Nos. 1 and 10). Both had difficulties later in their relationships with others, whilst in the case of the single woman who adopted, the childhood of the adopted girl (No. 30), was very abnormal and restricted.

Of the 6 foster-children two were brought up by widows, and, as a result, they both had very restricted childhoods and they both later had difficulties in their relationships with others of the opposite sex (Nos. 54 and 57), whereas the 4 foster-children, reared in homes with a foster-mother and father, though they had other problems, were all able to achieve happy marriages and reasonably good relationships with others. In this series then adoption by one parent was never associated with good adjustment. This is not really surprising when related to theories of child development, all of which stress the need for two parent-figures for the child to identify with at different stages of development, so that, when they come later to make relationships in the adult world, they have this experience to equip them for making discriminating relationships with people of both sexes.

Analysis of Histories

Death of Adoptive Parent and Known Health of Adoptive Parents related to Adjustment Classification

In adoptions now it is frequently stressed that no child should be placed with adopters who, because of an illness or infirmity, will not be able to provide fully for a child until they reach the age of self-support.[4] An analysis was made of the known health records of all the adopting parents in this group and also of the date at which any adoptive parent died, and this was related to the adjustment classification. The age of self-support was taken in all cases as 18, the age after which this study viewed people as adults. No details, therefore, are used of illnesses or deaths which occurred after the child was 18, although as was shown in the individual histories, parental ill-health after this age was a vital factor in several adoptive homes. Illnesses have been taken to include hypochondriasis on the part of adoptive parents.

In Group A, two adoptive fathers died, one when a child was aged 3, but a year later she acquired a substitute father (No. 11), and one when the child was aged 10 (No. 34). In Group B there were no parental deaths. In Group C one lost her adoptive mother when she was aged one, and three lost their fathers when aged 7, 16 and 17. In two cases both parents died before the child reached the age of 18, in one case when the child was 14 and 17, and in the other case both parents died when the child was aged 15. In this group it was clear from the histories that the death of a mother when the child was aged one had added to her problems (No. 36), as too in the case where the father died when the child was 17 (No. 16) and similarly in the case where both parents died when the child was aged 14 and 17 (No. 51). In the case where both parents died when the child was 15, this was in fact the beginning of problems where previously there had been none (No. 32). In the other cases the death of a father at 7 and 16 was in both cases that of a very critical father and in the second case this death was the beginning of a better adjustment for the boy (No. 52).

In Group B there were no parental deaths and in Group E, one foster-child lost a kind foster-mother at age 7 (No. 55),

Analysis of Histories and of Adoption Situation

but one gained freedom from a critical foster-father at age 16 (No. 56).

It would seem then that where there are other positive factors for good adjustment in the home, a child can still make a good adjustment in spite of parental deaths but that in some cases the removal of beloved and understanding adoptive parents could leave a child in a vulnerable position, or could increase its chances of maladjustment.

TABLE 3. KNOWN HEALTH OF PARENTS DURING CHILDHOOD OF ADOPTED PERSON TO AGE 18 RELATED TO ADJUSTMENT CLASSIFICATION

	Group A	Group B	Group C	Group D
	%	%	%	%
Both Parents—No Health Problems or Disabilities	33·3		23·8	60
Father—Health Problems or Disability	20		4·8	
Mother—Health Problems or Disability	33·3	50	38·1	40
Both Parents—Health Problems or Disability		50	9·2	
Where one parent died, health of remaining parent or health of parents before death { No Problem	13·3		23·8	
Health Problem				

When the health record of the adoptive parents was examined (Table 3) it was found that the percentage of parents who both had had no health problems was higher in Group D than in Group A and that there was quite a large proportion in each group where the mother had had some health problem. Paternal ill-health was in fact highest in Group A and non-existent in Group D. From this it would seem that ill-health of parents as such need not lead to bad adjustment and in the same way excellent health need not lead to good adjustment.

Analysis of Histories

An examination of the histories shows, however, that although in Group A, there were serious medical problems or disabilities such as tuberculosis of the spine with psoas ulcer, leg amputation, congenital malformation, and severe deafness, there was only one instance of known ill-health which was viewed as probably psychogenic. In Group D of the four cases of maternal ill-health, two were hypochondriacal, one suffered from unspecified chronic ill-health, and the other from severely crippling arthritis, whilst in Group C of the eight cases of known maternal ill-health, five were either hypochondriacal, neurotic, or had been so disturbed as to require admission to a mental hospital.

Financial Circumstances related to Adjustment Classification

Since all adoption societies enquire into the financial position of adopters and examine the material standards of their homes, and since many others placing children for adoption stress that adopters can frequently offer a good home materially, the financial circumstances of the adopting parents in these 52 histories have been analysed in relation to the adjustment classification. Actual figures of income were obviously not obtainable and also would not have been comparable as between different decades. Instead an analysis (Table 4) was made of financial security and adequacy as appropriate to the occupational status of the adoptive father.

In groups A, C and D it was found that a very high proportion in all groups fell into the 'adequate' category, while in group B there was a higher proportion with some financial difficulty at some time. In the group of those reared in poverty, although the proportion is high in Group B this represents only one history as does the 4·8% in Group C. Taking the total 52, it was found that 36 or 69·2% were reared in homes where finances were adequate throughout their childhood, 14 in homes where there was some financial strain at some time during their childhood and 2 in homes which were very poor materially. Financial circumstances as such then did not vary with the wide range of adjustment found, although financial strain particularly when it occurred after the child was the age of 12, influenced several in their choice of further education

Analysis of Histories and of Adoption Situation

and career. The motives, however, here were always mixed and finances could be used as a rationalisation for wanting to be independent of adoptive parents. In the case of the two reared in very poor material circumstances, again some interpretation is needed. In the case of the one in Group C (No. 47)

TABLE 4. FINANCIAL CIRCUMSTANCES DURING CHILDHOOD OF ADOPTED PERSON TO THE AGE OF 18 RELATED TO ADJUSTMENT CLASSIFICATION

Financial Circumstances	Group A	Group B	Group C	Group D	Total
Adequate	11 or 73·3%	1 or 16·7%	16 or 76·2%	8 or 80%	36
Some financial strain and difficulties throughout	3 or 20%	2 or 33·3%	2 or 9·5%	2 or 20%	9
Poverty and poor material standards	0	1 or 16·7%	1 or 4·8%		2
Financial difficulties after age of 12 having been adequate prior to 12	1 or 6·7%	2 or 33·3%	2 or 9·5%		5

the poverty of the home was due initially to lack of income caused by the severe ill-health of the adoptive father, whereas similar material standards of the Group B case (No. 31) arose in a home where the adoptive father was in regular employment with an adequate wage but the adoptive mother was an incompetent housewife and there were frequent quarrels between the parents over finance, with the father from time to time refusing to give the mother a regular sum for housekeeping. In the first case the poverty added considerably to the problems for the child, and in the second case, the child adjusted fairly well in spite of the poverty.

Analysis of Histories

Occupational Classification related to Adjustment Classification

In adoption work there is now much stress laid on the importance of 'matching'[5] the child and the adoptive parents in the sense that the occupational status of the biological parents is related to the occupational status of the adopters. In this series, it was possible to relate the occupational status of the adopted person to that of the adoptive parents, but frequently information about the biological parents was completely lacking, inadequate or in part even only surmise.

Where an occupation was given as a student, this cannot be given an occupational status under the Census 1951 Classification of Occupations, where they would be classified as 'not gainfully occupied'. For the purposes of this study, however, it was important to present this information in a way similar to that available for tradesmen and those established in their occupations. Where therefore a biological parent was described as a student, this has been classified according to the group they would fall into once their training was complete. This, of course, pre-supposes that they completed their course of training successfully. Also of relevance is the fact that all non-commissioned members of the armed forces are classified in the Census as in Class III D, irrespective of the work they were doing in the forces.

The occupational status of the adoptive father or mother at the time of placement, or, if the adopter were a widow, of her late husband, and that of the adopted person was related to the adjustment classification (Table 5). In five cases where the occupational status of the adopted adult had varied, the one used in this analysis was the one most appropriate to their level of social functioning as evidenced from their history.

When the occupational status of the adoptive father was related to the adjustment classification (Table 6), it was found that in Groups A and B there were no representatives of Class I or of Class V and the largest proportion fell into Classes III and IV. If the latter classes are amalgamated, for these 2 groups, it was found that in fact 90·5% fell into these classes. The comparable figure for Groups C and D is 64·5,% with 29% in Classes I and II, and 6·5% in Class V. This could be

TABLE 5. OCCUPATIONAL CLASSIFICATION RELATED TO ADJUSTMENT CLASSIFICATION

Occupational Class	Group A		Group B		Group C		Group D		Group E	
	Adoptive Father	Adopted Adult	Adoptive Father	Adopted Adult	Adoptive Father	Adopted Adult	Adoptive Father	Adopted Adult	Adoptive Father	Adopted Adult
I	1	1	1	1	4	1	5	3		
II					0	5	4	6	2	3
III	7	13	2	5	12	12	0		1	1
IV	7	0	3		4	3		1	3	2
V		1			1		1			

Analysis of Histories

seen as an indication that the adoptive parents in Classes I and II and Class V were less likely to make good adoptive parents than those in Classes III and IV. The figures, however, are not large enough for any such prediction and also it seems more relevant to examine the histories and to see what other factors were involved. Thus amongst the maladjusted group in Classes I and II there were three where the child was reared in a home with only one adoptive parent, an adoptive mother. This situation was most likely to arise in the occupational Classes I and II, where finances would make it possible for a

TABLE 6. OCCUPATIONAL CLASSIFICATION OF ADOPTIVE FATHER RELATED TO ADJUSTMENT CLASSIFICATION

Occupational Classes	Groups A and B	Groups C and D
I and II	2 or 9·5%	9 or 29%
III and IV	19 or 90·5%	20 or 64·5%
V		2 or 6·5%

woman to undertake to care for a child single-handed, and it has already been seen that the lack of a second parent-figure influenced adjustment. Also amongst the maladjusted group in Classes I and II there was one where the problems arose only after the death of understanding adoptive parents. This still, however, leaves 5 in the maladjusted group in Classes I and II with an equivalent percentage of 16% as opposed to 9·5% in the Groups A and B.

When the occupational status of the adopted person and the adoptive father was related to the adjustment classification it was found that in Groups A and B, there appeared to be a shift towards slightly higher occupational status for the adopted person than the occupational status of the adoptive parents. Thus there were 18 in Class III amongst the adopted adults and only 9 in this class amongst the parents, with none in Class IV amongst the adopted persons, and 10 in this class amongst the parents.

Analysis of Histories and of Adoption Situation

In Groups C and D, the main shift appears to have been towards adopted adults achieving less than their adoptive parents if one looks at Classes I and II, and this is particularly striking in two histories where the adoptive parents were in Class I, and the child's occupational status was in Classes III and IV. In other cases, the class was only one lower. On the other hand the one adult in these Groups represented in Class I, had adoptive parents in occupational Class III.

This lower level of achievement, however, would be what one would expect amongst a maladjusted group since the emotional problems could prevent the full use of abilities. In this particular study, however there is also the further factor of the biological parents from whom the child may or may not have inherited its potential abilities. Also the criterion on which the occupational classification was based must be borne in mind. This classification was carried out in such a way as to secure in so far as was practically possible that each 'category is homogeneous in relation to the basic criterion of the general standing within the community of the occupations concerned. This criterion is naturally correlated with (and the application of criterion conditioned by) other factors such as education and economic environment. . . .'[6] The classification then is not necessarily equated with the degree of intelligence needed to perform any particular occupation since questions of social prestige and the value the community places on occupation influence the classification. It must also be remembered that the term occupational class refers to what has been achieved and this does not necessarily correspond with inherent ability or intelligence.

The information available then in this study cannot be used for any valid conclusions about the question of the respective achievement of the three parties to any adoption placement, the biological parents, the child and the adopting parents.

The only comment which it appears valid to make is that in Groups A and B, there was only one instance of an adopted child achieving less than its adoptive father and she did so by two classes, but her level of achievement was similar to that of her biological mother. Similarly there were two instances where the adopted person's achievement was different by two classes from what was known about the biological parents, but

Analysis of Histories

in both these cases the adopted person's class corresponded with that of their adoptive father. In Groups C and D, two achieved more than their adoptive parents by two classes and one less by 2 classes, and another less by 3 classes. When this was related to the known details about their biological parents, in both cases of higher achievement, it was found that this was also two classes higher than the biological parents, whilst in the two cases of markedly less achievement, this was equally less than the biological parents' classification in one case, whereas nothing was accurately known about the biological parents in the other. In the foster-children group, of the four where details were known about the biological parents, the adopted person achieved less than their biological parents by 2 or 3 classes, but with one exception all six achieved a classification at least one above that of their foster-parents.

The only other point to make here is that difference in social class was given in 6 cases for the non-marriage of the biological parents and this is represented in so far as occupational classification is concerned by a difference in 2 cases of one class, in 3 of 2 classes and in one of 3 classes.

Religion in the Adoptive Home related to Adjustment Classification

One of the aspects stressed in Adoption Law is the right of the biological parents to choose the religion in which their child shall be reared, and most adoption societies in this country insist on church membership for all applicants.[7]

When the religious affiliation or otherwise of the adoptive parents was related to the adjustment classification (Table 7), it was found that in Group A in 8 adoptive homes the parents were members of the Church of Scotland, and fairly closely connected with church activities. In a further 4 homes the parents were nominally Church of Scotland members but they seldom attended church. In one adoptive home, the parents were Baptist, in one other Church of England, and in a third Roman Catholic.

In Group B only one family was closely associated with the Church of Scotland, although in the other 5 the parents were nominally members.

In Group C, there were 9 adoptive homes where parents

Analysis of Histories and of Adoption Situation

were both members of the Church of Scotland and closely associated with its activities, while there was one adoptive home which was nominally Church of Scotland. There was one home with a close affiliation to the Congregational Church and one affiliated to the Baptist Church. In four others the adoptive parents were members of the Church of England, but in two cases there was little or no church attendance. Four were Roman Catholic but in two cases there was no active church influence. In only one case, however, in this group was there no church connection.

TABLE 7. RELIGION IN THE ADOPTIVE HOME RELATED TO ADJUSTMENT CLASSIFICATION

	Group A	Group B	Group C	Group D
Active Church Membership	10 or 67%	1 or 17%	14 or 66·5%	9 or 90%
Church Membership	5 or 33%	5 or 83%	6 or 28·5%	
No Church Connections			1 or 5%	1 or 10%

In Group D, there were 5 adoptive homes where parents were active members of the Church of Scotland and there was one with a strong affiliation to the Congregational Church. In three homes the parents were devout Roman Catholics and there was only one home where the parents had no church connection.

If denomination is ignored an analysis could be made of how many adoptive parents in each group were actively attached to a church and how many were nominally members, which, with only two exceptions, meant occasional church attendance and that the children were sent to Sunday School and also in many cases to youth activities attached to the church.

From this it will be seen that the highest proportion in all groups except B fell into the active church membership group and of the total 52, only 2 homes were without any church connection, and a further two, though nominally Roman Catholic, had no church connection through their homes. Thus,

Analysis of Histories

although these particular 4 were in Groups C and D, it was also clear that religious influence in the home was as likely to be associated with good adjustment as with bad. In fact, in Group D, the poorly adjusted group, 90% were brought up in homes with active church membership.

Referral to the histories themselves revealed the fact that church membership as such need not be associated with warmth, sympathy and an understanding outlook towards children. On the contrary, there were several instances of children resenting the very religious atmosphere in their adoptive home, especially when strong religious convictions were held by possessive and dominating adoptive parents. Resentment and revolt against the religious convictions of the adoptive parents could, of course, be a projection of a more fundamental revolt simply against the parents. There was, however, also the problem of the Puritanical and Calvinistic outlook associated with some religious beliefs, perhaps particularly prevalent in Scotland, which made adoptive parents critical of illegitimately pregnant mothers (and in two cases this meant they adopted legitimate children, Nos. 30 and 46), and fearful about any inherent tendency in the child to 'weakness of will' (No. 50), to promiscuity (Nos. 25 and 37) or to the consumption of alcohol, especially where it was known that this had occurred in the biological family (No. 46).

There were two instances where religion entered into the adoption situation itself. In one case the adoptive mother saw no reason for giving her adopted daughter, who was curious, information about her biological parents since it was 'God's will' that she and her husband had adopted her (No. 46) and in another case the parents felt they need not tell a child of his adoption since his birth certificate had been endorsed by a priest (No. 41).

Age at Placement related to Adjustment Classification

One of the topics which causes almost more discussion than any other in the field of adoption, is the age at which a child should be placed in its adoptive home. The different theories about this can relate to what is thought to be best for the biological mother, for the child, or for the adopters, and

Analysis of Histories and of Adoption Situation

different answers emerge dependent to a large extent on how far the person discussing this identifies himself with the biological parents, the adopting parents or the child. In so far as the law is concerned, under the Adoption Act, 1950 and the Adoption Act, 1958, the biological parents cannot officially, in the legal sense, give consent to the adoption of their child until it is at least 6 weeks old. This, however, need not of course prevent the child from being placed with adopting parents before that age, except that for these placed now through registered adoption societies, possibly only 20% or 25%, a medical examination of the baby is required, which because of a particular medical test, that for congenital syphilis, is usually not done before the child is 6 weeks old.[8] Many children are, of course, not placed for adoption until well past early infancy for a wide range of reasons usually associated with the social circumstances of the biological parents.

The age at placement was related to the adjustment classifications (Table 8). The age divisions used are those of Gesell and Amatruda who hold that in relation to a child's development 'in terms of behaviour patterns, maturity stages and growth trends' there are in the first three years of life 'eight strategic points or key ages, namely 4, 16, 28 and 40 weeks; 12, 18, 24 and 36 months'.[9]

At 4 weeks a child's responses have a 'generalised character' and his 'countenance is impassive'. He becomes more discriminating in his response to his environment by the age of 8 weeks and by 16 weeks he has developed a 'spontaneous social smile'[10] in response to a face and he can recognise certain situations in his environment, but he is 24 weeks old before he normally discriminates strangers. At 28 weeks 'He knows what is going on around the house . . . shows familiarity and anticipation in the routines of the household. He recognises strangers and tolerates them if they do not disappoint his expectancies.'[11]

Changes then before 4 weeks will be appreciated by the child at a very physical level. He will become progressively more aware of any changes between 4 and 24 weeks but again rather in terms of how he is handled, fed and stimulated rather than by whom. Thereafter if one thinks of a child's emotional development in terms of building up a relationship with parent-figures, the 'who' in the situation becomes progressively more

Analysis of Histories

TABLE 8. AGE OF CHILD AT PLACEMENT RELATED TO ADJUSTMENT CLASSIFICATION

Age at Placement	Group A	Group B	Group C	Group D	Group E
Birth to 10 days	4	2	6	2	2
10 days to under 4 weeks		1	5	1	1
4 weeks to under 16 weeks	7		3	2	
16 weeks to under 28 weeks	1	1	2		
28 weeks to under 40 weeks	1	1	1	1	
40 weeks to under 12 months				1	
12 months to under 18 months	2		2	1	
18 months to under 24 months			1		
24 months to under 36 months		1	1		1
3 years and over				2	2

important and the child after recognising strangers at 28 weeks is likely to be more and more adversely affected by any change of mother-figure. This is in line with Bowlby's[12] thesis and those of Goldfarb[13], Spitz[14] and others, that separation from a mother, or frequent changes of mother-figure, in early childhood can lead to personality problems in later life. For this analysis

Analysis of Histories and of Adoption Situation

an extra age division beyond those used by Gesell and Amatruda, was introduced,—from birth to 10 days. This was to cover the group who experienced no change in environment at all, before going to their adoptive homes.

If one assumes that there begins for a child to be a danger of being disturbed by a change of care after Gesell's key age of 16 weeks, when the child is already beginning to show signs of being sociable, and if one amalgamated the figures for placements under this age, the following picture emerges. In Group A, 11 out of 15 or 73% were placed under 16 weeks. The equivalent percentage in Group B was 50%, in Group C, 67% and in Group D, 50%. Taking the two extremes of adjustment, this gave a higher proportion placed under 16 weeks amongst the well-adjusted than amongst these poorly adjusted. On the other hand it remains significant that 3 children placed as early as 4 weeks were later severely maladjusted and that of the 5 not placed until they were at least a year old, 2 later made a good adjustment and the two here classified as in Group C were in the sub-group whose adjustment was viewed as improving.

There were, however, no well-adjusted adults amongst the 7 in this total series of 58 who were placed when aged 2 and over. Although one falls into Group B (No. 26), the history showed that this late placement made for insecurity for her as a child. In the case of the two in Group D, who were aged 4 at placement, these were the two in the sub-group who had never been able to lead full, normal lives and who both clung to their adoptive homes for security. The more intelligent of the two (No. 50) commented that to have had another home which she could remember even vaguely and where she had been happy had added to her problems and to her feeling that she never had 'belonged' in her adoptive home.

From this series then it would seem that although age at placement as such did not correspondingly vary with the wide variety of adjustment found, yet amongst those well-adjusted there was a larger proportion placed before 16 weeks than amongst those poorly adjusted, and after the age of 2, there was some evidence, particularly from the histories, of insecurity being caused by late placement.

Analysis of Histories

Experience Prior to Placement and Separation from Adoptive Home and Changes of Mother-Figure

As the histories were compiled, information was gathered on experience prior to placement, on separations from the adoptive home and on changes of mother-figure. It was found, however, that, although fairly accurate information was obtainable about separations from the adoptive home after placement, there was frequently no information or only vague surmise about previous experience, changes of foster-homes and the like. This was so in 15 cases out of the 52 adopted children and in 3 cases out of the 6 foster-children. As the details about later separations were also not necessarily always known, any analysis here was not possible. Any information of this kind where it was significant was incorporated into the individual histories and their interpretation.

Family Pattern in Adoptive Home related to Adjustment Classification

There is much discussion and divergence of opinion as to what constitutes the family pattern in the adoptive home most likely to lead to successful adoption placement. Thus some adoption societies favour the adoption of more than one child, others will not place adopted children into homes where there are already children born to the parents or where there may be children born to them later. Others have no such specific rulings and in many instances the decision about family pattern is influenced by the laws of supply and demand. If there are more adopters than babies available for adoption, then the decision is to satisfy the wishes for parenthood of as many childless couples as possible.

The family pattern was analysed in relation to the adjustment classification (Table 9). The term 'biological child' is used to refer to children born to the adoptive parents.

When family pattern and adjustment classification were compared it was seen that the largest proportion in all groups were reared as only children, under 50% in Group A and over 50% in all other groups, with a particularly high percentage in Group B. If Groups A and B and Groups C and D are taken

Analysis of Histories and of Adoption Situation

together, then the proportion of only children well or fairly well adjusted is 52·5% (11 out of 21) and the proportion with problems is 61·9% (19 out of 31). Such quantitative comparisons then yield no information for prediction, and one has to look to other factors in the situation to be able to assess that in any particular home an adopted child brought up as an only child was likely to adjust well or badly. One of the particular

TABLE 9. FAMILY PATTERN IN ADOPTIVE HOME
RELATED TO ADJUSTMENT CLASSIFICATION

Where the adopted child was:	Group A	Group B	Group C	Group D	Total of 52	Group E
1. Only child	6 or 40%	5 or 83·3%	13 or 61·9%	6 or 60%	30	
2. One of 2 or more adopted children	2 or 13·3%		1 or 4·8%	1 or 10%	4	
3. Older than any biological children	1 or 6·7%		1 or 4·8%		2	
4. Younger than any biological children	4 or 26·7%		5 or 23·7%	3 or 30%	12	6
5. In between biological children who were older and younger	2 or 13·3%	1 or 16·7%	1 or 4·8%		4	

problems for the unhappy adopted only child was the feeling of isolation, and the feeling that they were different from all others. They frequently expressed a desire for an adopted brother or sister. What is of value in these groupings, however, is to note that a good adjustment was possible in all five family patterns mentioned, as also was a poor adjustment and an intermediate adjustment.

A frequent pattern now met in adoption society work, that of the family of adopted children, is represented by 4 histories, two in Group A (Nos. 11 and 29) and two in Groups C and D (Nos. 8 and 50). Another pattern often reported is that where

Analysis of Histories

a couple adopt a child and then later have a child of their own. This pattern is represented by two histories, again divided equally between those who had no problems (No. 38) and those with problems (No. 52). Another history (No. 47) could also be included in this pattern although classified as amongst those in the middle of a biological family. This was the history of a girl who was adopted by a couple who were advised they would have no more children and then almost at once conceived another child. Her adjustment was classified as falling into Group C.

An examination of the histories where these last two mentioned patterns occurred showed that in the well-adjusted group, these adopted children were accepted for themselves by their adoptive parents, whereas in the poor adjustment group, the children had to conform to particular specifications in the adoptive parents' minds and this resulted in emotional rejection of them in two cases (Nos. 47 and 52), when a biological child was later born who could be felt to be more truly the child of the adopting parents.

The pattern of the adopted child being younger than the biological children is represented by 12 in this series and here 4 or 33·3% had no problems, whereas 8 or 66·7% had problems. An examination of the histories showed that the adopted children reared in this family pattern and who were unhappy in their adoptive home interpreted behaviour towards them in terms of parental preference for older children born to the adoptive parents. Any sign of any difference in treatment was at once seized upon and magnified. Even amongst those who were well-adjusted, there had been moments when the child interpreted the parents' behaviour in terms of discrimination against him or her because he or she was adopted, for example, when the child had been scolded by its parents, or it had quarrelled with its adoptive sibling, born to the parents, and the parents had rightly taken the sibling's part.

Also from the histories of the 8 who were poorly adjusted or had problems, there was evidence of actual preferential treatment towards biological children in 3 cases (Nos. 12, 47, 51) whereas in two cases (Nos. 4, 17) the fact that the adopted child was given more materially than the biological children had been given as children, made for jealousy on the part of the

Analysis of Histories and of Adoption Situation

biological children, which in its turn could be seen as largely responsible in at least one case (No. 4) for the adopted person's poor adjustment.

The situation of a 'mixed' family in the sense of a family composed of biological or adopted children and foster-children was seen to be associated also with poor adjustment in the group of fostered children. This was particularly marked in five cases and the histories show how much insecurity and resentment was engendered in the fostered child by the preferential treatment by parents of biological children.

The situation then of a mixed family in the sense of a family of biological and adopted children can be fraught with dangers, and these include what the parents do and say, what they omit to do and say, and how the adopted person and others in the family interpret this. On the other hand, in adoptive homes where the children are all individually given emotional security and acceptance then the adopted child identifies completely with the adoptive family, its adoptive parents and its adoptive siblings, and the siblings in turn look on him or her as a brother or a sister. In the group of those well-adjusted there were in fact 7 out of the 15 in this position of being reared in a mixed family. Given the right circumstances then this family pattern can be associated with good adjustment whereas given other circumstances it can lead to severe maladjustment.

Relatedness and Personal Knowledge of Biological Parents related to Adjustment Classification

It was mentioned in Chapter Two under 'Method of Referral' that in eight cases it emerged that the adoptive parents were related in some way to the biological parents. When these eight histories were analysed in relation to the adjustment classifications it was found that 3 were in Group A, 1 in Group B, 2 in Group C and 2 in Group D. There were eight further cases where the adopting couple knew the biological mother or father before there was any question of their adopting their child. These, when related to the adjustment classifications showed that 3 were in Group A, 4 in Group 3 and 1 in Group D. This together with an examination of the histories showed that relatedness and personal knowledge of biological parents could

Analysis of Histories

be related both to good adjustment and to poor, and that what emerged as important was first, the adoptive parents' attitude and feelings towards the biological parents, and secondly whether they transferred these same feelings to the child Thus in Group A it was known that one adoptive mother was very fond of the child's biological father, who was one of her siblings, and that she also had very strong positive feelings for the illegitimately born baby. Equally, however, in Group A there were adoptive parents critical of the biological mother but not transferring any of this criticism on to the child. In the one case (No. 26) in Group B, the adoptive parents were critical of the biological parents and they occasionally used the information they had about them to be somewhat critical of the child. In Group C, of the 6 histories involved, there were three where the adoptive parents were approving in their attitude to the biological parents and two where they were openly critical. One of these latter cases was the history (No. 51) where there was constant reference to the biological mother's behaviour and to the fear that the child would behave in the same way. In another of these six Group C cases is a history (No. 39) where the adoptive mother was very approving of the biological mother and very critical of the child when she did not conform exactly to the picture the adoptive mother had of her biological mother.

Of the three in Group D there was one case where the adoptive parents were accepting in their attitudes to the biological parents, but critical of the illegitimate child; in one case they were critical of the biological parents although this never implied criticism of the child; and in one case no clear picture emerged of their real attitudes.

This then would suggest that relatedness and personal knowledge of biological parents can aid or hinder adjustment in so far as it aids or hinders the adoptive parents having a warm and accepting attitude towards their adopted child, and that though the actual content of what is known about the biological parents' behaviour can influence this situation, so too can the adoptive parents' attitude towards this information and their assumption or otherwise that the child is likely to, or will necessarily, follow the same pattern of behaviour as its biological parent.

Analysis of Histories and of Adoption Situation

Attitude in the Home Area to Adoption

An attempt was made to assess the attitudes to adoption in the different geographical areas and at the period in time when the adopted adult was a child. It was found, however, that such community attitudes were too nebulous to be defined accurately. Where appropriate they have been inserted in the individual histories.

On the whole, however, it was found that country areas and small towns were generally accepting of adoption as too were working-class areas of the city. Fishing communities, however, tended to have prejudices. In lower middle-class and middle-class areas some evidence emerged that to be an adopted child was very unusual 20 to 50 years ago.

What emerged more definitely in such an attempt to obtain a picture of community attitudes was that, in every community, no matter how generally accepting it was of adoption, there were individual members in it who had prejudices and doubts about adoption and about adopted children, and that they frequently communicated these feelings either to the children or the adoptive parents. These comments varied from remarks to the adopted child that they would have to repay all that their parents had done for them, and that no one knew what their antecedents had been, to remarks to the adoptive parents about their courage or foolhardiness in bringing up someone else's child.

Patterns which emerged

So far all the factors discussed related to particular facts or circumstances about the adopters or child and very little has been said about attitudes and feelings. An analysis of the histories, however, showed that it was the emotional attitudes and relationships within the adoptive home and the attitudes in the adoption situation itself which accounted to a large extent for the wide range in adjustment found.

Analysis of Histories

Histories in Group A

When the 15 histories in the well-adjusted group were examined it was found that in all cases there was a very good marital relationship between the adoptive parents. Each was satisfied with the other as a partner and there was mutual understanding. The children in this group had all been given affection, emotional security and consistent discipline from their parents, but they had all also been accepted for themselves, encouraged to follow their own interests, to do as well as they could at school without pressure, to have careers of their own choosing, friends of their own age, and later to join in adolescent activities and to have friendships with those of the opposite sex. Many of the parents had had difficulty in giving any guidance about sex and the different sexual rôles of men and women, but this could be viewed as normal for parents at the present time as much as for those of two or more decades ago. This relaxed attitude to their children applied whether the children were legitimately or illegitimately born and the particular relevance of commenting on this attitude will become apparent when the attitudes are described in the poorly adjusted histories.

There were only three instances of tension in the home between the child and its parents. In two cases (Nos. 9 and 44) girls had had poor relationships with their adoptive fathers but very good relationships with their mothers, and the girls accepted without anxiety that it was fairly usual for a daughter not to get along so well with her father. In the third case (No. 14) there was evidence of a slightly triangular situation with the adoptive mother perhaps somewhat over-anxious to encourage the daughter to have boy-friends and so leave home and not compete with her for the adoptive father's attention. This was in fact the one adoptive mother in this group to have an illness of a psychogenic nature.

Where there were other children in the family the adopted child was treated exactly as if it had been born to the adopting couple. When the wider family of relations was considered it was found that, in eleven cases, all uncles, aunts and so on had accepted the child completely into the family. In one case (No.

Analysis of Histories and of Adoption Situation

34), contact with relatives had to be dropped because it would have made for difficulties for the child since it would have brought her into touch with her biological mother. In one case (No. 44) there was an uncle and in another case (No. 14) an aunt who was opposed to the idea of adoption. In the latter case the adoptive parents, because of distance, did not see the aunt, and in the other case the parents, after quarrelling with the uncle over his opposition to adoption, had no further contact with him. In a third case (No. 11) again a break in contact following a quarrel prevented what might have been a difficult situation for the child—an aunt who also had adopted a child and who tended to compare the two adopted children in their hearing. The only other relatives problem in this group (No. 28) came from a sister-in-law who, on hearing that one of the family was adopted, became very critical of her. This hurt the adopted person but her adoptive father supported her in this situation.

When the adoption situation itself was examined, it was found that four reported that they had always known they were adopted. In fact in three of these cases there had been incidents when the child was about nine when other children had said they were adopted. Their adoptive mothers had told them at that time that this was so and had described their adopted status in a re-assuring way, for example, that the child had been chosen by them, or that the child's biological mother had asked them to look after him or her.

In three further cases, outside incidents with other children led the children to discuss adoption with their parents. The age range was 9, 11 and 12, but only in one case (No. 21) did the parents agree that the child was adopted and give re-assuring details about their love for the child. In another case (No. 29) the girl asked her adoptive mother persistently about adoption (there was a marked physical difference) and eventually the mother agreed that she was. In the third case (No. 28) the mother was somewhat non-committal but gave a definite confirmation of adoption when the girl was 14. In seven cases the children were given the information spontaneously by their adoptive mother, without some outside comment precipitating this, two when aged 4 or 5 and just about to go to school, one when aged 13, two when aged 14 and about to go to work,

Analysis of Histories

one aged 17 and one when aged 29, when about to be married. Of the two told at 4 or 5, both met comments from school children when they were 7 or 8 and aged 9, and these they shared with their adoptive parents and were told again in a re-assuring way about their adoption. The one told at 13 had known since age 12 that she was probably adopted but she had not asked her parents saying to herself that if there were anything in it her parents would tell her.

Of the two told spontaneously by their mothers at 14, one (No. 22) had overheard a conversation when she was 7 or 8 which had made her wonder if she were adopted, but she did not ask her mother, feeling again that any information of that kind would come from her mother. In the other case (No. 11), the girl had had no idea she was adopted until she was told. This information gave her a shock and since her adoptive mother did not give her much detail of her biological parents, she worried in case her mother had been unmarried and this, to her at age 14, would have caused her concern and have made her feel adoption was something of which to be ashamed. From what she had been told, however, she gradually realised her parents must have been married and she quickly recovered from her initial feeling of shock, although it took her several months to become used to the idea of adoption.

In the case of the girl told at 17 (No. 14), there had been two incidents for her when aged 12 when girls at school had said she was adopted. She wondered and worried, but again did not ask her adoptive mother who it transpired had worried for years about how to tell her. Of interest here is the fact that this girl was the only one in this group to have a generally acknowledged psychosomatic condition—dermatitis from which she suffered for 6 months at the age of 12.

In the seventh case (No. 38) the adopted person did not know that she was adopted until the day before her marriage at 29. This was a shock at the time but she denied that it had worried her for any length of time, saying that she was a person, irrespective of her antecedents, and that as it had all happened so long ago there was no point in enquiring further. She also commented that temperamentally she accepted things without questioning them. Again the picture emerged that, had she wondered at the time, she could not have asked her adoptive

Analysis of Histories and of Adoption Situation

mother. The information would have had to come from her adopted mother. Obtaining however an accurate picture of this particular one was complicated, it will be remembered, by the fact that this adult was now an adoptive parent herself.

In this group of 15 then there were only 3 cases where there was no report of adoption having been mentioned to the child by people outside the family. In one of these three cases the adopted adult (No. 5) said she had always known (she had used her biological name at school), and in the other two cases secrecy was maintained until 14 and 29. Exactly how this was possible cannot, of course, be accurately assessed, but it may not have been without significance that in one case (No. 11) the family moved to a completely new area when the adopted child was 10, and at the same time lost contact with the relative, already mentioned, who made comparisons between her adopted child and the one in this series, whilst in the other case (No. 38) the family moved to a new area when the adopted child was a few weeks old.

Except in the two cases where the first and only intimation of their adoption came from their adoptive mothers, all other 13 were emphatic that a child should be told of adoption by its parents. It was then in a position to deal with any comments from outsiders. In the three cases where the child's first intimation that it was adopted had come from outsiders but where the child had not shared this with its adoptive mother, two felt very strongly that they should have been told by their parents when much younger and not left to wonder for so long—5 years in one case and 6 in the other. This was the comment too of the girl who only obtained confirmation of her adoption by persistent questioning of her adoptive mother. Until it was confirmed the uncertainty had worried her.

In this group of 15, there was only one case where it was known that the adoptive parents were critical of the biological mother, but this never became criticism of the child. In nine cases it was clear that the adoptive parents either liked what they knew about the biological mother or were sympathetic to her particular position as an unmarried mother. There were three cases where there was no evidence for such positive feelings towards the particular unmarried mothers but there

Analysis of Histories

was lack of criticism of unmarried mothers in general. In two cases it was not known what parental attitudes were here.

Histories in Group D

When the ten histories in the group with a poor or abnormal adjustment were examined a very different picture emerged.

There were five instances of unhappy marriages with tensions between the adoptive parents and in some cases bitter quarrels. There was one child brought up by an embittered ego-orientated widow who had quarrelled with all her relatives and who had no friends. There were three brought up by couples, happy in their marriage but where the adoptive mother was strict and punitive towards the child. They were also all over 40 years in age. In a tenth case (No. 4) the adoptive parents' marriage was a happy one and the child was pampered and spoiled as the youngest in a large family. The problems here arose out of jealousies with other siblings in the family.

In the relationships between the parents and children only one (No. 4) was given emotional security and encouragement to have interests and friends of her own. In one case (No. 45) the parents were totally indifferent to what the child did. In all other cases, the parents were possessive, restrictive or dominating, or a mixture of all three. In four cases there was considerable educational pressure put on the child and the motive in this was in order that the child would be a credit to the adoptive parents. This was also the tenor in three further homes.

When the motive in adopting was analysed it was found that two had adopted to have someone to look after them in their old age, whilst in a third case this was again probably the motive. One adopted out of pity. In two cases it emerged that the mother had been the prime mover in wanting to adopt, with the father agreeing simply to please her. In one of these two cases (No. 25) the child had been viewed as company for the mother while the father was away a great deal on business, and in the other (No. 7) the child was used by the mother as a protection against sexual relationships with the adoptive father. In both cases this led to later rejection of the child by the father and to divided discipline in the home.

Analysis of Histories and of Adoption Situation

The wider family here too was not always accepting. In five cases they were accepting, but in one of these cases (No. 46) the child never felt she belonged in the wider family. In one case (No. 10) most of the family was accepting but the maternal grandmother had been very opposed to the adoption. In one case (No. 45) uncles were unaccepting and in another two (Nos. 7 and 33) it was aunts who visited the adoptive home who did not accept the child. In this latter situation cousins also, of course, did not accept the child. In the tenth case (No. 4) it was siblings and their children who were jealous of the child's place in the family.

When the adoption situation itself was examined it was found that how the child had been told of its adoption and the attitudes within the adoption situation itself had made for poor adjustment or had added to the tensions and problems in the adoptive home. One (No. 45) was told in anger by his parents when he was 9 or 10, the emphasis being made that he was unwanted and illegitimate, and would have been destitute but for them. In another case (No. 4) a jealous niece told the child along similar lines when she was aged 15, her adoptive mother having denied to her that she was adopted following an incident at school when she was 9 or 10. For four cases (Nos. 7, 10, 33, 46), there were years of doubts and uncertainty about whether or not they were adopted, with the respective adoptive mothers denying that they were adopted or evading answering relevant allied questions. The same picture emerged here as in the good adjustment cases. Although worried by their doubts and the uncertainty none felt they could ask their adoptive parents. The information about this had to come from the parents on the parents' initiative. These doubts arose out of incidents at age 9, 10, 12 and 15.

In one case (No. 48) the comments of outsiders made a child ask if she were adopted when aged 13, but, though the adoptive father admitted she was adopted, he gave no information about her early history. This led her to worry about possible illegitimacy. In another case (No. 25) the child had experience of hearing that a particular child was an adopted child in such a way as to imply this child was different from others, having even a different body. When the child in this series later learnt from an outsider that she herself was also adopted, this was a

Analysis of Histories

severe shock to her. It made her feel that she too must be quite different from other children. One (No. 41) was told that he was adopted when he was 17 and about to leave home for the Merchant Navy. His reaction was that if lies had been told about this basic fact of parenthood, then he should doubt the veracity of all that his parents had told him. Another (No. 50) always knew that she was adopted and that she had a previous home where she was given affection and acceptance instead of being constantly expected to conform to a particular pattern of behaviour. Her adoptive mother told her of her adoption when she was 14.

In eight of these ten histories then, the child knew definitely that he or she was adopted before they were out of their teens, the age range being from 9 to 17. In two cases (Nos. 7 and 33), however, they continued to live with their doubts until they were aged 32 and 42 — doubts which had repercussions on their adjustment. When one considered the other eight cases it was found that in seven the relationships between parents and child had never been without tensions and problems. Once the child knew it was adopted or it was acknowledged openly that it was adopted, then the relationships deteriorated further, with behaviour problems arising in the one home where previously there had been none. In this last case (No. 4) the child became aggressive, felt inferior and had death wishes. In one case (No. 41), the man made a complete break with his adoptive home and with his adoptive parents' religion, with consequent deep feelings of guilt. In another case (No. 45), the boy from the age of 9 felt that he was on his own in the world and that he must be self-sufficient, with resulting inability to have close relationships with others. In a further case (No. 50), adoption constantly entered into the conflicts between mother and daughter, the mother saying that, as the daughter was not conforming to her wishes, she should have left her in her poor home, and the girl for her part feeling that her adoptive mother was not a mother to her and threatening to run away from home. In one case (No. 25), the girl felt that now she knew of adoption this explained her adoptive father's punitive attitude towards her. He had only adopted her to please her mother. He had never wanted her. This led to aggressive and attention-seeking behaviour. In one case (No. 48), hearing that she was adopted drew a girl closer to her adoptive father to whom she was already close and made her relationship with her adoptive mother a completely negative one. In this case, however, there may have been other factors operating since the adoptive father was also the child's biological uncle and in intelligence range and interests they were alike.

In one case (No. 46), a realisation at 16 that she was adopted, after two incidents when her mother had assured her she was not adopted and even implied that she had been born to her, led a girl to doubt everything she had ever been told by her adoptive mother, and she continued to doubt her thereafter. Feeling that her parents had deceived her, she revolted aggressively against their influence, particularly that of her adoptive mother. She also felt considerable frustration over her inability to obtain some factual information about her placement and her biological parents, because her adoptive mother viewed her adoption as 'God's will'. In another case (No. 10) the same feeling that an adoptive mother had deceived her led a girl to withdraw into herself, to become secretive and to hide things, even more than she had already been doing, from her adoptive mother. It is interesting to note, however, that this girl was the only one of the ten whose reaction on knowing she was adopted was to want to seek out her biological mother as someone who would understand her in a way that her adoptive mother did not.

All ten felt that they should have been told of their adoption by their adoptive parents. This included the one who was told in a cruel way by them. He still felt they should have told him but that they should not have been critical of his biological parents or of himself as an illegitimately born child. Those who met comments from outsiders about adoption, before they knew they were adopted, or while they were in doubt about being adopted, were hurt by such comments. Those who were told cruelly of their adoption, together with one other, continued throughout life to be hurt by any community comment about adoption in general, feeling that any such comment always applied to them.

When the attitude of adoptive parents to the biological parents was examined, a very different picture emerged from that seen in the well-adjusted group. In only one case was it

Analysis of Histories

known that the adoptive parents had been sympathetic towards the biological mother and towards the child thus born. In one case the adoptive mother, a widow, was not critical of unmarried parents, since she considered that the consequent children could be adopted by people who wanted someone to look after them in their old age. Two adoptive mothers viewed illegitimacy as something 'sordid', and one of them associated this with 'weak wills'. Both feared and expected that their adopted daughters would inherit the same weaknesses. This made for a very distrustful attitude towards them, particularly in adolescence. One equally feared inherited traits, which was however in this case an inclination towards the consumption of alcohol. Having a 'horror of illegitimacy' she had adopted a child born legitimately, and she thus had no fears about deviant sexual behaviour in adolescence. In one case the adopters were not critical of the biological parents but they were very critical of the child thus illegitimately born, and in one case the adoptive parents stressed the inadequacy of the biological parents and of their home.

In the three further cases it was not clear what the attitude of adopters to the biological parents had been. In both the cases here of girls (Nos. 7 and 33), they had had a very abnormal and restricted adolescence, but this could have been attributed to general parental attitudes of possessiveness and domination. Neither ever had friendships with others of the opposite sex; but one (No. 7) was openly obsessed by sex, and so, in a histrionic way, took pleasure in the immorality of her biological parents.

Histories in Group C

The picture in Group C histories, those classified as being in an intermediate position of adjustment, is much more mixed than in the two groups already discussed.

In 13 cases the marriages of the adoptive parents were happy or at least stable and mutually satisfying. In 6 cases the marriages were very unhappy with frequent quarrels, and in two cases children in this group were reared by only one adoptive parent.

In three cases children were given emotional acceptance and

Analysis of Histories and of Adoption Situation

security and encouragement to develop along their own individual lines right through from childhood until past adolescence. In 6 cases, they were given this acceptance and encouragement up to adolescence, after which the adoptive parents began to be restrictive or possessive towards the child. In 6 cases there was divided discipline in the home, with the child finding one parent understanding of a child's or adolescent's point of view, while the other parent was punitive and rejecting or over-possessive and demanding. In 4 cases the good relationship was with the father (2 boys and 2 girls), and in 2 cases it was with the mother (one boy and one girl). In the remaining 7 cases a variety of situations arose. In one case, the child was subjected to 3 parent-figures all competing for his affection and in another to an over-possessive single parent who put very considerable educational pressure on the child. In one further case there was considerable educational pressure put on a child by a very possessive mother to achieve a particular pattern, and in two cases both parents were immature and inadequate and could offer the child no emotional security or encouragement of any kind in any sphere. In two cases the child was rejected in the adoptive home,—a rejection made more obvious to the child because of there being other children in the home, biological or adopted, who were accepted and given affection and some emotional security.

As there are many patterns and nuances in this group of 21 and much overlap between different patterns, referral has to be made to the original histories to see the interplay in the various areas studied. What has been done here is simply to select those features in each history which emerged as most significant and as far as was possible similar patterns have been grouped together.

In this way, it was found that there was a group of 5 (Nos. 13, 15, 18, 24, 37) who had problems in their relationship with their adoptive mothers, all of whom were ego-orientated, three of them suffering from hypochondriasis, and one from early dementia. In only one case in this group was the marriage happy; in the other four cases there were constant quarrels. In 3 cases the mothers were excessively possessive, hoping in two cases to repeat the patterns of their own childhood when they had been very close to and dominated by their own

Analysis of Histories

mothers; in two cases they were inconsistent and rejecting. All the children heard about their adoption from outside the family. One (No. 18) heard comments from the age of 5 but was unable ever to obtain a definite and accurate picture from her adoptive mother. Two found documents at home when they were aged 12, and both were resentful and hurt about hearing in this way and one subsequently hid things in turn from her adoptive mother (No. 24). In one of these two cases (No. 15) the situation was made much worse for an intelligent and sensitive child by her having definite and preconceived ideas about illegitimacy after learning of its social disgrace. This led to an acute feeling of having been personally rejected when she in turn realised that she had been illegitimately born. The importance of previous attitudes to adoption occurred in another case in this group (No. 13) where a girl was not told until she was 15. By that time she had, from two incidents, built up a picture first that people made a difference to one if one were adopted, and secondly that some adopted children when told suddenly had a mental breakdown. She frequently feared subsequently that she was or would become ill mentally. She too, however, like the first mentioned (No. 15), also had to contend with continual uncertainty about her origins, and differing stories. This in both produced a feeling of considerable anxiety. They both tried to build up a possible explanation of their origin from various items in their surroundings which they interpreted as significant.

In two (Nos. 15 and 37) of these five, there was again the pattern seen already in the poorly adjusted group where adoptive mothers feared that their adopted daughters would repeat the pattern of their unmarried biological mothers and thus they distrusted them in adolescence with regard to evening activities and being friendly with members of the opposite sex. In one of these cases (No. 37) the mother had been determined that her daughter should not be told of adoption and when the father did tell her, became convinced erroneously that the girl hated them from that moment. Her subsequent constant reference to adoption reminded the girl of it when otherwise she felt she would have forgotten. Also in this same home was the triangular situation referred to in one case in the well-adjusted group, although here the adoptive

Analysis of Histories and of Adoption Situation

mother overtly accused the adoptive father and his non-biological daughter of having a close relationship with each other which was not that of a father to a daughter.

There was a further case (No. 3) of a possessive and dominating and very unstable adoptive mother whose daughter had to achieve a certain intellectual and social standard to conform to the mother's wishes. When the girl was unable to do this, possibly from inherent lack of ability, the adoptive mother, who in fact knew nothing about her biological parents, assumed that this lack of achievement related to her antecedents. The girl reacted to her very unstable and frequently changing environment in such an affectless way that she accepted the information at 18 that she was adopted in a way lacking any significant feeling.

There was one further instance (No. 39) of an adoptive mother who was possessive and restrictive in the child's adolescence but here the motivation was to repeat two patterns; first, that of her own childhood when she had been close to her own mother, and secondly, that of the biological mother. The latter, also an adopted person, had devotedly cared for her adoptive mother and put her adoptive parents before husband and children. The child here showed aggression and independence. She was determined not to be dominated, and her feelings of resentment against her adoptive mother had been aroused originally by what she viewed as an underhand way of dealing with the legalisation of her adoption. She felt that as the person involved it should at least have been discussed with her.

The next group is of three histories where it appeared that only one parent had really wanted to adopt a child and that the marriage partner had simply agreed to please them. This was a pattern found too in the poorly adjusted group. In two instances (Nos. 6 and 52) there was definite evidence of rejection of the child by the father, and in the other (No. 16) this was how the adopted child interpreted his mother's punitive and restrictive attitude towards him. In one of these three cases (No. 52), the adoptive mother told the boy he was adopted and something of his early history after an incident at school when he was 8 or 9, and she had chosen carefully what she would tell him so that he would not feel an unwanted or unacknowledged child. In the other case of paternal rejection

Analysis of Histories

(No. 6) the girl was completely unaware that she was adopted until her mother suddenly told her when she was 21. She was very resentful that she had been told and that her biological mother had rejected her. In telling her own adopted son of his adoption she was careful in her turn, as the mother quoted in the previous case, to give no information that implied he had been unwanted or unacknowledged by his biological parents. In the shock of thus hearing at 21, she had apparently contemplated leaving home, and had she done so, she contended that she would not have returned. In the third case in this group (No. 16), the adoptive father was understanding of the child's need for information about his adoption and his biological family but his adoptive mother was not.

Thirdly there was a group of three where members of the adoptive family, other than the adoptive parents, treated the child in such a way that they felt that they did not belong in the family or that they were inferior in some way because they were adopted. In one of these cases (No. 32) the atmosphere in the adoptive home itself had been as described in the group of well-adjusted cases and the child had been told of her adoption by her mother at 12 in a way to make her feel that she was wanted and that adoption was nothing of which to be ashamed. Problems only arose for her after the deaths of her adoptive parents because of her non-acceptance by an aunt who had never approved of her adoption. In another case (No. 8) again an aunt was critical of the adopted children in the family and her exclusion of these children from family invitations hurt the child, who participated in this series, more than anything else in his adoption situation. He was also aware that he was adopted from the age of 12 but was given no confirmation of this or information about his placement and biological parents until he was 28. His main reaction was one of acute resentment that others in his family and in his community knew details about his adoption which he had not known. He also had to contend with a very possessive adoptive mother who wanted to believe that her adopted children had been born to her, a pattern found amongst adoptive mothers and which is mentioned later. In the third case (No. 12) an adopted sister's comments and overheard whisperings had made the child feel insecure in her adoptive home. An incident at 10

Analysis of Histories and of Adoption Situation

when children had commented cruelly about her as an adopted child, and when also she found a document at home, confirmed for her what she had feared. She interpreted later happenings in the house in terms of a brother deserting her, her parents not wanting her, and in her unhappiness she wanted to find her biological mother. A further pattern in this case was again the fear that an illegitimately born child was more likely to become illegitimately pregnant.

This last mentioned pattern was illustrated to excess in one of the two homes where adopted children were apparently always rejected by adult members of the household. In this case (No. 51), the constant mistrust and constant referral to the illegitimate pregnancies of the biological mother nearly drove this adopted child, not into becoming illegitimately pregnant, which she was determined to avoid, but into delinquency of another kind in order to escape from this constant criticism. In the other case of total rejection (No. 47), this appeared to have been related to the fact that a further child was unexpectedly born and that ill-health made for increasing poverty in the home. The child was deeply and permanently damaged by hearing of her adoption in a vindictive way from another girl when she was aged 14. Confirmation for her that her parents rejected her as an adopted child and preferred the children born to them, came when her adoptive mother introduced her as, not her daughter but 'just adopted'.

The problems in two cases (Nos. 35 and 36) sprang mainly from when or how they were told of their adoption. In one case (No. 35) the adopted person was not consciously fully aware that she was adopted until she was 31 when she needed her birth certificate for the first time, although there had been an incident at 9 or 10, when her adoptive mother had denied that she was adopted. The child noted thereafter, however, that her mother was evasive in answering questions about where she was born and whether she was like her. Sensitive and shy, she was very upset to learn of her status. She was particularly resentful to realise, first that she had met her biological maternal grandmother unknown to her, and secondly, that the family and others had known of her adoption for years whilst she had not.

In the other case (No. 36), a girl who had lost her adoptive

Analysis of Histories

mother when one year old, was told of her adopted status by her adoptive father and stepmother when she was 14. By this time she knew about the social stigma of illegitimacy from books (at least one of which was given to her by her adoptive father), and although no one ever did treat her any differently, she always feared that they might. She was ashamed of her illegitimate and adopted status. These problems were accentuated for her by her biological name being used unnecessarily for insurance purposes, and so later for National Service.

There was the group of two girls adopted by one adoptive parent—a widow and an unmarried woman. In the first case (No. 1), the child was accepted as one of the family although an aunt again made for problems by her disapproval of adoption. The crux, however, for this intelligent girl was again that she was not told of her adoption, but that she found out about it and then was unable to obtain accurate information about her early history and biological parents. This situation, as has already been mentioned, led to resentment towards her adoptive mother and aggressive behaviour. Added to this was a feeling of isolation derived from her erroneous belief that her two adoptive siblings, as well as her mother, knew the details of her adoption whereas she did not. She then interpreted ordinary happenings in the family in terms of the rest of the family wanting to hide things from her and in terms of preferential treatment of the two biological children. In the other case here (No. 30) the single adoptive mother was seeking all her personal emotional satisfactions and sense of fulfilment from the child, and the emotional pressure put on the child was excessive. Although the child was expected to call the adoptive mother 'mother', the child herself was never referred to as a daughter but simply by her first name, presumably to avoid difficulties for the adoptive mother of being an unmarried woman with a child. There was also the added difficulty that, following an incident at school when the child was 9 and her mother reluctantly admitted she was adopted, she became resentful, feeling that she had been deceived. She in turn deceived her mother whenever she could. She observed that her mother tried also to deceive people as to her unmarried status. The child also resented her adoptive mother's evasion of

Analysis of Histories and of Adoption Situation

giving her straightforward factual information about her biological parents and her placement, and in fact the situation here was an incongruous one with an unmarried woman, known in the community as unmarried, expected an adopted child to identify completely with her as a mother and to ask no questions.

The problems in the remaining two cases (Nos. 20 and 17), arose mainly out of relationships in the adoptive home and the personalities of the adoptive parents rather than the adoption situation itself, although in both cases it could also be argued that the child was adopted for unsuitable reasons. In one case (No. 20) this was to add satisfaction to an infertile and rather inadequate marriage, and in the other (No. 17) it was to give company and later companionship to an elderly couple living on an isolated farm. In both cases there was a lack of spontaneous parental affection for the child, and in the first case the problems were accentuated by there being three 'parents' competing for the affection of a child considerably more intelligent than any of them. Both these children later had a neurotic attitude to having children themselves. One found a document about his adoption when he was 12, his adoptive mother not mentioning it directly until he was 16. The other was told she was adopted following an incident at school when she was 8. She asked again for details when she was 12 or 13.

Histories in Group B

In this group again a rather mixed picture emerged, but they can be put roughly into three groups.

In the first group of two, the marriage relationship in one adoptive home was very good but less good in the other. The main difficulties in the first mentioned (No. 26) were the late age of placement and the frequent use by the adoptive parents of the implied threat that the child might be returned to its much poorer biological home if it did not behave. Relatives also were jealous here of the child and did not acknowledge its adopted status. In the second case mentioned (No. 40), a sensitive child was very aware that her dominating adoptive mother feared others in the community would discriminate against her because she was adopted, which emphasised for

Analysis of Histories

her that adopted children are different and inferior. The fact that the adoptive parents were also elderly meant that the child felt she had to explain to outsiders that she was adopted. She had known from her adoptive mother that she was adopted from the age of 5½ after having heard the word used but not knowing its meaning.

In two other cases the adult, though well-adjusted, had had to contend with very possessive adoptive mothers, neither of whom wanted to tell the child that he was adopted in case he would want to go back to his biological parents. In both these cases the marriage relationship of the adoptive parents was stable and reasonably harmonious with the adoptive mother as the dominant partner. In one case (No. 49), the child was told of his adoption at 24, having for the first time at 20 heard that he might be adopted, and in the other case (No. 42) his mother mentioned the subject first when he was 18 although he had wondered about it since children at school had commented upon it when he was aged 6. Since then he had looked out for anything which could confirm this for him. He interpreted happenings in his childhood as significant in relation to his adoption and he fantasied as to who his parents might be, seeing them as possibly in very different social circumstances from his adoptive parents.

In the last two cases, there was tension in the marriage relationships, and in one case (No. 31), there was evidence that the marriage had seldom been consummated, this having led to constant quarrels and recriminations. In this case the child had been told when he was 12 by his adoptive mother fairly reassuringly that he was adopted. In the other case (No. 27), a child became involved in family tensions, being told at 6 or 7 of her adoption by a grandmother who hoped thereby to hurt the adoptive mother. Further difficulties arose for this child through the use of her biological name to the age of 12. Lack of explanation of this caused her to feel insecure and to make her look for explanations not directly from her adoptive parents, but by reading books about adopted children.

Analysis of Histories and of Adoption Situation

Histories in Group E

In the case of the six fostered children, although the motive of monetary reward entered into the original decision about acting as foster-parents to these children, many of the patterns already described appeared here too.

Only one (No. 56) was reared in a home where the marriage of the foster-parents was reasonably happy and stable. Two (Nos. 54 and 57) were reared by elderly embittered women, of whom one was a widow and the other separated from her husband. All, except one (No. 57), were differentiated against in the family because they were only foster-children and not like the biological children, and in four cases they were very aware of being viewed as inferior by other members of the family.

In one case (No. 56), the child always knew he was a fostered or adopted child but there was no reference to this in the home, and, although not treated as if he were a biological child, this particular child did identify with his adoptive home and felt that he had been happy there. He was completely accepted by relatives as one of the family. In all other five cases the children were consciously aware of being unhappy in their foster-homes, and of having been adversely affected by them.

In three cases (Nos. 53, 55 and 58), there was constant reference in the home to the fact that the child was a foster-child and that it should remember its status as such. In one case (No. 53), this was made more obvious to the outside world by the use on some occasions of the biological name and by a marked difference in physical characteristics between the adopted child and the biological children. In one of these three cases (No. 58), a boy longed for his biological mother to trace him. There was in this group two instances of the pattern, already mentioned in Group C, of isolated items of information about the placement and the biological parents being given or being learned, which caused great confusion to the child. The child was again unable to ask for accurate information. One (No. 54) learned the whole story after a very traumatic incident with an adoptive sister when she was aged 18, but for

Analysis of Histories

the other (No. 55) the actual facts about her antecedents constantly eluded her. The many allusions and ambiguous comments which she had heard were all remembered, but they had never been sorted out or put into any kind of perspective by her. In the sixth case (No. 57), the boy did not definitely know he was adopted until he was 15 when he was told in an unsympathetic way by his foster-mother. He was bitterly ashamed of finding he was illegitimately born. This, together with being told unsympathetically, and the fact that, from the age of 15, he was made to use his biological name, which he felt emphasised to the world his illegitimate status, all conspired to make this man feel socially inferior.

This attitude of not wanting the outside world to know that they were fostered or adopted children occurred frequently amongst these fostered children. Thus one of the local authority boarded-out children felt keenly that his clothes were provided for him in a way differently from his school fellows. The girl physically different from her adoptive siblings found what hurt her most was discussion of her by her parents with strangers and their use of the term 'adopted' child. Another (No. 55) found it difficult to accept that sometimes her siblings acknowledged her as their sister and sometimes they did not.

Again the pattern was found of foster-parents being critical of biological parents and saying in relation to a girl that she would repeat the pattern of her unmarried mother (No. 53). There was for one girl one slight variation of this theme, which was her feeling that, as an illegitimately born child, no man would want to marry her (No. 54). As a result both of these girls found it impossible to have easy and relaxed relationships with others of their own age in adolescence and later. Except for the one foster-child (No. 56) reared in the home where there was a reasonably happy relationship between the foster-parents, where all relatives accepted him as one of the family and where his adoption or fostered status was acknowledged but not constantly referred to, all other five had had marked feelings of inferiority which they retained throughout their lives. The one fostered child, without overt signs of feeling inferior, may in fact have been able adequately to compensate by his prowess in the athletic field, which secured him considerable kudos and social prestige in the community.

Analysis of Histories and of Adoption Situation

2. ANALYSIS OF ADOPTION SITUATION IN 58 HISTORIES

Finally an analysis was made of different factors which occurred exclusively in the adoption situation and which were not intermingled with factors related to the situation of parents bringing up children. Here, of course, any very clear-cut division was difficult to make since there was bound to be some overlap. All 58 histories were analysed here since the factors discussed related to the situation of children being reared by parents to whom they had not been born and the consequent problems of communication between parents and children on this very question.

How and When the Adopted Person learned of Being Adopted

First considered is how, when and by whom the child was told of its adoption. Except in the two cases (Nos. 3 and 38) where adopted children denied having strong feelings at all about being told of their adoption, and in the four cases (Nos. 26, 50, 56 and 58) where, because of remembered previous experience, they always knew they had been adopted, all were emphatic that the source of information that they were adopted should be their parents and not outsiders. As already mentioned there were many instances of children being resentful and upset because they learned initially about their adopted status from finding a document or letter at home, from an overheard snatch of conversation, or from the comment of another child or children of their own age. There was considerable evidence that the comments of other children were cruel and often vindictive, and that other children informed the adopted of their adopted status frequently following a quarrel, or when jealous of them, or when they wanted to be the rather special one in a group who had a piece of information which the others did not have. Then they would confide in the others in the group about the particular child's adopted status and those with this knowledge became temporarily a group from which the adopted child, because of being different, was excluded. This kind of group behaviour and the exclusion of the one that is in any way different is very common amongst children. It is generally acknowledged too that children need

Analysis of Adoption Situation in 58 Histories

to be accepted by their peers and so any feeling that they were different on the fundamental question of whether their mother was their real mother or not was certain to be felt very acutely by them.

An analysis was made of the ages at which children were told or learned of their adoption. There are 6 not included in this analysis since, for various reasons, they always knew of their adoption. Eighteen heard initially of their adoption from their adoptive parents, and at the time this information was given to them, 3 were aged 5, 1 was aged 7, 3 were aged 9 or 10, 2 were aged 12, and 5 were told when they first needed their birth certificate for work at 14 or 15, and a further one when he joined one of the Armed Services at 17. One was told at 18, one at 21, and one just before her marriage at 29. From this it will be seen that in most cases, some external occurrence in the child's life precipitated the adoptive parents into telling them of their adopted status, such as going to school, an incident of another adopted child at school, a chance meeting, going to work or being married. In only 5 cases was there no such occurrence. The remainder learned initially from another source that they might be adopted. 18 asked their parents if this were true, but 16 did not mention it, although one did so later. Of those who asked, 9 were told at once that it was true, and they were given an explanation of their adoption. In one case the girl asked persistently until her adoptive mother admitted the truth of her adoption. In 8 cases, however, the fact of adoption was denied by the adoptive mother and where this denial persisted, as already shown, problems arose for the child.

What emerged forcibly in this study was that every child, at some point in its life, is likely to learn that it is adopted. This can happen in ways not even considered possible by their adoptive parents, and children will not necessarily communicate such discoveries to their adoptive parents. It is obvious that only children who knew they were adopted were included in this study, and so it may be that many go through life without realising it. An examination, however, of the individual histories showed the wide variety of everyday occurrences which could bring the fact of adoption to light. First, there was the question of a birth certificate which could be required

Analysis of Histories and of Adoption Situation

at many points during a child's life, sometimes when starting school, frequently when entering senior secondary school, when starting work, entering insurance or superannuation schemes, at marriage and so on. These situations still require birth certificates and the full birth certificate currently used for the adopted child shows that it is an Extract from the Adopted Children Register. Another item of information frequently needed was place of birth, for example, for a passport, and when the child had not been given some factual information this blank in their basic information about themselves presented them with problems. When they were given simply the information of their place of birth, frequently in a town other than their adoptive home, but no further explanation, they became very puzzled as to how the placement had been made. The request for a full family health record could again reveal that the child was not the parents' biological child. Simple things too in the home could be noted by the child as strange. For example, from a mother's cookery book a girl learned that her adoptive mother had gone to her usual cookery class three days after the child was born, whereas mothers usually spent ten days in hospital after the birth of babies. Then there were also the child's normal questions to its adoptive mother about how babies are born, which would reveal to the observant child that his or her mother was not personally very conversant with such things. There was also the chance of finding some relevant letter at home, possibly a lawyer's letter referring to the adoption. Finally, there were the comments of other children which was by far the most common way for a child to learn that it might be adopted. Such comments were reported in 26 cases. The most common age for this to happen was given as between 9 and 10, and 13 met comments during this time. Two reported the age as 7 or 8, whilst two mentioned 6. One, who met comments at 9, had also heard her adoption referred to when she was 5. One met comments when she was 11. The next most likely age, however, after 9 or 10 was 12, when 5 experienced comments. The remaining three did not know of their adoption until outsiders referred to it when they were 14, 15 and 20.

Given then that children need to know of their adopted status and that they infinitely prefer to hear of this from their

Analysis of Adoption Situation in 58 Histories

adoptive parents, and can be resentful and emotionally damaged if they hear of it in other ways, then it is clear that they should certainly be told before they reach the age of 9 and that there are risks that others will tell them from the age of 5 onwards.

How Much Information was Wanted by the Adopted Person about the Details of his or her Adoption

The second question which arose was how much an adopted child wanted to know about its biological parents and about how its adoption had been arranged. The policy of those arranging adoptions varies very much here with an emphasis in many cases on not giving much information.[15] Many adopting parents also do not want to know much about the antecedents of the child they are adopting. From the adopted child's point of view, however, there was no doubt that the majority of those in this study wanted to have information which would give them a clear picture of their biological parents, particularly of their mother, and of how their adoption had been arranged. There were, however, certain kinds of information which they did not want to have or which they feared they would learn if they started to make enquiries.

Thus of the total 58, only 9 stated at interview that they were not curious about their biological parents or interested in them. In 7 of these cases, however, they had learned by that time some factual information about them from the comments of their adoptive mother or others. In fact by the time of interview most knew the age and occupation of their biological mother, something of her personality, and even in some instances what she looked like. Except in one case they also knew something of how the actual placement had been made. In two cases, Nos. 38 and 50, they knew, however, no details about their biological mother and they stated they had no desire to know. They were aged 60 and 46 at the time of interview. In all other cases the adopted child had been curious at some point in their life or still remained curious about their biological parents, although there were considerable variations here depending apparently to some extent on their adjustment.

Analysis of Histories and of Adoption Situation

Thus of those who were well-adjusted, excluding 3 who were amongst those who stated as above that they were not interested, there were six who had been given or had learned some factual information about their biological mother and how they were adopted but three were still curious and would like to have known more about the personality of their mother or their father. The remaining six knew little or nothing about their biological parents. The two men were only mildly curious and one had mixed feelings about being curious at all since he felt there might be something here he was better not to know. The wife of the other was very curious. All the remaining 4 girls said they were curious and that they would probably want to have definite information when they married. Two went so far as to say they would like to meet their biological parents but not as parents, simply out of curiosity and in such a way that these biological parents would not know who they were.

This curiosity was apparent in all the other adjustment classifications and there were several constantly recurring themes. Where the adopted individuals were not given details when they asked for them, or where they were told reluctantly or given conflicting stories, then they felt there was something of great significance in their antecedents which was being hidden. Many felt they wanted to know 'what stock I came from' or they wanted 'to know enough to establish my identity'. They wanted to know the age, occupation and personality of their biological parents, why they had been placed for adoption and how the adoption had been arranged. Many thought they would like to meet their biological parents 'out of curiosity', but in this purely curious group they all made it clear that they were not looking for a mother in their biological mother. She was remote and a stranger to them, but they remained curious about her. Such curiosity frequently occurred when marriage was thought of, or when a woman was pregnant, and several in this position took steps to try to obtain more information. On the whole, the men were less curious than the women, but when this was so, their wives were more curious and one went so far as to trace the biological mother unknown to the adopted person himself (No. 45).

Where there was insecurity in the adoptive home and the

Analysis of Adoption Situation in 58 Histories

adopted child had been given isolated fragments of information about its biological parents and early history, the frustration caused by such information being hidden accentuated feelings of insecurity. They talked of feeling 'rootless', and of 'being in a vacuum', if they did not know their antecedents (Nos. 25 and 46). They felt they could accept and adjust to any story, 'no matter how sordid', since any certainty was better than the flood of uncertainty which surrounded them. Others, lacking factual information, became neurotic about the risks of inherited disease, for example No. 47. Those, however, who were less disturbed and less insecure, frequently had mixed feelings about making enquiries saying that they might find out something they would rather not know, that they had a respectable home now and it might be better to 'let sleeping dogs lie', and so on. They also feared hearing of why they had been placed for adoption by their biological parents. There were in fact instances in this series of adopted adults being given information which they would rather not have had. One (No. 6) would have liked to forget all she had been told about her biological mother's rejection of her. Another (No. 12) wished she had not been told her biological mother had spent money intended for her. One (No. 53) felt it was very cruel to be told her biological mother had thought she was an ugly baby. Another (No. 35) wondered what there could be about her biological father that made her biological mother not want to marry him. Yet another (No. 8) felt that he would have been better not to know that his biological father had possibly been a doctor, since this contrasted so much with the social circumstances of the home in which he was reared.

By contrast others found it helpful and satisfying to know that their biological parents had been 'respectable', 'normal' and so on, and that they had been concerned for them as babies. As one (No. 57) said, to know that his biological mother had visited him for some time as a baby gave him respect for himself.

From all this it emerged that the adopted children in this series of 58 almost without exception wanted factual information about their biological parents, and why and how they were placed for adoption. They feared, however, to hear that, as children, they had been unwanted or rejected by their

Analysis of Histories and of Adoption Situation

biological parents and they saw no point in being given information which suggested that there were wide social and material differences between their biological origins and adoptive homes. Although many talked of wanting to meet their biological parents out of curiosity and without these parents knowing who they were, there were only five who looked on such a meeting as a way of finding a mother who would perhaps understand them in a way that their adoptive parents did not. This occurred in two of the very unhappy fostering arrangements (Nos. 55 and 58), in the one adoption by a widow in Group D (No. 10), and in two cases in Group C (Nos. 12 and 51). In the first of these last two cases, however, it was a desire of only relatively short duration coinciding with a period of acute unhappiness in the adoptive home. In all other cases, whether well-adjusted and happy, or the opposite, the adopted person looked on the adoptive parents as their mother and father and they continued to do so long after they knew they were adopted and also after years of estrangement from them. Relevant comments ranged from 'bearing a child does not make a mother' to the frequent statement that 'it is the people who bring you up who are your parents'. In the six instances (Nos. 16, 20, 24, 34, 41 and 45) where adopted children later met their biological mother or father, all commented on how they were strangers to them, 'just another human being', for whom they had no positive or negative feeling.

The final point made here by many was that, although they were curious about their antecedents, they would not have wanted constant reference made to them. In 3 cases there was clear evidence of adopted children not wanting their adoptive mothers to go on talking about their biological mothers as 'mothers', since they found it confusing to think of two sets of parents.

Communication regarding Adoption within the Adoptive Family

The third main subject in this part of the analysis is the question of communication between the adopted child and other members of the family on the question of adoption. There was repeated evidence that the lines of communication

Analysis of Adoption Situation in 58 Histories

between parent and child were on the whole only one way. The child could not ask for information, but wanted information to come from the adoptive parents. This linked with their general feeling that it should be their parents who told them of adoption and, as already mentioned, 16 learned of their adoption in one way or another from sources other than their parents, but they did not tell their parents of their discovery either at the time or in many instances later. They frequently reported their attitudes as . . . 'If there is anything in it my mother will tell me' or 'she will tell me in her own way'. In the 8 cases where in fact a child had asked about its adoption and this had been denied, this again shut the door to any further questions from the child. They might still have doubts and they were on the look-out for any clues, any change of expression even, but with only one exception (No. 29) they did not ask again. In this exceptional case the girl felt there was something in it because of a very marked physical difference in appearance between herself and her parents, and she did not want to be in the position of believing that her mother was telling lies.

Of the 9 who asked their parents after an incident in their childhood whether they were adopted, and who were given an affirmative reply, only three later asked their mothers further questions. One (No. 21) was given satisfying answers about her place of birth and how she was adopted, but in the other two cases the mothers evaded answering. In one case (No. 25), the child gave up after this one attempt, but the other (No. 30) went ahead persistently rather as No. 29 had done, though without gaining straightforward answers. Of the others in this series of 58, one (No. 13) tried to trick her less intelligent mother into giving her some factually reliable information to replace the differing stories she had previously been given, and four others asked once for information about their biological parents or the arrangements made for their fostering. Of these four, one (No. 52) received factual information from an understanding adoptive mother, but the other three (Nos. 47, 54 and 58) were told it was no concern of theirs, or were asked why they wanted to know since their mother had not wanted them anyway.

Apart from these last eight exceptions, however, the rest of

Analysis of Histories and of Adoption Situation

this series did not tell their adoptive parents of their doubts and queries, nor did they ask for information. In the same way, although curious about their biological parents and about how their adoption had been arranged, they could not introduce the subject. Their reasons here were given as being that it might have hurt or upset their adoptive parents or that it would have seemed disloyal to them. Even when and if the subject were introduced by their adoptive parents, although the child might be curious and waiting, and even eager to be told, they would not ask and in some cases feigned indifference, so that their adoptive mother would not know how much they were upset by the whole question of adoption. Looking at all this from the point of view of the parents, they, at their end of the line of communication, could not know the turmoil that was frequently occurring in the child. If the child never asked, they would assume that they were not curious.

It was interesting to note, however, that in 8 cases where children were unable to communicate their doubts to their adoptive mother and ask her directly for information, they were able to ask instead someone else with whom they had a close relationship. In two instances this was an adoptive aunt, and in three a much older adoptive sibling who in two of these cases had really been also a sympathetic mother-figure. In three cases, the person asked was a family friend.

In so far as talking of adoption with siblings was concerned, although of the 52 adopted children, 22 had adoptive siblings, some who were also adopted and some who were the biological children of the adoptive parents, there were only 5 cases where adoption was ever discussed with them. Two of these were cases mentioned in the previous paragraph. In two others, siblings were protective towards their adopted sister, and in one case they were very critical. In all other 15 cases this question of adoption, although known about by siblings, was never referred to in any way. This same pattern occurred in an equally striking way in the case of two cousins who were both adopted about the same time from the same mother and baby home. They were very good friends and when the one (No. 21) who participated in this study was married, the other was her bridesmaid. Each knew they were adopted but they had never once referred to the fact.

Analysis of Adoption Situation in 58 Histories

This leads on to another facet which emerged when studying the adoption situation from the viewpoint of the child. It emerged that the child viewed his adoption as something personal, as something which could be talked of occasionally within the intimate family, but which he did not wish to hear discussed with relatives or others further outside the family circle. He himself might not want to tell people of it at all. A man or woman would always want to tell anyone he or she hoped to marry, although sometimes somewhat fearful of what their response might be. They might also find they wanted to tell a special friend, either when the subject arose in the course of general conversation or in some personal crisis, as when mourning an adoptive parent's death, but they all stressed that this was not something they wanted either to 'broadcast' themselves or their parents or relatives to 'broadcast'. Thus they were emphatic that they did not want to be introduced as an 'adopted' son or an 'adopted' daughter. They wanted to feel they belonged in the family and were completely accepted there as a son or a daughter. Those two (Nos. 47 and 53) who had actually had experience of such an introduction stressed that it was this particular aspect of their already unhappy adoption situation which caused them most pain.

None of these adopted children wanted their adoptive status shrouded in complete secrecy. Such secrecy they found irritating and unrealistic since it led themselves and their adoptive parents into situations where they had to tell lies, as, for example, when any specific discussion arose about details of the mother's pregnancy, the child's early feeding and so on. Equally, however, they did not want constant reference to it. They wanted something in between, where their adopted status was acknowledged without embarrassment and then overtly apparently forgotten, so that they were treated exactly as if they were the biological son or daughter of the adoptive parents.

Where information was not readily available or was refused to a child, it was interesting to note in these histories the use the child made of clues or incidents in its environment to try to piece together a story. Thus, one (No. 39), studied all the snapshot albums of families and friends and asked who everyone

Analysis of Histories and of Adoption Situation

was, hoping thus to learn who was her biological mother. Two others (Nos. 44 and 49) worked out the age they thought they must have attained when placed in their adoptive home from the youngest age they found in any photographs in their home. Another (No. 7) assumed her biological parents were wealthy because she had heard in an indirect way that she had very lovely clothes as a baby when she was placed in her adoptive home.

Others pieced together a possible story about their early history from fragmentary comments collected over the years whilst watching their parents and others for even expressions which they could then have used as clues. There were four instances of interpreting other events as significant to their adoption. One (No. 18) wondered why a particularly well-dressed person in her home town appeared to take an interest in her. One (No. 42) wondered why a soldier had once given him, an unknown small boy, half a crown. One (No. 24) fantasied that a strange couple whom she saw approaching the block of flats where she lived had come to take her away, and another (No. 48), on hearing of someone else of the same biological name as herself, wondered if they might be related. Yet another (No. 13), noting a certain similarity between herself and her adoptive father and also observing that her adoptive mother became confused when she asked for details about her biological father, interpreted this as meaning that perhaps she was the illegitimate child of her adoptive father whom he and his wife subsequently adopted.

These incidents, presumably in most cases of little significance in themselves, became significant in the child's eyes, and illustrate the dangers of leaving adopted children with indeterminate information and no reality on which to base their concept of their origins and their very early history.

When one considered together, first the question of how much children want to know about their biological parents and about their placement, and, secondly of how this could be communicated to them, it was clear that they wanted factual information and that this information had to be offered to them by their adoptive parents. They wanted a clear picture and not isolated fragmentary pieces of information. They wanted information which portrayed their biological parents

Analysis of Adoption Situation in 58 Histories

in a favourable light and which did not imply that they were unwanted children who had been rejected by their biological parents. They did not think of their biological parents as parents unless they were acutely unhappy in their adoptive home, but they remained curious about their antecedents and could be particularly so when becoming engaged, when marrying, when having children of their own, or when asked for a familial health record.

Some Adoptive Parental Attitudes in the Adoption Situation

That adoptive parents on their side found it difficult to tell their children of their adopted status emerged in many of the histories. A full picture, however, of attitudes here was not possible because not all communicated their attitudes here to the child. Some, however, did so, and also the adoptive situation was discussed in 8 cases with adoptive parents. From these two sources details emerged about some attitudes of adoptive parents in the adoption situation.

It emerged that four had been reluctant to mention adoption or to give requested information about biological parents. In two cases (Nos. 9 and 30), this arose from anxiety that the child might not be satisfied with them as a mother or as a father. In one case (No. 29), the mother feared that the child would think less of her as a mother if she knew she were not her biological mother, and in another (No. 42), it was feared that the boy might want to go back to the biological parents.

In two cases (Nos. 46 and 50), adoptive mothers were ashamed of not having been able to have children of their own, and so they wanted to hide the fact of adoption. Four mothers (of cases 8, 15, 25 and 26) wanted so desperately to have children that they wanted to persuade themselves and also therefore others that these children had been born to them. In one case (No. 8), this led to an adoptive mother frequently seeking physical resemblances in her adoptive grandchildren although by that time it had been acknowledged that her children were all adopted.

One adoptive mother (of No. 22) gave as her reason for not telling a child of her adopted status that it was difficult for her to say that she was not the child's own mother, and two others (of Nos. 14 and 19), although wanting to tell the child, found it difficult to know how to begin and so put off telling the child until this was a constant anxiety to them. Once they had found an opportunity to tell the child they found as they said that 'a weight was lifted off their mind'.

In two instances once a child knew of its adopted status, one mother (of No. 37) was certain that her daughter hated her adoptive parents from then on, and another (of No. 35) felt that an essential element in the close mother–daughter relationship had gone once her daughter knew. In another case (No. 10), a mother had reported that she had been afraid to tell a daughter of her adoption since friends had said she would be angry when she knew.

In another group 4 in number (Nos. 16, 18, 20 and 24), the adoptive mothers implied that it was disloyal of the child to be curious about its biological parents. It was the child's duty to care for, to be grateful to, and to be loyal to those parents who had brought him or her up. An enquiry about biological parents was met with the comment 'Have we not done enough for you?'.

In three other cases, difficulties arose with regard to the adoptive parents' feelings about illegitimacy. In one case (No. 52), it was this aspect which a mother found most difficult to explain because of her own attitude of prudery. In one case (No. 4), the adoptive mother wanted to shield the child from knowing she was illegitimate, and thus she denied that the child was adopted. In another case (No. 40), the adoptive mother expected the child would be discriminated against because she was adopted and illegitimate. In another two cases, which have already been mentioned as appearing under the patterns of parents wanting to deny that the child was adopted, illegitimacy was viewed either as something of which to be socially ashamed and so to hide (No. 50), or something which in itself was sordid (No. 25).

In one case (No. 2), the adoptive mother commented that she had found it an advantage to have known the biological parents. Two other mothers (of Nos. 14 and 15), who knew only about the biological mother's family, remarked that as their adopted daughter was so intelligent it would have been helpful to them in bringing up the child to have known some-

Analysis of Adoption Situation in 58 Histories

thing about the biological father and his level of intelligence. The adopted child in both these cases was more intelligent than the adoptive mother.

This then gives a glimpse of the kind of parental attitudes which can occur in the adoption situation particularly in relation to telling the child of its adoption. To assess these attitudes fully, however, a full study would have to be done from the viewpoint of adoptive parents.[16] Enough, however, emerged here to show that telling the child of his or her adoption is no easy and straightforward task for adoptive parents and that giving the parents advice that they should do so will not by itself necessarily help. This question is related to the parents' very basic emotional attitudes to rearing children not biologically their own, in some cases apparently to their feelings about their own infertility and in others to their feelings about illegitimacy.

Physical Resemblances and Differences

A final aspect noted in the adoption situation was the question of physical similarity or otherwise between the adopted child and the rest of the adoptive family. This was an area of enquiry added later in the study after it had emerged to be of considerable importance from taking two of the later histories. Full information was thus not available in all cases. The analysis here applies to the 52 adopted children. Seven offered no comment on this aspect of their adoption situation although they might have done so had more details been requested as in interviews later in the series. In 5 cases the parents were so much older than the adopted child that the question of comparing physical characteristics was unlikely to arise.

In 18 cases the children were not dissimilar from one or other of their adoptive parents or siblings. In 16 cases the children reported that they were like one or other of the adoptive parents or like siblings, and in 12 of these cases this was due to pure chance, since in only 4 cases was it known that the child was biologically related in some way to the adoptive parents. In one case, a girl (No. 13), who was unable to obtain details about her biological father, interpreted an observable likeness between herself and her adoptive father as an indi-

Analysis of Histories and of Adoption Situation

cation that he might in fact be her biological father. In 8 cases, adopted children reported that they were pleased when they heard outsiders comment on how like their adoptive parents they were. One here (No. 26) who never felt she really belonged in her adoptive family said comments of this kind were helpful to her since they reduced her feelings of isolation from her adoptive parents. One (No. 9) in Group A reacted with amusement to such comments, but two, both in Group C, became irritated by them. One of these two (No. 36) felt that such a comment was absurd in the circumstances, and the other (No. 15) felt that it was a sign of insincerity, although she realised intellectually that these outsiders did not know she was an adopted child. Her feelings in fact about her adoptive mother were very ambivalent and she both wanted to identify with her and yet deeply resented her. These feelings then she projected on to outsiders when they commented that she was like her adoptive mother.

In 6 cases among the adopted children and in one case among the 6 foster-children, there was a marked difference in physical characteristics, stature, build or colouring. In 2 cases this was observed by the adopted children before they knew they were adopted. In one case (No. 28), this in itself caused the child to wonder if it were adopted, whilst in the other case (No. 8) a child observed not only how different temperamentally he was from his adoptive mother's whole family but also that one of his aunts excluded him in her family invitations. The physical difference in this latter case then was possibly only an additional factor, perhaps in fact even a later interpretation. The persistent comments of outsiders on the marked physical dissimilarity worried two further children. One of these (No. 29) questioned her mother until she admitted that she was adopted, but in the other case (No. 33), the child was unable to ask her parents and also unable to cope with the persistent comments of her workmates. She withdrew into herself, and from much social contact. In one case (No. 12), although the child was dissimilar to the adoptive parents in appearance, outsiders sought similarities, to which the adoptive mother responded by saying in a whisper that the child could not be like them since she was not their child. This reaction proved very hurtful to the

Analysis of Adoption Situation in 58 Histories

adopted child. In the case of one adopted child (No. 47) and one fostered child (No. 53), their reaction to the observable physical difference between themselves and their adoptive siblings was to feel that this made their adopted status obvious to outsiders. In both cases, however, they were in addition rejected in their adoptive home and made to feel different from their siblings.

From these details and from the histories, it emerged therefore that adopted children found physical similarity to their adoptive parents a positive factor for them in their adoption situation unless their feelings for their adoptive parents were so ambivalent that they projected such feelings onto comments by outsiders about family likenesses. Marked physical dissimilarity could be associated with good adjustment (Nos. 28 and 29—Group A) where other factors in the situation were favourable, and with poor adjustment (No. 8—Group C, and No. 33—Group D) where other factors were unfavourable. In only one instance (No. 12) did an adoptive parent respond to the comments of outsiders regarding appearance by telling them the fact that the child was adopted. This public discussion of her adoption was deeply resented by the child. In all other cases the adoptive parents accepted the comments of outsiders without comment or in some cases by showing pleasure.

Although there were many in this series, as shown in the individual histories, who found themselves out of harmony with their adoptive parents or temperamentally different from them, particularly strong feelings of difference were described only in two cases in the adopted series and in one case in the fostered series. These three adults, all men, reported that before they knew they were adopted they had very strong feelings of being different from their adoptive parents and family. They each stressed this throughout the interviews, wondering if others too had experienced the same. One (No. 45) had always found the drunkenness of his adoptive father something totally repulsive and he later, of course, related this to being an adopted son. In another case (No. 41), a child reacted very strongly against the superstitious and religious attitude of his Irish adoptive parents and again, when he learned of adoption, he felt that this related to being born from a different cultural group. In the case of the fostered child (No. 57),

Analysis of Histories and of Adoption Situation

although he always identified with his foster-family, he had always found that their extrovert attitudes and their rough language and behaviour contrasted with his more introvert nature and his more aesthetic sensibilities. When he later learned of being a foster-child and of how the social circumstances of his biological father differed from those of his foster-parents, he too regarded this as the explanation of his difference in temperament.

No further discussion of these reported findings is possible however, as there is not enough accurate data available about the biological families. There is also the possibility here of subsequent retrospective falsification in recalling former attitudes after these adopted children knew, first that they had been adopted, and secondly the social circumstances and level of intelligence of their biological parents, which in two cases were apparently very different from their adoptive parents.

Chapter Five

CONCLUSIONS

THE main conclusions to be drawn from this particular study of adoption can be seen as fourfold. First, the present series of 58 histories, 52 of adopted children and 6 of fostered children, showed that a wide range of social circumstances and adjustment was possible for such children in adulthood. Secondly, this study indicated that a great many factors could influence the ultimate outcome for each individual adjustment and that these multifarious factors were often less questions of overt fact or circumstance than of subtle emotional attitudes. Thirdly, it was clear that in the adoption situation itself certain basic patterns recurred throughout the whole series. Finally, from the evidence available under the second and third conclusions, it was evident that this situation of a child being brought up by parents who did not bear him can be 'a complicated experiment beset with problems for the child and parent', and it is not, as is often assumed one 'with no more problems than those potentially inherent in any parent–child relationship'.[1]

Conclusions can be drawn and tendencies indicated from the patterns described in the last chapter. These will be related to the findings of the other studies on adoption problems which were described in Chapter One. Before this is done, however, the specific limitations which are inevitable in any study of adoption at a point in time should again be stated.

First, this study used details which were made available through the retrospective introspection of adults adopted as children. These details were confirmed, and in some cases elaborated further, by the family doctor. Full details, however, were not always available in all cases. This could be so either because these were not known to the adopted person or because the information related to occurrences at such an early

Conclusions

age that these could not be recalled by the adopted person.

Secondly, this was an exploratory study, and as such it cannot be known whether it has covered all the family and other patterns possible within the adoption situation. It certainly covered all major patterns about which there is current controversy from the point of view of making adoption placements.

Thirdly, this was a study of environmental factors. The adopted person's individual inherited predispositions in so far as these could have been assessed by a detailed study of the history of the biological family, were of necessity excluded since the detailed history of the biological family was inevitably not available. Particular patterns, however, both in the environment and in the adopted adults' reactions to facets of the adoption situation recurred in the histories, and conclusions can be drawn from these.

When the age of the adoptive mother at the time of placement was examined in relation to the adjustment classification, it was found that there was a larger percentage of adoptive mothers under 40 amongst the well-adjusted group than the percentage of those of similar age in the poor adjustment group. Differences in age as such, however, did not account for the wide range of adjustment found. Much more important was the personality and stability of the adoptive mother and her attitudes to the child.

Michaels and Brenner in their study[2] found that there was no significant connection between the age of the adoptive parents and the success or otherwise of the placement. In this present study, however, it was clear that, other things being equal, there was advantage to the child in being brought up in a home where the adoptive mother was under 40 rather than over 40. Adoption by couples of normal child-bearing age had an additional advantage that this aroused no comments from outsiders about the elderliness of the child's parents.

The death of adoptive parents could leave an adopted child in a vulnerable position, but provided that the rest of the adoptive family were accepting in their attitudes towards the child this need not in itself lead to poor adjustment.

Health problems in adoptive parents could be associated with all degrees of adjustment but ill-health of a psychogenic or

Conclusions

hypochondriacal nature was particularly associated with the parents of those who had an 'intermediate' or 'poor' adjustment. The histories showed that adoptive mothers with such illnesses were possessive, restrictive and inconsistent towards their adopted children. Because of their own egocentric needs and problems they had no insight into the adoption situation from the point of view of the child.

Good adjustment in this series was never associated with the situation where one parent was bringing up a child and in fact it could lead to a particularly incongruous situation for the child.

The adequacy of the financial circumstances of adopters did not vary in relation to the adjustment classification, although it was found that there was a slightly higher proportion of adoptive parents in the two highest occupational classes amongst those with a poor adjustment than amongst those with a good adjustment. It will be remembered that Michaels and Brenner concluded from their study that it was dangerous to assume that those couples who were better educated and who were in the higher income groups necessarily provided a richer home emotionally for an adopted child. On the other hand, one of the conclusions of the survey done by the National Association for Mental Health[3] was that there was no evidence in those adoptions studied by them of a higher proportion of failures amongst the higher work status groups. The findings of the present research led to conclusions similar to those of Michaels and Brenner. It must be remembered, however, that the universal popularity of adoption in the middle and professional classes in Great Britain dates only from the Second World War. Previously it was viewed as rather unusual in these social groups. This in itself may have created additional problems for those interviewed in this series, and so in part may have contributed to their 'poor' or 'intermediate' adjustment. The histories, however, showed the kind of social and educational pressures which can be put on an adopted child in such a home. Shaw, whose study[4] was concerned mainly with middle-class families, also commented on the fact that the less intelligent adopted child was a disappointment to its parents and that adopting couples had stressed the importance of matching the achievement background of the biological parents and of the adoptive parents in order to avoid such disappointment.

Conclusions

Michaels and Brenner showed in their study, however, that prediction by intelligence testing and by the background of biological parents gave only 50% accuracy. Their conclusion was to stress the need to select adopters who were not primarily concerned with the intellectual status of the child.

All, however, that can be concluded from the present study is that factors other than high material standards and good educational opportunities are essential for good adjustment.

Reference has already been made to the conditions laid down by most adoption societies about religious affiliation for prospective adopters. This study showed that again other factors are important here, and that it should not be assumed that because adopters are members of a Church they would be sympathetic adoptive parents. In fact it would seem important to assess particularly carefully the attitudes of those who hold very rigid religious beliefs since these, if unduly puritanical, might lead them to finding difficulty in accepting illegitimacy and the child born to unmarried parents.

The age of the child at placement was found in this study to be apparently important only within certain limits. There was a larger proportion placed under four months amongst the well-adjusted than amongst the poorly adjusted, but good adjustment could be associated with placement as late as eighteen months, and poor adjustment with very early placement. After the age of two, however, there was clear evidence of feelings of insecurity in the child resulting from such late placement.

When the family pattern in which the adopted child was brought up was examined it was found that a good and a poor adjustment could be associated with all five family patterns described. There was no evidence to support the finding reported in the National Association for Mental Health study that the chances of success were increased when the adopted child was an only child as compared with the situation where there were other children in the family. There was also no evidence to support Shaw's tentative finding that there appeared to be a slight advantage when the child was adopted to complete rather than to create a family.

In this study, it emerged that much more important than family pattern as such were the basic attitudes in the family to

Conclusions

all the children, whether adopted or biological. These attitudes related to the many factors which could be seen as collectively contributing to the total situation where a good adjustment was possible. These will be discussed later in this chapter. It is important, however, to note that the mixed family, in the sense of mixed biological and adopted children, is potentially fraught with difficulties, since the adopted child can always interpret differences in parental behaviour, whether or not justifiably different, in terms of preferential treatment for the biological child.

The question of whether it is helpful or unhelpful in the adoption situation if the adoptive parents already knew the biological parents was seen to relate more to the adoptive parents' attitude to what they knew of the biological parents rather than the actual content of what they knew. Of prime importance here was whether or not the adoptive parents transferred any critical feelings they might have towards the biological parents to their feelings and attitudes towards the adopted child.

For an adoptive home to be an environment conducive to good adjustment in later life for a child placed there, a wide range of factors was seen to be necessary. First it emerged as essential that the marriage relationship between the adoptive parents should be stable, essentially happy and mutually satisfying. There was evidence that the adoption of a child could put extra strains on a marriage relationship, as where an adoptive mother became jealous of the relationship between the adoptive father and a non-biological daughter. There was evidence too that some couples seeking to adopt a child did so because of incompatibilities in the marriage.

Secondly it was seen as important that both adoptive parents should be able to offer children emotional security and acceptance, consistent discipline, together with encouragement, but also freedom for the child to develop along its own individual lines. The neurotic hypochondriacal mother was unlikely to be able to offer this. These conditions too would not be available unless both parents had been equally enthusiastic in the first instance about adopting a child. They would also not be available in situations where consequent on the birth later of a biological child into the family, both parents did not maintain such attitudes to the adopted child. A further situation where these essential conditions would not be available was where the child was adopted for a reason other than a spontaneous and genuine love of children or because of a real concern for the future of an individual child. When the reasons for adoption by married couples or others was examined, it was found that in certain circumstances the child would not be accepted for itself but only in so far as it met the specific needs of those who adopted it. Such circumstances were found to be where the reasons for adoption were: to have someone who belonged to the adoptive parent or parents or who would offer them company; to have someone to care for them in their old age; or to repeat the pattern of their own early childhood.

Thirdly, it was clear that the attitudes of adoptive parents towards the biological parents, either as people or as unmarried parents, and their attitudes towards illegitimacy and to the illegitimately born child they had adopted, could all influence their basic attitude of acceptance towards their adopted son or daughter. For the child it was important that its adoptive parents should not transfer to it feelings of criticism or envy which they might have towards unmarried parents who had borne children when they themselves had been unable to do this. Fears and strong feelings about the inheritance of particular behaviour patterns was a frequent pattern in this series, and one which was never associated with good adjustment.

This finding has had confirmation in subsequent research. First, in a study by Humphrey and Ounsted of a series of adoptive families referred for psychiatric advice,[5] there was also similar evidence of 'genetic anxiety' on the part of adoptive parents. Secondly, in a survey by Goodacre of the practice of adoption agencies and of the attitudes of adoptive parents,[6] it emerged that some adopters had been given a great deal of information about the biological background which they felt was adverse and they had experienced difficulty in living with this.

Fourthly, adopted children resented the attitude found in several adoptive homes that the children should be grateful to the adoptive parents because they had been cared for and adopted by them. This attitude produced a feeling of resentful obligation towards these parents, or alternatively a resentful rebellion against them since the children felt that they had had

Conclusions

no opportunity to participate in the decision that these particular parents would adopt them.

It emerged as important that in any assessment of an adoptive home due regard should be paid to the attitudes of the whole family and not simply to those of the prospective adopters themselves, since the child placed into a home acquired not only new parents, but adoptive siblings, grandparents, uncles, aunts and cousins. The critical attitude of any of these could be sensed by an adopted child.

When the question was examined of how the adopted person had heard of his or her adopted status, it emerged that this was information which they considered should come to them on the initiative of their adoptive parents and not from outsiders. The comments of outsiders could frequently be critical and cruel and could occur in situations which made the adopted child feel different and isolated from its peers. The age in childhood when peers were most likely to comment on the child's adopted status was nine, although there could be comments from as early as five. Children could also learn of their adoption in many ways and they did not necessarily communicate their discoveries to their parents. They disliked uncertainty about their status. It emerged therefore that in order to avoid the risk of trauma, a child should be told by its adoptive parents of its adopted status before the age of five. Thereafter there were risks in the situation for the child, from outsiders' comments or from chance discovery. Another risk in delaying telling a child was that in the interval he or she might acquire attitudes and ideas about adoption or about adopted children which implied that they were set apart and different from other children. In acquiring such attitudes the adopted child would have assumed that he or she was in the group of non-adopted children. A further risk in delaying was that when the child was ultimately told it would feel that the parents had deceived it. This could lead to the child losing confidence in its parents, in their reliability and in their veracity.

Although there were individual differences, the adopted and fostered children in this series wanted on the whole to have factual information about their biological parents and about why and how they had been placed for adoption. Inadequate, incomplete or varying information here led to difficulties. For

Conclusions

example, if they were not given information, or were given conflicting details, then they fantasied about what the true story might be, and in most cases their fantasies made their biological parents and the circumstances of their birth less socially acceptable than they were in reality.

There was evidence that, although these adopted and fostered children wanted to know about their antecedents, they did not want to be given information which implied rejection of them by their biological parents, or which suggested that there were wide social and material differences between the circumstances and homes of their biological and adoptive parents.

The men were less curious than the women. The women found themselves curious when contemplating marriage or when they themselves became mothers. Although they were curious, either always or at some point in their lives, in only five cases did they view such biological parents potentially as parents. In all other cases their interest in their biological parents arose more simply out of a desire not to be without information about their antecedents. It was the adoptive parents whom they viewed as their 'real' parents. Even in the five cases where the biological mother would have been actively sought as a mother, the adopted person felt some filial obligation to the adoptive parents. This relationship with the adoptive parents appeared in individual histories to be in fact a particularly compelling one in that it could be either a particularly strong positive feeling towards the adoptive parents, or a particularly strong negative feeling against them. Those who were happy in their adoptive homes felt that they wanted to give more to their adoptive parents once they knew that they were adopted. Of those who were unhappy in their adoptive homes, some talked of wanting to make a complete break with their adoptive parents and homes, whilst others talked of feeling even more obligated to their adoptive parents once they knew of their status.

An important and unexpected finding was the pattern which emerged about communication within the adoptive family. This showed that communication about adoption was on the whole one-way, from the adoptive parents to the child. The child, though wanting to be told of its adopted status and to be

Conclusions

given information about its biological parents, about why and how its adoption was arranged, could not ask its adoptive parents. Even when the subject was raised on the initiative of adoptive parents, the child frequently feigned indifference.

Although those interviewed wanted to be told of their status, they did not want frequent discussion of it at home. They did not want reference to be made to it with relatives or with those outside the family. They wanted to feel that their position in their adoptive family was exactly that of a biological son or daughter.

This whole question of discussing adoption within the adoptive family showed a lack of communication between the world of adults and that of children. A frequent adult attitude to children is that as children they are different from adults. In this attitude it is assumed that children cannot understand certain situations, that they should not be given answers to some of their questions, since in this way they will forget about the wonderings which gave rise to their questions, and also that children do not hear the comments of adults nor observe happenings between adults or in the home. The histories here however showed children to be extremely observant of the happenings and comments in a home and to be very sensitive to these. They frequently, however, feigned indifference and they often did not communicate to their adoptive parents the fact that they had observed or heard, or that they had remembered. They also emerged as being much more logical and having more understanding than their adoptive parents assumed. They resented parental attitudes which implied that they could not understand the adoption situation and that details about this were no concern of theirs.

Another frequently recurring pattern in these histories was where the fact of adoption was something which was generally known within the family and which was recognised tacitly by members both of the intimate and of the wider family, and yet this remained a subject which was never referred to openly.

With regard to this whole question of telling a child of his or her adoption, this present study confirms the findings of the studies by Michaels and Brenner and by Shaw that this is a problem for adoptive parents. Further confirmation of this comes from the subsequent survey made by Goodacre of the

Conclusions

attitudes of adoptive parents. Michaels and Brenner commented that although all adoptive parents in their series had originally been advised to tell their adopted children of their adoption, it had not been realised by the adoption workers that there were emotional problems inherent in this for the adoptive parents. That there were emotional problems emerged when these families were studied later. This present study, although focused on the adopted person's reactions to the adoption situation, revealed also that adoption was frequently something which adoptive parents found very difficult to discuss. For example, even in most of the cases where parents had taken the initiative in telling their children of their adopted status, this had not been done spontaneously but because of some other event in the child's life. It emerged that parental difficulties in discussing adoption could be related to parental fears about their adequacy as parents, to their feelings about their own infertility, and to their feelings about the illegitimacy of the child whom they had adopted.

This conclusion can now also be related to the findings in other subsequent research studies. Kirk[7], making a comparative study of fertile and non-fertile couples, has shown that non-fertile couples tend to have 'feelings of inadequacy,' and to feel alienated from other couples. Such feelings of inadequacy, which he found were particularly strong in the women, lead to various types of compensation, for example rejecting that there is a difference between adopting and bearing a child, and so avoidance and delay in telling a child that he is adopted.

The question of physical similarity between the adopted child and its adoptive family was examined. The presence of such similarity could be a positive factor for an adopted child but was not essential to good adjustment. When this question, however, is linked with the adopted and fostered child's great desire that it should be viewed as one of the adoptive family and that no reference should be made of its adopted status to outsiders, then it is clear that striking differences in physique and colouring can be seen as accentuating the child's adopted status both to itself and to outsiders. It will be remembered that Michaels and Brenner concluded on this question that there was a general advantage for the child to bear some resemblance to its adoptive parents but that this was not stressed by the

Conclusions

adoptive parents. This present study suggested that it was the children rather than the adoptive parents who were more aware of these similarities and differences.

When these conclusions are considered in relation to the assessment of couples as prospective adopters, it will be seen that to assess couples for such parenthood requires very careful and detailed interviewing and assessment. As mentioned in the Introduction, the interviewing and assessments currently carried out by Adoption Societies and Local Authority Children's Departments in Great Britain vary widely, depending upon the training and experience of those doing this work. It is clear, however, that interviewing done by anyone other than a skilled interviewer would be likely to reveal little of the subtle attitudes discussed here. Also the reliance which is frequently placed on community standing and material provision would not necessarily lead to the selection of adopters who would provide an environment conducive to good adjustment for the adopted child.

As mentioned in the Introduction, many workers in this field and sometimes the presiding judge, magistrate or sheriff in the court where the adoption is legalised, will advise the adopters to tell the child of its adopted status. The Hurst Committee[8] went so far as to recommend that there should be an entry in the form of application for an adoption order to the effect that the adopters had told the child of its adoption or undertook 'to bring up the child in the knowledge that he is adopted'.[9] It appears however that little individual help is given on these occasions. Generalised statements are used.[10] The assumption is that adopters should have little difficulty in accepting or following such advice and that, if children are curious about their antecedents, they will ask. This present study showed, however, that this whole question of communication between adoptive parents and their adopted children and vice versa, is fraught with emotional implications and problems peculiar to this adoptive relationship, and different in kind from natural parent–child relationships.

There is divergence of opinion about whether or not children should be told details of their biological parents. Some adoption workers[11] imply that adopters should give such information, but only if and when the child asks for it. Others have

Conclusions

written, 'Generally the court encourages adopters to say little or nothing about the natural parents to their adopted children when they grow up. It is no good fostering any sentiment which could compete with loyalty to the home they are to enter'.[12] This present study showed that neither of these attitudes corresponds to the needs of the adopted child. If the conclusions of this study are accepted then it is clear that it is not in the interests of the adopted person that they should be precluded, as they are in England, from having ready access to factual information about their biological parents.

Whilst, as discussed in the Introduction, it is at present possible in Scotland for an adopted child on reaching the age of 17 to apply to Register House for information about his or her biological parents from the original birth entry, in England a Court Order is still required before such information is made available to the adopted person. This present study clearly suggests that such needs of the adopted person should be recognised by a change in the law of England.

In the Introduction it was also shown how in Great Britain the protection of current adoption law lies, first, in the regulation of placements made by adoption societies and by local authorities, secondly, in the supervision by the local authority of third party placements after the child has been placed in an adoptive home, and finally and ultimately, in the investigation of the curator and guardian *ad litem*.

This study shows that much more should be enquired into than is specified in the regulations and in the duties of the curator and guardian *ad litem* [13], [14], where enquiries relate mainly to material circumstances and to overt facts and to ascertaining that all parties have in fact truly consented to relinquishing the child for adoption. It would also seem that even this protection of the law comes into operation much too late since a child will already have been in an adoptive home for at least three months before an application for legalisation is made to the court. At this stage it would be very difficult to make a sufficiently adequate assessment of the more subtle nuances inherent in a couple's motivation for and emotional attitudes towards becoming adoptive parents. This is borne out by the experience of Children's Officers and others supervising adoption placements during the three months' probationary

Conclusions

period before an adoption is legalised. Furthermore, even if a home is considered to be unsuitable, adoptions are often legalised because there is no better alternative provision available for the particular child concerned. Real protection for the child must come then at an earlier stage in the process of adoption placement. This should be at the stage of initial assessment of the child and of the prospective adopters. As discussed in the Introduction, however, the standards of adoption assessment work vary greatly and there is evidence[15] that interviewing and assessment can be very hurried and superficial.

Since, however, a child's whole future happiness and ultimate adult adjustment can depend on such assessments, there would thus seem to be urgent need for a critical re-appraisal of the methods and supervision of organisations undertaking adoption work, as well as investigations into the standards of those who make third party placements of children. Shortage of trained social work personnel has been a limiting factor in the past, but special training could now be provided for many already in the field, if there were a full realisation of the inadequacies of the present service. We have, as a community, assumed that British law gave adequate protection to adopted children. This in fact, however, is far from true, and the only real protection for the child comes from the effectiveness of the assessment of the total situation, in relation to both external facts and intrinsic attitudes, prior to the time of his or her placement in an adoptive home.

Although our sum of social work knowledge is gradually increasing, much remains unknown, particularly in this field of child adoption. The present study considered adoption from the viewpoint of the adopted person, and further detailed exploratory studies are needed into other aspects of the adoption situation. It is only in this way that we can hope to acquire objective knowledge to replace vague generalisations and surmise. Then we may be able to follow Bacon's dictum[16] . . . 'It cannot be that axioms discovered by argumentations should avail for the discovery of new works. . . . We must lead men to the particulars themselves, while men on their side must force themselves for a while to lay their notions by and begin to familiarise themselves with the facts.'

NOTES

Introduction

1. Sophocles, *The Theban Plays*. Translated by E. F. Watling, London, 1947.
2. Sir James Frazer, *The Golden Bough*, London, 1890 and 1922.
3. Mary Ellison, *The Adopted Child*, London, 1958, Chapter 2.
4. Ibid.
5. Estimated by Society for the Protection of Infant Life. See Mary Hopkirk, *Nobody Wanted Sam*, London, 1948, p. 92.
6. Margaret Waters, a notorious baby-farmer was tried and executed, 16 babies having been found dead within a month in the immediate neighbourhood of her home in Brixton. She had obtained these and many other infants by advertising adoption with 'a good home and a mother's love and care', in return for £5 and on condition that no questions were asked. Although this was an extreme case, it was by no means unique. In 1870, 276 bodies, mostly of infants less than a week old, were found in London alone. See Mary Hopkirk, op. cit., p. 93.
7. H. P. Tait, in *Child Health and Development*, ed. R. W. B. Ellis, London, 1956, p. 273.
8. Children and Young Persons Act, 1932. (The consolidating Act of the same name in England was passed in 1933 and in Scotland in 1937.)
9. Children Act, 1948.
10. Child Adoption Committee. Third Report, 1926.
11. This was opened by one of the original rescue societies, 'The Female Mission to the Fallen', which '... from 1858 employed women missionaries to seek out erring young ladies, give them tracts and find homes and employment for them'. See Mary Hopkirk, op. cit., p. 152.
12. Josephine Butler, wife of Canon Butler, Principal of Liverpool College, was largely responsible for the change in emphasis in rescue work from personal salvation to social reform. 'The Josephine Butler Memorial House, Training House for Moral Welfare Workers at Home and Abroad' is active at the present time in training workers.
13. Deaths of infants under one year of age per 1,000 live births in England and Wales
    1914—Legitimate, 100; Illegitimate, 207
    1918—   „   91;   „   186
14. 'It is no use talking about "How can we help the girl to leave her immoral life" unless we are prepared to say what is right conduct, and we can only say what is right in relation to what we believe to be true to our religion. Unless the people who are doing this work have something to give on these lines they are not meeting the girl's funda-

Notes to pages 5–7

mental need.' Miss E. M. Steel, Organising Secretary, Church of England Moral Welfare Council, quoted by M. Penelope Hall in *The Social Services of Modern England*, London, 1955, p. 158, f.n. 4.

15. See L. Retallack, 'The Changes and Chances of Moral Welfare', *Social Work*, October 1942.
16. The relevant object in 1918 states: 'To secure the provision of adequate accommodation to meet the varying needs of mothers and babies throughout the country, with the special aim of keeping mother and child together.' See *Twenty-one Years and After* by Lettice Fisher (Nat. Counc. Unmarried Mother and Child, 1946). The same object in 1963 reads: 'The Council tries to promote and encourage hostels, homes and other suitable accommodation to meet the varying needs of mothers and babies throughout the country with the special aim of making it possible to keep mother and child together.' (See Annual Report, 1962–1963.)
17. Education (Administrative Provisions) Act, 1907, and Education (Scotland) Act, 1908.
18. Education Act, 1918, made such provision compulsory in England. It was permissive in Scotland.
19. For example, Maternity and Child Welfare Act, 1918.
20. Guardianship of Infants Act, 1886.
21. Birth Rate (Living Children). Rates per 1,000 of population.

	England & Wales	Scotland
1891–1900	29·9	31·4
1911–1915	23·6	25·4
1921	22·4	25·2
1931	15·8	19·0
1939	14·8	17·3

22. Report of the Departmental Committee on Adoption Societies and Agencies, 1937
23. *Name of Adoption Society*

	No. of Adoptions Arranged in 1936
The National Adoption Society, London	394
The National Children Adoption Association, London	333
The Homeless Children's Aid and Adoption Society, London	83
The Adoption Society (Church House) London	100
The National Children's Home and Orphanage, London	59
The Church of England Homes for Waifs and Strays, London (In period Nov. 1934 to Dec. 1935)	58
The Mission of Hope, Croydon	44
The Lancashire and Cheshire Child Adoption Council	42

24. *Illegitimate births per 1,000 live births in England and Wales*

1900	40		1938	42
1914	42		1942	56
1916	48		1945	93
1918	63		1947	53
1919	60		1949	51
1922	44			

Notes to pages 8–14

Illegitimate births given as percentage of live births in Scotland

1900	6·49	1938	6·15
1914	7·16	1942	7·18
1916	7·09	1945	8·66
1918	7·97	1947	5·58
1919	7·93		
1922	6·83		

25. Adoption Act, 1958, Part II, Section 52.
26. Report of the Committee on Child Adoption (Chairman: Mr Alfred Hopkinson), 1921.
27. Ibid., p. 5.
28. Ibid., p. 12.
29. Ibid., p. 12.
30. Child Adoption Committee, First Report (Chairman: Mr Justice Tomlin), 1925.
31. Ibid., p. 4.
32. Ibid., p. 8.
33. Ibid., p. 9.
34. Adoption of Children Act, 1926, Section 5(1).
35. Ibid., Section 2(3).
36. Ibid., Section 2(3)
37. Ibid., Section 3(b).
38. Ibid., Section 10.
39. Ibid., Section 8.
40. Particulars to be entered are given in the Schedule to the Adoption of Children Act, 1926.
41. Ibid., Section 11(5)
42. Ibid., Section 11(7)
43. Report of the Departmental Committee on Adoption Societies and Agencies, 1937.
44. Figures of Adoptions registered in England and Wales show increase:

| 1927 | 2,943 | 1933 | 4,524 |
| 1930 | 4,511 | 1936 | 5,180 |

45. Ibid., p. 4.
46. Ibid., pp. 5, 6.
47. The report estimated that 'more than 1,200 children were placed with adopters every year by societies describing themselves as adoption societies and probably several hundred by other agencies', p. 6.
48. Ibid., p. 9.
49. Between 1932 and 1936, it had arranged 72 completed adoptions.
50. Ibid., p. 9.
51. Ibid., p. 10.
52. Ibid., p. 11.
53. Ibid., p. 11.
54. Ibid., p. 14.
55. Ibid., p. 14.

Notes to pages 15–24

56. These sums ranged from £5 to £150.
57. The Adoption Societies Regulations, 1943 (Second Schedule), and The Adoption Societies (Scotland) Regulations, 1943 (Third Schedule).
58. Report of the Care of Children Committee, 1946.
59. Ibid., p. 23.
60. Ibid., p. 148.
61. Report of the Committee on Homeless Children, 1945.
62. Report of the Care of Children Committee, 1946, p. 5.
63. See Summary of Recommendations, para, 15.
64. See The Succession (Scotland) Act, 1964, Sections 23 and 24.
65. M. Penelope Hall, *The Social Services of Modern England*, London, 1955, p. 164.
66. The Adoption of Children (Summary Jurisdiction) Rules, 1949, Section 7, and similarly in the County Court and High Court Rules, 1949 and 1950.
67. See Act of Sederunt (Adoption of Children), 1950, Section 4.
68. Report of the Departmental Committee on the Adoption of Children (Chairman: Sir Gerald Hurst), 1954.
69. Adoption Act, 1958, Section 5 (2).
70. Adoption Act, 1958, Part II, Section 52.
71. The Adoption Agencies Regulations, 1959, Section 9, and The Adoption Agencies (Scotland) Regulations, 1959, Section 9.
72. See Act of Sederunt (Adoption of Children), 1959, for Sheriff Court, Scotland, and, for England, The Adoption Rules, 1959, for Juvenile Court, County Court and High Court.
73. See Second Schedule, Part I of the Adoption of Children Rules. 1950, for Juvenile, County and High Court.
74. See The Adoption Societies Regulations, 1943, for England and Scotland.
75. Report of the Departmental Committee on the Adoption of Children, 1954, p. 53.
76. Register House in Edinburgh report that in 1958 and 1959 they received enquiries of this kind from approximately 30 persons in each of these years.
77. Reported speech of Dr Somerville Hastings in the House of Commons in 1949. See Margaret Kornitzer, *Child Adoption in the Modern World*, London, 1952, p. 15.
78. M. Penelope Hall, op. cit., p. 164.
79. Ibid., p. 164.
80. Adoption Act, 1958, Section 35 (3).
81. Report of the Care of Children Committee, 1946, p. 148.
82. Joint U.N./W.H.O. Meeting of Experts on the Mental Health Aspects of Adoption. Final Report, 1953, pp. 3–4.
83. Report of the Care of Children Committee, 1946, p. 148.
84. John Bowlby, *Maternal Care and Mental Health*, Geneva, 1952, p. 100.
85. Total annual figures of registration of Adoption Orders, from 1927 to 1962 in England and from 1930 to 1962 in Scotland appear in the Appendix.

Notes to pages 24–43

86. See (a) Report of the Residential Conference of the Standing Conference of Societies Registered for Adoption, 1953, p. 13.
    (b) Report of the Departmental Committee on the Adoption of Children, 1954, para. 45.
87. See Report of Departmental Committee on the Adoption of Children, 1954, para. 45.
88. *Child Adoption*, No. 43, Autumn/Winter, 1963–4, p. 2.
89. John Bowlby, op. cit., p. 100.
90. Iris Goodacre, 'Adoption Agencies and their Clients', *Child Adoption*, No. 43, Autumn/Winter, 1963–4.
91. Lulie A. Shaw, 'Following-up Adoptions', *British Journal of Psychiatric Social Work*, Vol. 2, No. 8, November 1953.
92. The Report of the Departmental Committee on Adoption Societies and Agencies, 1937, p. 14.
93. Joint U.N./W.H.O. Meeting of Experts on the Mental Health Aspects of Adoption. Final Report, 1953, p. 4.
94. Its original object was stated as being: 'to afford an asylum for women who, after deviation from the paths of virtue express and manifest a desire to reform; and the Society's endeavours shall be directed to assist them in the attainment of this object by moral religious and industrial training'.
95. The Midwives and Maternity Homes (Scotland) Act, 1927.
96. Under a Regulation made by the Registrar-General in Scotland in 1918, this practice stopped.

Chapter One: Previous Research Studies in Relation to the Present Research Project

1. Report of the Departmental Committee on Adoption Societies and Agencies, 1937, pp. 1 and 2.
2. A complete list of subsequent research is given in the Bibliography.
3. Sophie van Senden Theis, *How Foster-Children Turn Out*, New York, 1924.
4. Wm. Healy, et al., *Reconstructing Behaviour in Youth—A Study of Problem Children in Foster-Families*, Boston, 1929.
5. Lulie A. Shaw, 'Following-up Adoptions', *British Journal of Psychiatric Social Work*, Vol. 2, No. 8, November 1953.
6. *A Survey based on Adoption Case Records*, N.A.M.H., 1956, p. 24.
7. Classifications used were:
    (A) Professional class (including managerial and executive).
    (B) Supervisory clerical and other more non-manual.
    (C) Skilled and semi-skilled manual.
    (D) Unskilled.
8. Ibid., pp. 24–5.
9. Ibid., p. 25.

Notes to pages 43–53

10. C. A. Moser, *Survey Methods in Social Investigation*, London, 1958, p. 10.
11. M. E. Edwards, 'Failure and Success in the Adoption of Toddlers', *Case Conference*, November 1954.
12. E. W. Burgess and L. S. Cottrell, *Predicting Success or Failure in Marriage*, New York, 1939.
13. See study by R. Michaels and R. F. Brenner, *A Follow-up Study of Adoptive Families*, New York, 1951.
14. See study by Lulie A. Shaw, 'Following-up Adoptions', *British Journal of Psychiatric Social Work*, Vol. 2, No. 8, November 1953.

Chapter Two; Method of Research Used in this Study

1. Adolf Meyer, 'A Short Sketch of the Problems of Psychiatry', *American Journal of Insanity*, Vol. 53, 1897.
2. Adolf Meyer, 'The Rôle of the Mental Factors in Psychiatry', *American Journal of Insanity*, Vol. 65, 1908.
3. Such as the experiments of Cannon (1939) who described the 'alarm reaction' in animals, the views of Selye (1950) on the General Adaptation Syndrome, the classical observations of Wolf and Wolff, and the reviews of the literature in this field by Dunbar.
4. O. L. Zangwill, *An Introduction to Modern Psychology*, London, 1950, p. 198.
5. E.g. Studies by Bowlby, Goldfarb, Spitz, and others, and also work of social anthropologists who have related character to different methods of child-rearing in different primitive cultures, such as A. Kardiner. *The Psychological Frontiers of Society*, New York, 1947.
6. John Bowlby, *Maternal Care and Mental Health*, Geneva, 1952, p. 59.
7. D. R. MacCalman, Foreword to A. Bowley's *The Natural Development of the Child*, Edinburgh, 1954, p. ix.
8. Ibid.
9. Barbara Wootton, *Testament for Social Science*, London, 1950, p. 21.
10. John Madge, *The Tools of Social Science*, London, 1953, p. 22.
11. L. S. Penrose, *Heredity and Environment in Human Affairs* (The Convocation Lecture, 1955, of the National Children's Home), p. 9.
12. F. Galton, 'The History of Twins as a Criterion of the Relative Powers of Nature and Nurture', *Journal of Royal Anthropological Institute*, Vol. 5, 1875, p. 391.
13. Johannes Lange, *Crime as Destiny* (1929). Translated by Charlotte Haldane, first published in Great Britain in 1931.
14. H. H. Newman, F. N. Freeman, K. J. Holzinger, *Twins: A Study of Heredity and Environment*, Chicago, 1937.
15. F. J. Kallman, Results published in a number of papers. See Report to International Congress of Psychiatry, 1950.
16. Eliot Slater, *Psychotic and Neurotic Illnesses in Twins*, London, 1953, pp. 88–9.

Notes to pages 53–67

17. F. N. Freeman, K. J. Holzinger, B. C. Mitchell, 'The Influence of Environment on the Intelligence, School Achievement, and Conduct of Foster-children', *Twenty-seventh Yearbook*, Vol. I, Nat. Soc. Stud. Educ., 1928, pp. 101–217.
18. B. S. Burks, 'The Relative Influence of Nature and Nurture upon Mental Development', *Twenty-seventh Yearbook*, Vol. I, Nat. Soc. Stud. Educ., 1928, pp. 235–55.
19. A. M. Leahy, 'Nature—Nurture and Intelligence', *Genetic Psychology Monographs*, Vol. 17, 1935, pp. 235–308.
20. (i) H. M. Skeels and E. A. Fillamore, 'The Mental Development of Children from Underprivileged Homes', *Journal of Genetic Psychology*, Vol. 50, 1937.
   (ii) H. M. Skeels and T. Harms, 'Children with Inferior Social Histories: Their Mental Development in Adoptive Homes', *Journal of Genetic Psychology*, Vol. LXXII, 1948, pp. 283–9.
   (iii) M. Skodak and H. M. Skeels, 'A Final Follow-up Study of One Hundred Adopted Children', *Journal of Genetic Psychology*, Vol. LXXV, 1949, pp. 82–125.
21. H. Kalmus, *Variation and Heredity*, London, 1958, p. 68.
22. A. M. Carr Saunders and D. C. Jones, 'Relation between Intelligence and Social Status among Orphan Children', *British Journal of Psychology*, Vol. 17, 1927, p. 343.
23. John Bowlby, *Maternal Care and Mental Health*, Geneva, 1952, p. 14.
24. Ibid., p. 14.
25. H. Kalmus, op. cit., p. 21.
26. S. A. Barnet, Editor's note to *Variations and Heredity* by H. Kalmus.
27. Ibid.
28. H. Kalmus, op. cit., p. 65.
29. C. P. Blacker, *Eugenics: Galton and After*, London, 1952, p. 266.
30. Swithun Bowers, 'The Nature and Definition of Social Casework: Part III', *Journal of Social Casework*, Vol. 30, December 1949, p. 417.
31. Clare Britton, 'Casework Techniques in the Child Care Services', *Case Conference*, January 1955, p. 6.
32. Ibid., p. 6.
33. Florence Hollis, 'Principles and Assumptions Underlying Casework Practice', *Social Work*, April 1955.
34. John Bowlby, *Maternal Care and Mental Health*, Geneva, 1952, p. 126.
35. Florence Hollis, art. cit., p. 49.
36. Ibid., p. 49.
37. Mary B. Sayles, *Substitute Parents. A Study of Foster Families*, New York, 1936, Preface.
38. Sophie van Senden Theis, *How Foster Children Turn Out*, New York, 1924.
39. Annual Report of the Registrar-General for Scotland, 1955, H.M.S.O., 1956.
40. This number refers to those where legalisation took place after age of 5.
41. See page 24.
42. Census 1951. Classification of Occupations, H.M.S.O. 1956.

Notes to pages 68–182

43. Annual Report of the Registrar-General for Scotland, 1955, H.M.S.O 1956, p. 59.
44. Margaret Kornitzer, *Adoption*, London, 1959, p. 47.
45. (a) J. R. Wittenborn, *The Placement of Adoptive Children*, Springfield, Ill., 1957.
    (b) Charles E. Brown, 'The Adjustment of Adopted Children', *Child Adoption*, No. 31, Autumn 1959, pp. 6–20.
    (c) R. J. Goldman, 'Case Studies in Adoption', reported in *Child Adoption*, Nos. 34, 35 and 36, 1960–1.
46. John Madge, *The Tools of Social Science*, London, 1953, p. 177.
47. Ibid., p. 164.
48. C. A. Moser, *Survey Methods in Social Investigation*, London, 1958, p. 207.
49. Robert Merton and Patricia Kendall, 'The Focused Interview', *American Journal of Sociology*, Vol. 51, 1945–6, p. 545.
50. Annette Garrett, *Interviewing, Its Principles and Methods*, New York, 1942, p. 37.
51. C. A. Moser, op. cit., p. 206.
52. Robert Merton and Patricia Kendall, art. cit., p. 552.
53. O. A. Will, in Introduction to *The Psychiatric Interview*, by Harry Stack Sullivan, New York 1954 and London 1955, p. XXIII.
54. John Bowlby, op. cit., p. 61.
55. (a) Adoptive mother objected to a subsequent interview.
    (b) Pregnancy.
    (c) Removal from area.
56. John Madge, op. cit., p. 222.
57. Harry Stack Sullivan, op. cit., p. 51.

Chapter Three: Description of Histories

1. Census 1951, Classification of Occupations, H.M.S.O., 1956, p. vii.
2. These figures have been kept by the Registrar-General's Office since 1946. They were published for the first time for 1962. In that year of 1,621 adoptions, the proportions were 88·5% illegitimate, 9% legitimate, and 2·5% status unknown.
3. Adoption Act, 1950, Part I, para. 5.
4. John Bowlby, *Forty-Four Juvenile Thieves; Their Character and Home Life*, London, 1946.
   John Bowlby, *Maternal Care and Mental Health*, Geneva, 1952.
   John Bowlby, et al., 'The Effects of Mother–Child Separation, A Follow-up Study', *The British Journal of Medical Psychology*, Vol. 29, September 1956.
5. Ibid.
6. R. Hoggart, *The Uses of Literacy*, London, 1957, Chapter 10.
7. It can be assumed that such visits were undertaken under the Infant Life Protection provisions of the Children Act, 1908.

Notes to pages 196–259

Chapter Four: Analysis of Histories and of Adoption Situation

1. *Price's Textbook of the Practice of Medicine*, edited by Donald Hunter, London, 7th ed 1956, p. 492.
2. Adoption Act, 1958, Part I, Section 2.
3. Margaret Kornitzer, *Adoption*, London, 1959, p. 24.
4. Under an Act of Sederunt (Adoption of Children), 1959, a medical certificate on the health of adopters must now be presented to the court before an adoption is legalised.
5. See study by Lulie A. Shaw, 'Following up Adoptions', *British Journal of Psychiatric Social Work*, Vol. 2, No. 8, November 1953.
6. Census 1951, Classification of Occupations, H.M.S.O., 1956, p. vii.
7. (a) See article 'Is Religion Important', *Child Adoption*, No. 28, Autumn/Winter, 1958–59.
 (b) An Agnostics Adoption Bureau was formed in 1963, and in 1965 it became a registered adoption society for Agnostics.
8. See Children and Young Persons, The Adoption Agencies (Scotland) Regulations, 1959, Fifth Schedule. Medical Report as to Health of Infant.
9. Arnold Gesell and Catherine S. Amatruda, *Developmental Diagnosis* 2nd ed., London, 1947, p. 23.
10. Ibid., p. 39.
11. Ibid., p. 50.
12. John Bowlby, *Forty-Four Juvenile Thieves; Their Character and Home Life*, London, 1946.
 John Bowlby, *Maternal Care and Mental Health*, Geneva, 1952.
 John Bowlby, et al., 'The Effects of Mother–Child Separation, V Follow-up Study', *The British Journal of Medical Psychology*, Vol. 29, September 1956.
13. W. Goldfarb, Various articles in *American Journal of Orthopsychiatry*, 1943–9.
14. *Mental Health and Infant Development*, edited by K. Soddy. Proceedings of the international seminar held at Chichester, England. Published by World Federation for Mental Health in 2 vols. (1) *Papers and Discussions*, London, 1955; (2) *Case Histories*, New York, 1956.
15. See study by Lulie A. Shaw, 'Following-up Adoptions', *British Journal of Psychiatric Social Work*, Vol. 2, No. 8, November 1953.
16. Iris Goodacre, 'Adoption Agencies and their Clients', *Child Adoption*, No. 43, Autumn/Winter, 1963–4, pp. 17–20.

Chapter Five: Conclusions

1. See p. 45 of this book (Chapter One).
2. R. Michaels and R. F. Brenner, *A Follow-up Study of Adoptive Families*, New York, 1951.
3. A survey based on Adoption Case Records, N.A.M.H., 1956.

4. Lulie A. Shaw, 'Following-up Adoptions', *British Journal of Psychiatric Social Work*, Vol. 2, No. 8, November 1953.
5. (a) M. Humphrey and C. Ounsted, 'Adoptive Families Referred for Psychiatric Advice', *The British Journal of Psychiatry*, Vol. 109, September 1963, pp. 599-608.
   (b) M. Humphrey, 'Factors Associated with Maladjustment in Adoptive Families', *Child Adoption*, No. 43, Autumn/Winter, 1963-4, pp. 25-31.
6. Iris Goodacre, 'Adoption Agencies and their Clients', *Child Adoption*, No. 43, Autumn/Winter, 1963-4, pp. 17-20.
7. H. D. Kirk: (a) 'From Empirical Investigation—to Theory and Return', Annual Meeting, Canadian Political Science Association, Quebec, June 1963.
   (b) 'Non-Fecund People as Parents, Some Social and Psychological Considerations', *Fertility and Sterility*, May-June 1963 (American Society for Study of Sterility).
8. Report of the Departmental Committee on the Adoption of Children, 1954, para. 152.
9. Ibid.
10. See (1) *What Shall We Tell Our Adopted Child?* and *Adopting a Child*; pamphlets issued by the Standing Conference of Societies Registered for Adoption.
    (2) *Adopting the Older Child*, published by Northampton Diocesan Catholic Child Protection and Welfare Society.
    (3) *Adoption* by Margaret Kornitzer, London, 1959, Chapters XIV, XV and XVI.
11. See *Adopting a Child*, pamphlet issued by the Standing Conference of Societies Registered for Adoption, p. 11.
12. Sir Gerald Hurst, *Lincoln's Inn Essays*, London, 1949, p. 107.
13. See The Adoption (Juvenile Court) Rules, 1959, Second Schedule. (Particular duties of guardian *ad litem* contained in Statutory Instruments following the Adoption Act, 1958.)
14. See Act of Sederunt (Adoption of Children), 1959, Section 6. (Particular duties as above for curator *ad litem* in Scotland.)
15. See page 27 of this book (Introduction).
16. Quoted by John Madge, *The Tools of Social Science*, London, 1953, p. 60

BIBLIOGRAPHY

I BOOKS

ADDIS, ROBINA S., *Mental Health Aspects of Adoption*, London 1946.
AINSWORTH, MARY D. and BOWLBY, JOHN, *Research Strategy in the Study of Mother–Child Separation*, Paris 1954.
BENEDICT, RUTH, *Patterns of Culture*, London 1935.
BIESTEK, FELIX P., *The Casework Relationship*, Chicago 1957.
BLACKER, C. P., *Eugenics, Galton and After*, London 1952.
BOTT, ELIZABETH, *Family and Social Network*, London 1958.
BOWLBY, JOHN, *Forty-four Juvenile Thieves: Their Character and Home Life*, London 1946.
Maternal Care and Mental Health, Geneva 1952.
BOWLEY, AGATHA H., *The Psychology of the Unwanted Child*, Edinburgh 1947.
Problems of Family Life, Edinburgh 1948.
The Natural Development of the Child, Edinburgh 1954.
BRILL, KENNETH and THOMAS, RUTH, *Children in Homes*, London 1964.
BROOKS, L. M. and E. C., *Adventuring in Adoption*, Durham, N.C. 1939.
BURGESS, E. W. and COTTRELL, L. S., *Predicting Success and Failure in Marriage*, New York 1939.
BURLINGTON, DOROTHY and FREUD, ANNA, *Infants without Families*, London 1943.
CADY, ERNEST, *We Adopted Three*, London 1954.
DAVIDSON, AUDREY, *Phantasy in Childhood*, London 1952.
DEUTSCH, HELENE, *The Psychology of Women*, London 1947.
DRAWBELL, JAMES WEDGWOOD, *Experiment in Adoption*, London 1935.
DYSON, D. M., *The Foster Home*, London 1947.
ELLIS, R. W. B. (Editor), *Child Health and Development*, London 1956.
ELLISON, MARY, *The Adopted Child*, London 1958.
FLEMING, C. M., *Adolescence: Its Social Psychology*, London 1948.
(Editor), *Studies in the Social Psychology of Adolescence*, London 1951.
FRENCH, DAVID G., *An Approach to Measuring Results in Social Work*, New York 1952.
GARRETT, ANNETTE, *Interviewing, Its Principles and Methods*, New York 1942.
GESELL, ARNOLD and AMATRUDA, CATHERINE S., *Developmental Diagnosis*, London 1947.
GESELL, ARNOLD and ILG, F. L., *The Child from Five to Ten*, London 1946.
GILES, F. T., *Children and the Law*, London 1959.
GREENWOOD, ERNEST, *Experimental Sociology: A Study in Method*, New York 1945.
GRIFFITHS, RUTH, *A Study in Imagination in Early Childhood*, London 1940.
HALL, M. PENELOPE, *The Social Services of Modern England*, London 1952.
HALMERS, PAUL, *Towards a Measure of Man*, London 1957.

Bibliography

HAMILTON, GORDON, *Theory and Practice of Social Casework*, Columbia 1940.
Principles of Social Case Recording, New York 1946.
HEALY, WM., et al., *Reconstructing Behaviour in Youth—A Study of Problem Children in Foster Homes*, Boston 1929.
HEYWOOD, JEAN S., *Children in Care*, London 1959.
HICKLIN, MARGOT, *War-damaged Children*, London 1946.
HOCHFELD, EUGENIE and VALK, MARGARET A., *Experience in Inter-Country Adoptions*, New York 1954.
HOGGART, RICHARD, *The Uses of Literacy*, London 1957.
HOPKIRK, MARY, *Nobody Wanted Sam*, London 1948.
HOWELLS, JOHN G. (Editor), *Modern Perspectives in Child Psychiatry*, Edinburgh 1965.
HUTCHISON, DOROTHY, *In Quest of Foster Parents*, New York 1943.
ILG, FRANCES L. and AMES, LOUISE BATES, *Child Behaviour*, New York 1955
ISAACS, SUSAN, *Intellectual Growth in Young Children*, London 1930.
Social Development in Young Children, London 1933.
JEPHCOTT, A. P., *Girls Growing up*, London 1942.
KALMUS, H., *Variation and Heredity*, London 1958.
KASIUS, CORA (Editor), *Principles and Techniques in Social Casework: Selected Articles 1940–1950*, New York 1953.
KASTELL, JEAN, *Casework in Child Care*, London 1962.
KORNITZER, MARGARET, *Child Adoption in the Modern World*, London 1952.
Adoption, London 1959.
LANGE, JOHANNES, *Crime as Destiny*, London 1931.
LEWIS, HILDA, *Deprived Children*, London 1954.
LOCKRIDGE, FRANCES with the assistance of THEIS, SOPHIE V. S., *Adopting a Child*, New York 1947.
MADGE, JOHN, *The Tools of Social Science*, London 1953.
MEAD, MARGARET, *Coming of Age in Samoa*, London 1929.
Sex and Temperament in Three Primitive Societies, London 1935.
Growing up in New Guinea, London 1942.
MEEHL, PAUL E., *Clinical versus Statistical Prediction*, Minneapolis 1954.
MICHAELS, R. and BRENNER, R. F., *A Follow-up Study of Adoptive Families*, New York 1951.
MOSER, C. A., *Survey Methods in Social Investigation*, London 1958.
MYRDAL, GUNNAR, *Value in Social Theory*, London 1958.
NEWMAN, H. H., et al., *Twins: A Study of Heredity and Environment*, Chicago 1937.
OLDFIELD, R. C., *The Psychology of the Interview*, London 1941.
OSBORN, FREDERICK, *Preface to Eugenics*, New York 1940.
PERLMAN, HELEN H., *Social Casework: A Problem-Solving Process*, Chicago 1957.
PRENTICE, CAROL S., *An Adopted Child looks at Adoption*, New York 1940.
RAYMOND, LOUISE, *Adoption and After*, New York 1955.
RICKMAN, J. (Editor), *On the Bringing-up of Children*, London 1936.
RONDELL, FLORENCE and MICHAELS, RUTH, *The Adopted Family*, New York 1951.
ROWE, JANE, *Yours by Choice*, London 1959.
Parents, Children and Adoption, London 1966.

Bibliography

SAYLES, MARY BUELL, *Substitute Parents: A Study of Foster Families*, New York 1936.
SLATER, ELIOT, *Psychotic and Neurotic Illnesses in Twins*, London 1953.
SPINLEY, B. M., *The Deprived and the Privileged: Personality Development in English Society*, London 1953.
SULLIVAN, HARRY STACK, *The Psychiatric Interview*, New York 1954 and London 1955.
THEIS, SOPHIE VAN S., *How Foster Children Turn Out*, New York 1924.
TIMMS, NOEL, *Casework in the Child Care Service*, London 1962.
TRASLER, GORDON, *In Place of Parents*, London 1960.
WIMPERIS, VIRGINIA, *The Unmarried Mother and her Child*, London 1960.
WINNICOTT, D. W., *The Ordinary Devoted Mother and her Child*, London 1953. *The Child and the Outside World*, London 1957.
WOODWORTH, ROBERT S., *Heredity and Environment*, New York 1941.
WOOTTON, BARBARA, *Testament for Social Science*, London 1950. *Social Science and Social Pathology*, London 1959.
WYNN, MARGARET, *Fatherless Children*, London 1964.
YOUNG, MICHAEL and WILLMOTT, PETER, *Family and Kinship in East London*, London 1958.
YOUNG, LEONTINE, *Personality Patterns in Unmarried Mothers*, New York 1945 *Out of Wedlock*, New York 1954.
YOUNGHUSBAND, EILEEN, *Social Work and Social Change*, London 1964.

II SUBSEQUENT RESEARCH STUDIES AND SURVEYS

GOODACRE, I., 'Adoption Agencies and their Clients', *Child Adoption*, No. 43, 1963–4.
HUMPHREY, M., 'Factors associated with maladjustment in adoptive families', *Child Adoption*, No. 43, 1963–4.
KIRK, H. D., (a) 'From Empirical Investigation to Theory and Return', Annual Meeting of Canadian Political Science Assoc., 1963.
(b) 'Non-fecund people as parents: Some social and psychological considerations', *Fertility and Sterility*, Vol. 14, No. 3, 1963.
(c) *Shared Fate, A Theory of Adoption and Mental Health*, London 1964.
OUNSTED, C. and HUMPHREY, M., 'Adoptive Families Referred For Psychiatric Advice', *The British Journal of Psychiatry*, Vol. 109, 1963, pp. 599–608 and Vol. 110, 1964, pp. 549–55.
WITMER, HERZOG, WEINSTEIN and SULLIVAN, *Independent Adoptions in the State of Florida: A Follow-up Study*, The Russell Sage Foundation, U.S.A., 1963.
WITTENBORN, J. R., *The Placement of Adoptive Children*, Springfield, Ill., 1957.

III PAPERS AND ARTICLES IN SOCIAL WORK, SOCIOLOGICAL, PSYCHOLOGICAL AND OTHER JOURNALS

ASHLEY, ANNE (Editor), *Illegitimate Children and their Parents in Scotland* Scottish Council for the Unmarried Mother and her Child, 1955.
BLACK, J. A. and STONE, F. H., 'Medical Aspects of Adoption', *The Lancet*, ii, p. 1272, 1958.

Bibliography

BLOM-COOPER, L. J., 'Historical Development of Legal Adoption', *Child Adoption*, No. 20, Autumn 1956.

BODMAN, FRANK, et al., 'The Social Adaptation of Institution Children', *The Lancet*, Jan./June 1950.

BOWLBY, JOHN, AINSWORTH, MARY, BOSTON, MARY and ROSENBLUTH, DINA, 'The Effects of Mother–Child Separation. A Follow-up Study', *British Journal of Medical Psychology*, Sept. 1956.

BOWLEY, AGATHA, 'The Unmarried Mother and her Child', *The Fortnightly*, June 1950.

BRITTON, CLARE, 'Casework Techniques in the Child Care Services', *Case Conference*, Jan. 1955.

BROWN, FLORENCE, 'What do we seek in Adoptive Parents?', *Social Casework*, April 1951.

BURKS, B. S., 'The Relative Influence of Nature and Nurture upon Mental Development', *Twenty-seventh Yearbook*, Nat. Soc. Stud. Educ., 1928.

Child Adoption, No. 2, 'Adoption—The Parents' Point of View', Jan. 1952.

Child Adoption, No. 18, 'The Hearing of Adoption Applications', Spring 1956.

Child Adoption, No. 28, 'Is Religion Important?' Autumn/Winter, 1958–59.

Child Adoption, No. 30, 'Investigating a Marriage', Summer 1959.

CLOTHIER, FLORENCE, 'Placing the Child for Adoption', *Mental Hygiene*, April 1942.

'Problems of Illegitimacy as they concern the Worker in the Field of Adoption,' *Mental Hygiene*, October 1941.

'The Psychology of the Adopted Child', *Mental Hygiene*, April 1943.

COWAN, EDWINA S., 'Some Emotional Problems besetting the Lives of Foster Children', *Mental Hygiene*, July 1938.

DUKETTE, RITA, 'Some Casework Implications in Adoptive Home Intake Procedures', *Child Welfare*, Jan. 1954.

DICK, KENNETH, 'Towards earlier placement for Adoption,' *Social Casework*, Jan. 1955.

EDWARDS, M. E., 'Failure and Success in the Adoption of Toddlers', *Case Conference*, Nov. 1954.

FISHER, LETTICE, *Twenty-one Years and After. 1918–1946*, National Council for the Unmarried Mother and her Child, 1946.

FRANKLIN, A. WHITE, 'A Study of 460 girls in a Service Hostel having out-of-wedlock babies,' *Child Adoption*, No. 14, Feb. 1955.

FREEMAN, et al, 'The Influence of Environment on the intelligence, school achievement and conduct of foster children,' *Twenty-seventh Yearbook*, Nat. Soc. Stud. Educ. 1928.

GALTON, F., 'The History of Twins as a Criterion of the relative Powers of Nature and Nurture', *Journal of Royal Anthropological Institute*, Vol. 5, 1875.

GOLDFARB, W., *American Journal of Orthopsychiatry*—various articles, 1943–1949.

HOLLIS, FLORENCE, 'Principles and Assumptions underlying Casework Practice,' *Social Work*, April 1955.

INTERNATIONAL CHILD WELFARE REVIEW, 'Adoption as an International Problem,' 1949–50, Vols. 3–4.

Bibliography

JOSSELYN, IRENE, 'Evaluating Motives of Foster Parents', *Child Welfare*, Feb. 1952.

KNIGHT, ROBERT P., 'Some Problems in Selecting and Rearing Adopted Children,' *Bulletin of the Menninger Clinic*, May 1951.

LEAHY, A. M., 'Nature-Nurture and Intelligence', *Genetic Psychology Monographs*, Vol. 17, 1935.

LEVY, DOROTHY, 'A Follow-up Study of Unmarried Mothers', *Social Casework*, Jan. 1955.

LEWIS, HILDA, 'Follow-up of Adoption in the U.S.A.', *Child Adoption*, No. 42, 1963.

'Some Recent Studies of Adoption', *Child Adoption*, No. 44, 1964.

MCWHINNIE, Alexina M., 'Adoption Work of a Scottish Society', *Child Adoption*, No. 45, 1964.

'Adoption Placements', *Child Adoption*, No. 46, 1964–65.

MERTON, ROBERT K. and KENDALL, PATRICIA L., 'The Focused Interview', *American Journal of Sociology*, Vol. 51, 1945–46.

NEWSHOLME, H. P., *The Illegitimate Child: A Challenge to Society*, National Council for the Unmarried Mother and her Child, 1946.

PENROSE, L. S., 'Hereditary Influences in relation to the Problem of Child Adoption', *Bulletin of World Health Organisation*, 1953.

Heredity and Environment in Human Affairs, The Convocation Lecture 1955 of the National Children's Home.

RATHBUN, CONSTANCE, 'Psycho-Physical Reactions to Placement', *Journal of Social Casework*, Vol. 28, Feb. 1947.

RETALLACK, L., 'The Changes and Chances of Moral Welfare', *Social Work*, Oct. 1942

SHAW, LULIE A., 'Following up Adoptions', *Brit. Journal of Psychiatric Social Work*, Vol. 2, No. 8, Nov. 1953.

SHIELDS, JAMES, 'The Social Development of Twins', *Case Conference*, August 1954.

'Twins Brought Up Apart', *Eugenics Review*, July 1958.

SKEELS, H. M. and DYE, H. B., *Proceedings of American Association of Mental Deficiency*, Vol. XLIV, 1939.

SKEELS, H. M. and HARMS, T., 'Children with Inferior Social Histories; Their Mental Development in Adoptive Homes', *Journal of Genetic Psychology*, Vol. LXXII, 1948.

SKODAK, M., and SKEELS, H. M., 'A Final Follow-up Study of 100 Adopted Children', *Journal of Genetic Psychology*, Vol. LXXV, 1949.

TAIT, H. P., 'Follow-up of Illegitimate Children', *The Medical Officer*, Dec. 1956.

TORRIE, A. with BRILL, K. and MELFORD A., 'The Problems of Placement of Children for Adoption', *Journal of Royal Sanitary Institute*, Vol. 71, No. 4, July 1961.

WATSON, JOHN, 'Notes by a Magistrate', *Child Adoption*, No. 16, August 1955.

WOLKIMIR, BELLE, 'The Unadoptable Baby Achieves Adoption', *Child Welfare*, Feb. 1947.

Bibliography

IV SYMPOSIA, MEMORANDA, REPORTS

Child Welfare League of America, *Adoption of Children with Pathology in their Backgrounds*, 1949.
Adoption Practices, Procedures and Problems, 1951.
Citizens' Committee on Adoption of Children in California, *A Three Years' Study 1949 to 1952*, 1953.
Family Service Association of America, *Adoption Principles and Services*, 1953. *Research Programmes and Projects in Social Work*, 1953.
National Association for Mental Health, *A Survey based on Adoption Case Records*, 1956.
Royal College of Obstetricians and Gynaecologists and Population Investigation Committee, *Maternity in Great Britain*, 1948.
Standing Conference of Societies Registered for Adoption, Reports of Residential Conferences, 1953, 1955, 1961, 1962, 1964 and of Day Conference, 1957: *Adopting a Child, Adopting the Older Child, If you are Adopted, What shall we tell our adopted Child?*
Toronto and District Unmarried Parenthood Committee, *A Study of the Adjustment of Teen Age Children born out of Wedlock who remained in the Custody of their Mothers or Relatives*, Toronto 1943.
United Nations Department of Social Affairs, *Study on Adoption of Children*, New York 1953.
World Health Organisation, General UN/WHO Meeting of Experts on the Mental Health Aspects of Adoption. Final Report, Geneva 1953.

V H.M.S.O. PUBLICATIONS

Report of the Committee on Child Adoption, 1921.
Child Adoption Committee, First Report, 1925, and Third Report, 1926.
Adoption of Children Act, 1926.
Adoption of Children (Scotland) Act, 1930.
Report of the Departmental Committee on Adoption Societies and Agencies, 1937.
The Adoption of Children (Regulation) Act, 1939.
The Adoption Societies Regulations, 1943.
The Adoption Societies (Scotland) Regulations, 1943.
Report of the Committee on Homeless Children, 1945.
Report of the Care of Children Committee, 1946.
Children Act, 1948.
Adoption of Children Act, 1949.
The Adoption of Children (Summary Jurisdiction), Rules, etc., 1949.
Act of Sederunt (Adoption of Children), 1950.
Adoption Act, 1950.
Report of the Departmental Committee on the Adoption of Children, 1954.
Census 1951. Classification of Occupations, 1955.
The Registrar-General's Statistical Review of England and Wales for the year 1962, Part II.
Annual Report of the Registrar General for Scotland, 1962.

Bibliography

Children Act, 1958.
Adoption Act, 1958.
The Adoption Agencies Regulations, 1959.
The Adoption Agencies (Scotland) Regulations, 1959.
The Adoption (Juvenile Court) Rules, etc., 1959.
Act of Sederunt (Adoption of Children), 1959.

APPENDIX

ANNUAL FIGURES OF LEGALISED ADOPTIONS IN ENGLAND AND SCOTLAND
(a) REGISTRATION OF ADOPTION ORDERS, 1927 TO 1962 (ENGLAND)

The Registrar General's Statistical Review of England and Wales for the year 1962. Part II, Table T 4. p. 90.

Year	Number of Adoption Orders dealt with:			
	Total	High Court	County Court	Court of Summary Jurisdiction
1927–30	14,026	403	961	12,662
1931–35	22,708	276	1,432	21,000
1936–40	31,521	349	2,511	28,661
1941–45	58,732	266	7,916	50,550
1946–50	88,123	870	19,225	68,028
1951–55	66,743	392	21,654	44,697
1951	13,850	114	3,757	9,979
1952	13,894	74	4,280	9,540
1953	12,995	75	4,297	8,623
1954	13,003	56	4,529	8,418
1955	13,001	73	4,791	8,137
1956	13,198	44	5,118	8,036
1957	13,401	44	5,553	7,804
1958	13,303	53	5,899	7,351
	Total*	Provisional	Total*	Provisional	Total*	Provisional	
1959	14,105	71	46	1	6,529	70	7,530
1960	15,099	207	42	2	7,602	205	7,455
1961	15,997	249	55	1	8,678	248	7,264
1962	16,894	280	53	4	9,592	276	7,269

*Provisional Adoption Orders, which were introduced on 1st April 1959, (see Adoption Act, 1958, section 53) are included in the total.
These Orders confer authority on a person not domiciled in Great Britain to take a child out of this country for adoption.

Appendix

(b)   ADOPTED CHILDREN REGISTER
NUMBER OF ADOPTIONS RECORDED ANNUALLY
(SCOTLAND)

Annual Report of the Registrar-General for Scotland, 1962. Chapter II. Page 61.

Year	No.	Year	No.
1930	3	1947	1,890
1931	347	1948	2,073
1932	492	1949	1,764
1933	437	1950	1,289
1934	602	1951	1,562
1935	683	1952	1,523
1936	704	1953	1,486
1937	820	1954	1,343
1938	812	1955	1,352
1939	1,100	1956	1,358
1940	1,424	1957	1,405
1941	1,222	1958	1,365
1942	1,563	1959	1,236
1943	1,747	1960	1,457
1944	1,681	1961	1,609
1945	1,876	1962	1,621
1946	2,292		

INDEX

Acceptance in social casework, 55–6
Act of Sederunt (Adoption of Children) 1950, 19 n. 67
Act of Sederunt (Adoption of Children) 1959, 20, 201 n. 4, 268 n. 14
Adopted child,
  adoptability, 26;
  primary emphasis on needs of child, 22
Adopted Children's Register, 12, 35, 103, 242
Adopted persons interviewed,
  age at time of placement, 88, 211–14, 260;
  age at time of research study, 69, 85;
  attitude to learning of adoption, 45, 246–51, 263–6;
  'community value', 37, 195–7;
  family patterns, 87–9, 215–18, 260–1;
  fantasies about origins, 249–50;
  health record, 196–7;
  legitimate or illegitimate birth, 86–7;
  marital status, 85–6;
  need for information about biological background, 45, 78, 226, 237–8, 240–51, 263–5;
  placement, how made, 87–8;
  placement, reasons for, 86–7;
  occupational classification, 86;
  sex distribution, 69, 85
Adoption,
  advocacy of, 23–4;
  community attitudes to, 6–8, 10, 21, 25–6, 31, 220, 259;
  definition of, 30, 36, 64, 66–7;
  statistics, 21, 24, 64, 289–90
Adoptions, 'de facto', 3, 6, 8–9, 11, 13, 65, 90, 159;
  third party, 8, 16, 18, 22–4, 28–9, 34, 41, 65, 87, 268–9
Adoption Act, 1950, 19–21, 23 n. 80, 100, 198 n. 2, 209, 212
Adoption Act, 1958, 8, 19, 198 n. 2
Adoption Agencies Regulations, 1959 (Section 9), 20 n. 71, 27
Adoption Agencies (Scotland) Regulations, 1959 (Section 9), 20 n. 71, 27
Adoption law,
  development of legalisation, 6–23;

Index

effectiveness of, 22–3, 268–9;
general provisions, 11–12, 18–21;
protective value too late, 268;
recommendation for change in English law, 268
Adoption of Children Act, 1926, 10–12, 15–16, 18, 34, 128
Adoption of Children (Scotland) Act, 1930, 10–12, 15, 33–4, 106, 159, 170
Adoption of Children (Regulation) Act, 1939 (brought into force 1943), 15
Adoption of Children Act, 1949, 18
Adoption of Children (Summary Jurisdiction) Rules, 1949, 19 n. 66, 20
Adoption of Children (County Court) Rules, 1949, 19 n. 66
Adoption of Children (High Court) Rules, 1950 (Second Schedule), 19 n. 66, 20 n. 73
Adoption of Children (Juvenile Court) Rules, 1959 (Second Schedule), 20 n. 72, 268 n. 13
Adoption of Children (Consolidating) Act, 1950, 18, 100, 212
Adoption order, failure to obtain, 23
Adoption situation, 45, 78, 222, 226, 240–56, 258
Adoption Societies,
control of, 16, 20 n. 74, 22–3, 269;
growth of, 6–8, 24, 33;
methods of, 10, 13–15, 26–9, 41, 267, 269
Adoption Societies Regulations, 1943 (Second Schedule), 16, 20 n. 74
Adoption Societies (Scotland) Regulations, 1943 (Third Schedule), 16 n. 57, 20 n. 74
Adoptive parenthood,
acceptability and social class, 9, 21, 220, 259
Adoptive parents,
age limits of, 27;
assessment of applicants, 26–8, 267;
attitudes to adoption situation, 198–256, 261–6;
motivation in adopting, 262;
number of applicants, 21
'Adult', definition of for research study, 59
Advertisement, of baby for adoption, 34, 87
'Advisory Council in Child Care', 17
Agnostics Adoption Bureau, 209 n. 7 (b)
Allport, G., 49
Amatruda, C. S., 212–14
Ancestor worship, 1
Aristotelian conception, 57

'Baby farming', evils of, 3–4, 33
Bacon, Francis, 48, 269
Dr Barnardo's Homes, 3, 7
Barnet, S. A., 53 n. 26
Biological background of child placed for adoption,
attitude of adoptive parents to

Index

background information, 224–5, 228–9, 231–2, 238–9, 240–51, 261–2, 266; availability to adopted person of information about background, 20–1, 30, 40, 268; availability to adoptive parents of information about background and advice about this, 28, 40–1, 267–8; secrecy about, 10, 15, 20, 249
Birth Certificates, 12, 35; for adopted child, 9, 34, 103; for illegitimate child, 35, 109; shortened form of Birth Certificate, 35
Birth Rate, 6, 68–9; illegitimate, rise in First and Second World Wars, 7
Births and Deaths Registration Act, 1874, 4
Blacker, C. P., 53, 54 n. 29
Bowers, Swithun, 54
Bowlby, John, *Maternal Care and Mental Health*, 24–6, 50 n. 5 & 6, 53 n. 23 & 24, 56 n. 34, 77, 116, 147, 213; *44 Juvenile Thieves*, 116 n. 4, 147 n. 5, 213 n. 12; 'The Effects of Mother-Child Separation', 116 n. 4, 147 n. 5, 213 n. 12
Bowley, Agatha, 51 n. 7 & 8
Brenner, R. F., 38, 40, 45 n. 13, 258–60, 265–6
British Penitent Female Refuge, 4
Britton, Clare 55 n. 31 & 32

Brown, Charles E., 71 n. 45 (b)
Burgess, E. W., 44 n. 12
Burks, B. S., 53 n. 18
Butler, Josephine, 5

Carnegie Trust for the Universities of Scotland, xvi
Case histories, adjustment classification, criteria for, 91–5; analysis chart, details and use of, 90–1; assessment and evaluation, 45, 54, 56–7, 81; compilation of, 75, 81–2; confirmation by discussion with medical practitioners, 79, 81–4, 257; individual initials, C.A. (No. 1), 158, 200, 235
E.A. (No. 2), 104, 252
J.A. (No. 16), 164, 201, 232–3, 246, 252
B.B. (No. 43), detailed history, 96–8
H.B. (No. 35), 171, 234, 245, 252
M.B. (No. 8), detailed history, 158–64, 196, 216, 233, 245, 251, 254–5
B.C. (No. 51), detailed history, 139–44, 195, 201, 217, 219, 234, 246
P.C. (No. 14), 105, 221–3, 252
C.D. (No. 27), 184–5, 237
G.D. (No. 55), 194, 196, 201, 238–9, 246

293

Index

individual initials—*cont.*
T.D. (No. 41), detailed
history, 112–17, 211,
297, 246, 255
G.F. (No. 19), 104, 252
M.F. (No. 13), 153, 230–1,
247, 250, 253
C.G. (No. 44), 104–5, 221–2,
250
H.G. (No. 20), detailed
history, 144–7, 196, 236,
246, 252
J.G. (No. 48), 138, 195,
226–7, 250
C.H. (No. 38), detailed
history, 107–11, 217,
223–4, 240, 243
G.H. (No. 21), detailed
history, 105–7, 222,
247–8
J.H. (No. 5), 107, 224
K.H. (No. 54), 194, 200,
238–9, 247
L.H. (No. 12), 153, 196,
217, 233, 245–6, 254–5
P.H. (No. 25), 138, 195,
211, 225–7, 245, 247,
251–2
R.H. (No. 39), 175, 219,
232, 249
N.J. (No. 22), 107, 223, 251
A.K. (No. 17), 144, 217, 236
M.K. (No. 26), 184–5, 214,
219, 236, 240, 251, 254
A.L. (No. 57), 189, 200,
238–9, 245, 255–6
E.L. (No. 23), 98
S.L. (No. 11), 107, 201, 216,
222–4
W.L. (No. 52), 147, 201,
217, 232, 247, 252
C.McD. (No. 45), 117,
225, 7, 211, 245, 255
G.McG. (No. 58), detailed
history, 185–9, 238,
240, 246–7
H.McG. (No. 56), 189, 202,
238–40
K.McI. (No. 10), 132, 200,
226, 228, 246, 252
B.M. (No. 24), 171, 230–1,
246, 250, 252
E.M. (No. 3), detailed
history, 171–5, 232,
240
G.M. (No. 40), detailed
history, 180–4, 236, 252
J.M. (No. 4), detailed
history, 132–8, 217–18,
225–7, 252
M.M. (No. 46), detailed
history, 124–32, 211,
226, 228, 245, 251
M.N. (No. 37), detailed
history, 147–53, 195,
211, 230–1, 252
T.N. (No. 31), 180, 204, 237
V.O. (No. 29), 105, 216,
222, 247, 251, 254–5
A.P. (No. 7), 132, 195,
225–7, 229, 250
P.P. (No. 30), detailed
history, 153–8, 200,
211, 235, 247, 251
S.R. (No. 47), 171, 204,
217, 234, 245, 247, 249,
255
C.S. (No. 9), detailed
history, 101–4, 221,
251, 254

Index

individual initials—*cont.*
E.S. (No. 6), detailed
history, 164–71, 195,
232–3, 245
F.S. (No. 32), 171, 201, 233
J.S. (No. 36), 171, 201,
234–5, 254
C.T. (No. 15), 171, 230–1,
251–2, 254
J.T. (No. 42), 179–80, 237,
250–1
M.T. (No. 34), 107, 201,
222, 246
P.T. (No. 28), detailed
history, 98–101, 222,
254–5
B.W. (No. 18), 153, 230–1,
250, 252
D.W. (No. 53), detailed
history, 189–94, 238–9,
245, 249, 255
T.W. (No. 50), detailed
history, 117–24, 211,
214, 216, 227, 240,
243, 251–2
B.Y. (No. 33), 124, 226–7,
229, 254–5
G.Y. (No. 49), detailed
history, 175–9, 237, 250;
numerical sequence,
No. 1, C.A., 158, 200, 235
No. 2, E.A., 104, 252
No. 3, E.M., detailed
history, 171–5, 232, 240
No. 4, J.M., detailed
history, 132–8, 217–18,
225–7, 252
No. 5, J.H., 107, 224
No. 6, E.S., detailed
history, 164–71, 195,
232–3, 245
No. 7, A.P., 132, 195,
225–7, 229, 250
No. 8, M.B., detailed
history, 158–64, 196,
216, 233, 245, 251,
254–5
No. 9, C.S., detailed
history, 101–4, 221,
251, 254
No. 10, K.McI., 132, 200,
226, 228, 246, 252
No. 11, S.L., 107, 201, 216,
222–4
No. 12, L.H., 153, 196, 217,
233, 245–6, 254–5
No. 13, M.F., 153, 230–1,
247, 250, 253
No. 14, P.C., 105, 221–3,
252
No. 15, C.T., 171, 230–1,
251–2, 254
No. 16, J.A., 164, 201,
232–3, 246, 252
No. 17, A.K., 144, 217, 236
No. 18, B.W., 153, 230–1,
250, 252
No. 19, G.F., 104, 252
No. 20, H.G., detailed
history, 144–7, 196,
236, 246, 252
No. 21, G.H., detailed
history, 105–7, 222,
247–8
No. 22, N.J., 107, 223, 251
No. 23, E.L., 98
No. 24, B.M., 171, 230–1,
246, 250, 252
No. 25, P.H., 138, 195, 211,
225–7, 245, 247, 251–2

Index

numerical sequence—*cont.*
No. 26, M.K., 184–5, 214, 219, 236, 240, 251, 254
No. 27, G.D., 184–5, 237
No. 28, P.T., detailed history, 98–101, 222, 254–5
No. 29, V.O., 105, 216, 222, 247, 251, 254–5
No. 30, P.P., detailed history, 153–8, 200, 211, 235, 247, 251
No. 31, T.N., 180, 204, 237
No. 32, F.S., 171, 201, 233
No. 33, B.Y., 124, 226–7, 229, 254–5
No. 34, M.T., 107, 201, 222, 246
No. 35, H.B., 171, 234, 245, 252
No. 36, J.S., 171, 201, 234–5, 254
No. 37, M.N., detailed history, 147–53, 195, 211, 230–1, 252
No. 38, C.H., detailed history, 107–11, 217, 223–4, 240, 243
No. 39, R.H., 175, 219, 232, 249
No. 40, G.M., detailed history, 180–4, 236, 252
No. 41, T.D., detailed history, 112–17, 211, 227, 246, 255
No. 42, J.T., 179–80, 237, 250–1
No. 43, B.B., detailed history, 96–8

No. 44, C.G., 104–5, 221–2, 250
No. 45, C.McD., 117, 225–7, 244, 246, 255
No. 46, M.M., detailed history, 124–32, 211, 226, 228, 245, 251
No. 47, S.R., 171, 204, 217, 234, 245, 247, 249, 255
No. 48, J.G., 138, 195, 226–7, 250
No. 49, G.Y., detailed history, 175–9, 237, 250
No. 50, T.W., detailed history, 117–24, 211, 214, 216, 227, 240, 243, 251–2
No. 51, B.C., detailed history, 139–44, 195, 201, 217, 219, 234, 246
No. 52, W.L., 147, 201, 217, 232, 247, 252
No. 53, D.W., detailed history, 189–94, 238–9, 245, 249, 255
No. 54, K.H., 194, 200, 238–9, 247
No. 55, G.D., 194, 196, 201, 238–9, 246
No. 56, H.McG., 189, 202, 238–40
No. 57, A.L., 189, 200, 238–9, 245, 255–6
No. 58, G.McG., detailed history, 185–9, 238, 240, 246–7
Catholic Enquiry Office, 33
Cattell, R. B., 39
Census 1951. Classification of Occupations, 1955, 67

Index

n. 42, 86 n. 1, 205, 208 n. 6
Central Training Council in Child Care, 17
Child adoption,
  in antiquity, 1;
  related to ancestor worship, 1;
  historical review of community attitudes in England and Scotland, 2-8
Child development,
  prediction of, 38-9;
  maturity stages of Gesell and Amatruda, 212-14
Child welfare legislation, 6, 17
Children Act, 1908 (the 'Children's Charter'), 4, 182 n. 7
Children Act, 1948, 4 n. 9, 7, 16-17, 278
Children and Young Persons Act, 1932, also consolidating Acts (England 1933) (Scotland 1937), 4 n. 8, 271
Children and Young Persons, The Adoption Agencies (Scotland) Regulations, 1959, Fifth Schedule. Medical Report as to Health of Infant, 212 n. 8
Children's Departments,
  adoption work of, 7-8, 17-19, 22-4, 26-7, 29, 267-9;
  setting up of, 17
Children's Officers, 17, 26, 268
Clyde Report (1945), 16 n. 61
College of General Practitioners, South-East Scotland Faculty of, 60
'Community value', 37, 195-7

Consanguinity, 11, 18
Consent to adoption, 11-12, 15, 18-19, 100
Control groups, discussion of, 43-4
County Court (England), 18-19
Court of Session (Scotland), 12, 18
Curator *ad litem*,
  appointment of, 12, 17, 100;
  duties of, 15, 18-23, 29, 268
Curtis Report (1946), 16-17, 23-4

Dalston Refuge, 4
Day Servants' Hostel, 5
Deed of declaration,
  change of name by, 34-5
Deed Poll,
  change of name by, 34-5, 173
Dickens, Charles, 3

Edinburgh Council of Social Service, 33
Edinburgh Home for Babies, 33
Edinburgh Home for Mothers and Infants, 32
Edinburgh Magdalene Asylum, later Springwell House, 31
Education (Administrative Provisions) Act, 1907, 272
Education (Scotland) Act, 1908, 272
Education Act, 1918, 272
Edwards, M. E., 43 n. 11
Ellison, Mary, 1-2
English Common Law (Rights of natural parents), 3, 6
Environment, influence of, 44, 50, 52-4, 258

Index

Environmental factors, research related to, 54, 258
Eysenck, H. J., 49

Female Mission to the Fallen, 4, 271
Fisher, Lettice, 5 n. 16
Foster-children, 30–3, 64–6, 85, 185–94, 238–9;
   age range at interview, 185;
   age range at placement, 89;
   research studies of, 37–8
Freeman, F. N., *et al.*, 53 n. 17
Freud, Sigmund, 49–50, 56–7, 72;
   influence of, 50

Galton, F., 53 n. 12
Garrett, Annette, 74 n. 50
General Register Office for England and Wales, 35
Gesell, A., 212–14
Goldfarb, W., 50 n. 5, 213 n. 13
Goldman, R. J., 71 n. 45(c)
Goodacre, Iris, 27 n. 90, 253 n. 16, 262, 265
Guardian *ad litem*,
   appointment of, 12, 17;
   duties of, 15, 18–23, 29, 268
Guardianship of Infants Act, 1886, 6, 272
Guardianship of Infants Act, 1925, 6
Guild of Service, 33

Haig Ferguson Memorial Home, 32
Hall, M. Penelope, 5 n. 14, 18 n. 65, 22 n. 78, 23 n. 79
Hastings, Dr Somerville, M.P., 21 n. 77

Health records, discussion of, 196–7
Healy, Wm., *et al.*, 37–8
Heredity, 44, 52–4, 258
High Court (England), 18
Hoggart, Richard, 147
Hollis, Florence, 56, 57 n. 35 & 36
Homes for Catholic Destitute Children, 3
Hopkinson Report, (1921), 8–9, 16, 21
Hopkirk, Mary, *Nobody Wanted Sam*, 3 n. 5
Horsburgh Report, (1937), 7 n. 22, 13–15, 22–3, 29, 36, 64
Humphrey, M., 262
Hurst, Sir Gerald, 268 n. 12
Hurst Report, (1954), 19–21, 24 n. 86 & 87, 267

Illegitimacy,
   adoption seen as cloak for, 10;
   attitudes of adoptive parents, 229, 262
Illegitimate child,
   adoption of second or subsequent child, 26;
   attitudes towards in Nineteenth Century, 3–5;
   certification of birth, 35;
   in feudal Britain, 2;
   in Roman Law, 2;
   in Tudor England, 2;
   influence of Industrial Revolution on attitudes towards, 3
Infant Life Protection Acts, 1872 & 1897, 4, 32, 34
Infant Mortality Rate, 5

Index

Inheritance by adopted children, 18
Intelligence Tests and Developmental assessment, 38–40, 48, 71–2
Interview Guide, 73, 77–8, 81, 90
Interviews and Interviewing, 54, 56, 267;
 definition of, 77;
 focused, 73, 76;
 length of, 79–80;
 number of, 80–1;
 recording of and note-taking, 80–1;
 rigidly structured, 72–3;
 unstructured and non-directive, 72–3;
 use of provocative statement, 74–5

Josephine Butler Memorial House, 5 n. 12
Juvenile Court, 18–19

Kallman, F. J., 53 n. 15
Kalmus, H., 53 n. 21, 25–8
Kardiner, A., 50 n. 5
Kirk, H. D., 266
Klein, M., 50
Kornitzer, Margaret, 21 n. 77, 69 n. 44, 199 n. 3, 267 n. 10
Kretschmer, E., 49

Lange, Johannes, 53 n. 13
Latent content of interviews, 57, 73
Leahy, A. M., 53 n. 19
Legislation in adoption,
 effectiveness of, 22–3, 268–9;
 general provisions, 11–12, 18–21;
 historical review and development of legalisation, 6–23;
 protectiveness too late, 268;
 recommendation for change in English law, 260
Life history,
 importance for assessment, 50, 54, 57;
 see also case histories
Local Government Board, 34
Local Medical Committees, 60
London County Council, 13
London Female Penitentiary, 4
London Society for the Prevention of Cruelty to Children, 3
Lord Lyon King of Arms, Office of, 34–5

MacCalman, D. R., 51 n. 7 & 8
Madge, John, 52 n. 10, 72 n. 46, 73 n. 47, 80, 269 n. 16
'Matching' adopted child and adoptive home, 29, 42, 205, 259–60
Maternity and Child Welfare Act, 1918, 6, 272
Medical examinations and certificates,
 regarding health of adopted child, 14–15, 20, 212;
 regarding health of adoptive parents, 14–15, 20–1, 28
Medical Officer for Child Welfare in Edinburgh, 33
Medical practitioners,
 consultation with, 79, 81–4, 257;
 referral by, 31, 58–64, 69–71
Mendelian Laws, 53

Index

Mental Health Aspects of Adoption, Final Report of Joint U.N./W.H.O. Meeting of Experts, 94 n. 82, 30 n. 93
Meyer, Adolf, 49 n. 1 & 2
Michaels, R., 38, 40, 45 n. 13, 258-60, 265-6
Midwives and Maternity Homes (Scotland) Act, 1927, 32 n. 95
Mixed family, 218, 261
Moral welfare organisations, 4-5
Moser, C. A., 43, 73 n. 48, 74 n. 51
Mother and Baby Homes (Scotland), 32-3

National Adoption Society, 7
National Association for Mental Health, *A Survey based on Adoption Case Records*, 42-3, 259-60
National Children Adoption Association, 7
National Children's Home and Orphanage, 7
National Council for the Unmarried Mother and her Child, 5, 33; Annual Report 1962-3, 272 n. 16
National Health Service, Administrative Areas of Edinburgh, the Lothians and Peebleshire, and the counties of Roxburgh, Berwick, and Selkirk, 30-1, 60
Natural (biological) parents, rights of, 3, 6, 8-9, 18-19, 21, 212
Newman, H. H., *et al.*, 53 n. 14
Northampton Diocesan Catholic Child Protection and Welfare Society, 267 n. 10

Objective appraisal, 25-6, 29
Occupational Classification, 67 n. 42, 86, 205-9, 259
Ounsted, C., 262
Oxford Penitentiary, 4

Parental responsibility, 6, 9
Parish Council Inspector of the Poor, 34
Pavlov, Ivan P., 49
Payments for adoption, 3-4, 14-15, 33-4, 185
Penitentiaries, 4, 31-2
Penrose, L. S., 52 n. 11
Personality tests, 71-2
Physical resemblances and differences, 40, 253-6, 266-7
Poor Law legislation, 2
Poor Law Act, 1930, 13
Probationary period, introduction of, 18
Professional relationship, in social case-work, 55
Psychiatry, influence of, 49-51, 53, 56, 72
Psychological and Social laws, 51-2
Psychosomatic conditions, discussion of, 196-7
Public Assistance Departments, 7, 13, 17, 32-4, 87, 159-60

Index

Questions and questioning in interviews,
 type used, 74–5;
 unstructured or 'open question,' 74
Questionnaires, 41, 72–3

Rating scale, 45
Register House (Edinburgh), 21, 35, 188, 268
Registrar-General for Scotland, Annual Reports of, 64 n. 39, 68 n. 43, 86 n. 2
Registrar-General, 12, 21, 35
Relatives,
 attitudes of to adopted person, 78, 81, 90, 218, 221, 226, 233–5, 237, 263, 265
Religious ideals and attitudes, 2, 5 n. 14, 25, 27–8, 209–11, 227, 260
Representative group, need for in research, 57–8, 63–4, 69
Research,
 methodology, 30, 47–8, 51–2, 71;
 need for discussed, 23–31;
 object of, 30, 45–6;
 paucity of studies, 25
Retallack, L., 5 n. 15
Retrospective introspection,
 concept of, 75–6;
 use of as research method, 83–4, 257
Retrospective life history,
 in research methodology, 30, 75
Royal Infirmary of Edinburgh Maternity Hospital, 32
Royal Society for the Prevention of Cruelty to Children, origins of, 3

St Andrew's Home, Joppa, 32
Salvation Army Mother and Baby Home, 32
Saunders, A. M. Carr, *et. al.*, 53 n. 22
Sayles, Mary Buell, 58 n. 37
School of Discipline for Destitute Girls, 4
School Medical Service, 6
Scottish Association for the Adoption of Children, 7, 33
Scottish Society for the Prevention of Cruelty to Children, 139
Self-determination in social case-work, 56
Shaw, Lulie A., 28 n. 91, 30 n. 93, 41, 45 n. 14, 205 n. 5, 243 n. 15, 259–60, 265
Sheldon, W. H., 49
Sheriff Court (Scottish), 12, 18
Skeels, H. M., *et al.*, 53 n. 20
Skodak, M., 53 n. 20
Slater, Eliot, 53 n. 16
Social case-work, 17, 49–50, 54–5;
 definition of, 54–5;
 methods of, 74;
 principles of, 55–7;
 ultimate aim or ideal of, 57
Social case-worker, 17, 49–50, 54;
 need for adequate training, 267;
 shortage of trained social workers, 14, 27, 269
Social class differences in attitudes to adoption, 9, 21, 220, 259

Index

Social class grouping, 67–9;
   See also Occupational Classification
Social histories,
   See under case histories
Social work attitudes, 4–5, 25–6, 33, 54–7
Social work provisions in Southeast Scotland from 1890 to 1939, 31–5
Society for the Protection of Infant Life, 271
Sociological research, 48, 51
Soddy, K., 213 n. 14, 279 n. 14
Spitz, R. A., 50 n. 5, 213 n. 14
Springwell House, formerly the Edinburgh Magdalene Asylum, 31
Standing Conference of Societies Registered for Adoption, 24 n. 86, 267 n. 10 & 11
Statistical correlation techniques, applicability of, 43
Steel, E. M., 272
Succession (Scotland) Act, 1964, 18
Sullivan, Harry Stack, 77, 80

Tait, H. P., 4 n. 7
Telling about adoption, 10, 28, 40, 42, 222–8, 231, 233–53, 263–7;
   one-way communication, 246–51, 264–6
Theis, Sophie van Senden, 37–0, 43, 45, 59, 195
Third party adoption placements, 8, 16, 18, 22–4, 28–9, 34, 41, 65, 87, 268–9
Tomlin Committee, 4, 9–10, 12, 16, 22
Twin studies, 44, 53

Unconscious motivation, importance of, 49, 72
Unmarried mothers,
   attitudes of adoptive parents, 224–5, 228–9, 231–2, 262;
   attitudes of community, 4–5, 31;
   social provisions for, 4–5, 31–3;
   social work attitudes to, 4–5, 25–6

Waifs and Strays Society, 3
Wards in Chancery, 3
Waters, Margaret, 271
Will, O. A., 77 n. 53
Wittenborn, J. R., 71 n. 45(a)
Wootton, Dame Barbara, 52 n. 9
World Federation for Mental Health, 279 n. 14

Zangwill, O. L., 50 n. 4

For Product Safety Concerns and Information please contact our EU representative GPSR@taylorandfrancis.com
Taylor & Francis Verlag GmbH, Kaufingerstraße 24, 80331 München, Germany

www.ingramcontent.com/pod-product-compliance
Lightning Source LLC
Chambersburg PA
CBHW071803300426
44116CB00009B/1188